Teaching the Young

The Early Childhood Development Profession in India

Teaching the Young

The Early Childhood Development Profession in India

Edited by
**Kinnari Pandya
Jigisha Shastri
Vrinda Datta**

All rights reserved. No part of this book may be modified, reproduced or utilised in any form, or by any means, electronic or mechanical, including photocopying, recording or by any information storage and retrieval system, in any form of binding or cover other than in which it is published, without permission in writing from the publisher.

TEACHING THE YOUNG: THE EARLY CHILDHOOD DEVELOPMENT PROFESSION IN INDIA

ORIENT BLACKSWAN PRIVATE LIMITED

Registered Office
3-6-752 Himayatnagar, Hyderabad 500 029, Telangana, India
e-mail: centraloffice@orientblackswan.com

Other Offices
Bengaluru, Chennai, Guwahati, Hyderabad,
Kolkata, Mumbai, New Delhi, Noida, Patna

© Orient Blackswan Private Limited 2024
First published by Orient Blackswan Private Limited 2024

ISBN 978-93-5442-283-6

Typeset in
Minion Pro 10.5/12.6pt *by*
Shine Graphics, Delhi 110 094

Illustrations: Stuti Pandya

Printed at
Rathna Offset Printers
Chennai 600 014

Published by
Orient Blackswan Private Limited
3-6-752, Himayatnagar, Hyderabad 500 029, Telangana, India
e-mail: info@orientblackswan.com

Contents

List of Acronyms	*ix*
Foreword	*xi*
Acknowledgements	*xiii*
Preface	*xv*
Introduction	*xvii*

Section 1
History and Policy of Early Years Teacher Preparation

1. Promising Policy Developments and Challenges for Teacher/Caregiver Education in ECCE — 3
   Venita Kaul

2. Higher Education in the Development of Early Childhood Professionals — 18
   Prerana Mohite

3. The Role of NGOs in Developing ECCE Professionals in India: Experiences of Mobile Crèches — 32
   Mridula Bajaj

4. Continued Relevance of Nai Talim's Pre-basic Teacher Education Curriculum — 51
   Varadarajan Narayanan and *Rajashree Srinivasan*

Section 2
Curriculum and Programmes for Pre-service Teacher Preparation

5. Curriculum and Pedagogy for Early Childhood Professional Development — 67
   Kinnari Pandya

6. An Early Educator's Professional Development: Insights from Bhutan — 83
   Karma Gayleg

7. Cultural Tools for Children's Literacy and Learning — 96
   Asha Singh

8. Role of Vocational Education in the Development of Early Childhood Professionals — 109
   Neela Dabir

9. Distance Education for Professional Development: IGNOU's Diploma Programme — 118
   Rekha Sharma Sen, Pankaj Khare and *Pranjali Dev*

10. The 5Ws and 1H of Teachers' Professional Development — 128
    Maya Menon

11. Implementing Inclusive Education in Early Childhood Settings: Preparing Teachers for the Role — 138
    Ankur Madan

12. Inclusive Classrooms: Challenges of Deaf Learners and their Teachers — 148
    Kanika M. Agarwal

Section 3

In-service Professional Development of Early Childhood Teachers

13. Role of DIETs in Training Preschool Teachers — 161
    Padma Yadav

14. Strengthening ECE in Anganwadis Through Ankur — 172
    Nilesh Nimkar

15. Professional Development Strategies: Akshara Foundation's Experience — 186
    Vaijayanti K. and *Gayatri Kiran*

16. A Multimodal Approach to In-Service Capacity Development of Anganwadi Teachers — 201
    Yogesh G. R., Kinnari Pandya and *M. Sreenivasa Rao*

17. A Community Approach to Early Childhood Care and Education — 221
    Mary Punnoose and *Shikha Kumari*

18. Ensuring Quality through Teacher Appraisals and In-Service Education — 238
    Gauravi Jadhav, Valentine Borges and *Elizabeth Mehta*

19. In-service Programme for Teacher Educators for Early Years Education — 252
    Jigisha Shastri and *Kinnari Pandya*

Section 4
Resources for Early Childhood Educators

20. ECD Toolkits for Quality Early Years Education — 271
    Gauravi Jadhav and *Jumana Rampurawala*

21. Anganwadi Teacher's Handbook: Azim Premji Foundation — 288

22. Pre-Basic Education: A Syllabus for Teacher Training — 303

Recommendations for Way Forward — 331
About the Contributors — 339

List of Acronyms

ASHA	Accredited Social Health Activists
AWC	Anganwadi Centre
AWCC	Anganwadi cum Creche
AWCW	Anganwadi Creche Worker
AWT	Anganwadi Teacher
AWW	Anganwadi Worker
CLR	Centre for Learning Resources
DPSE	Diploma in Preschool Education
ECCD	Early Childhood Care and Development
ECCE	Early Child Care and Education
ECCE Policy	Early Child Care and Education Policy 2013
ECD	Early Childhood Development
ECE	Early Childhood Education
GOI	Government of India
ICDS	Integrated Child Development Services
MC	Mobile Crèches
MHRD	Ministry of Human Resource Development
MNREGA	Mahatma Gandhi National Rural Employment Guarantee Act
MoH	Ministry of Health
MWCD	Ministry of Women and Child Development
NCERT	National Council of Educational Research and Training
NCTE	National Council for Teacher Education
NEP 2020	National Education Policy 2020
NFHS	National Family Health Survey
NHM	National Health Mission

NNM	National Nutrition Mission
NTTI	Nursery Teacher Training Institute
PHRN	Public Health Resource Network
PSE	Preschool Education
RTE	Right to Education
RTFS	Right to Food Security
SDGs	Sustainable Development Goals
SEWA	Self Employed Women's Association

Foreword

The National Education Policy 2020 (NEP 2020) has placed young children and their development as the foremost responsibility of the nation's education system. Without doubt this was needed and urgent. Research and experience over the past few decades confirm the critical and lifelong importance of education and care in early years. This must then be the decade of Early Childhood Care and Education in India, the platform for which has been set.

India is a complex society, and care and development of the young child is even more complex in the changing socioeconomic-technological context.

As the country prepares to provide high quality early childhood care and education to *all* children between 3 to 8 years of age, we need caregivers and teachers with appropriate capacities and commitment. The role of an early childhood educator is central and thus the quality of preparation and training of the teacher is of utmost importance. NEP 2020 rightly emphasises this and lays down its framework.

Teaching the Young—The Early Childhood Development Profession in India, edited by Kinnari Pandya, Jigisha Shastri and Vrinda Datta, is a timely resource in the current context. The book captures the context, implemented initiatives, programmes at universities and on-the-field realities for developing early childhood professionals. These examples and learnings illustrate that it is possible to develop high-capacity professionals for early childhood care and education through concerted efforts.

The editors have a rich background in developing and implementing ECCE programmes for higher education and with the public system of our country. We have observed them closely, developing these programmes, and we can see the invaluable imprint of their experience on this volume. This curated edited volume therefore provides a must-read view of the essential aspects for the professional development of Early Childhood Educators in the Indian context. It is a definite contribution to the discourse on professionalising the ECCE domain to help provide high quality education and care for all our children.

Indu Prasad   **Anurag Behar**
Vice-Chancellor   *Chief Executive Officer*
Azim Premji University, Bengaluru   *Azim Premji Foundation*

Acknowledgements

Our sincere gratitude to Azim Premji Foundation for their belief and support for this entire project.

We are thankful to S. Giridhar and Manoj P., without whose support and guidance, this project would have remained unfulfilled.

Our sincere appreciation to our authors for being with us on this journey.

Our special thanks to Padmaja Anant, Mahalakshmi Jayaram and the Orient BlackSwan team for their efforts in ensuring a high-quality publication.

Our appreciations and thanks to Stuti Pandya for the drawings and Ruchi Shewade for the overall editorial support.

To our colleagues, friends and families for being with us always.

To my boys—Ved and Dhruv—for their love and patience while watching me work behind the screen – Kinnari

Kinnari Pandya, Jigisha Shastri and Vrinda Datta

Preface

The birth to six years child population of India is about 163 million. The number of children attending day care centres and preschools has been rising steadily. The need for quality care leading to holistic development of children in early years is an urgent need for all children of our country.

The Early Childhood Care and Education Policy of India (2013) highlighted the significance of early years and care of young children, giving an impetus to the field of early childhood in India. The National Education Policy (NEP 2020) has strengthened the focus on early years and recommended systematic efforts to ensure quality opportunities for all children. The projection is of an increase in provision for Early Childhood Care and Education (ECCE) services, thus bringing the critical need for preparing of ECCE professionals to the forefront. ECCE professionals range from day care providers, caregivers within homes, anganwadi workers, helpers, teachers of preschools, administrators, supervisors and educators of teachers and caregivers.

Azim Premji University, Bengaluru, Association for Early Childhood Education and Development (AECED) and UNICEF had organised a two-day conference on *Re-defining Early Childhood Development Profession in India: Challenges and Potential* in November 2016. The aims of the conference were to bring to fore the need for re-imagining the field and deliberate on alternatives to current issues in all aspects of the early childhood development profession, debating and endorsing some non-negotiables such as quality teacher education, and finding strategies to meet the policy requirements regarding in-service capacity building of early years professionals. Towards this end, the conference was successful in bringing together policy-makers, teachers, teacher training institutes, academicians, researchers and representatives from all sectors—private, NGO and government—from ECCE domains. The conference led to a report with detailed recommendations for strengthening the ECCE domain, and preparation of the ECCE professionals, published by Azim Premji University in 2017.

This book includes select papers presented during the conference and a few invited papers. It aims to present the spectrum of efforts and practices in early childhood professional development in India so far, and the potential that the National Education Policy 2020 provides. This volume by no means is comprehensive of the range of efforts several individuals and organizations in the ecosystem have undertaken for the past several decades, to make the early years most significant in the development of young children of our country. This is a glimpse of the vast expanse of work happening on the ground, and the potential for further work.

Introduction

Globally, the last two decades have seen rising interest in and understanding of the early years and the significant role that early childhood programmes can play in optimising development of young children. Macro-level inputs in terms of care, nutrition, safety and education provisions, increased reach and access of services to the most marginalised population, programmes for parenting skills are getting the necessary thrust through policy emphasis at the international and national level. The Sustainable Development Goal 4 (SDG 2030) is to 'ensure lifelong learning—*Early stimulation increases duration of schooling, school performance, and adult income.*' National Education Policy 2020 (GOI), has identified early years as the most critical period of engagement, and brought it in the realm of overall education and schooling system of the country.

While the Early Childhood Care and Education (ECCE) field has emerged as a critical domain for intervention through neuroscience research evidence, returns on investment leading to prioritisation at the national and international policy level, efforts in professionalising the domain and investing in teacher development have been inadequate. In order to understand the urgency of reforming the early childhood profession in India, let us first deliberate on the concepts of *profession, professionalisation, professional development* and *teaching as a profession.*

The notion of 'profession' implies that there is a body of knowledge—a broad knowledge base that the profession aligns itself to. This knowledge base is exclusive, and therefore the role the professional plays is exclusive. Another characteristic that defines the idea of profession is the clear social function that the professional has to play—in the larger realm of contributing to society by the unique and valuable relationship the professional holds with the clients. These characteristics further imply the need for the professional to be 'educated' and not merely trained, and the knowledge base is such that it enables the professional to act independently and provides necessary autonomy to make decisions best in the interest of the clients. Further, the profession therefore operates within an articulated code of ethics and bound by legal obligations (Downie, 1990; Hoyle, 1982).

Professionalisation is the process whereby these attributes of a profession are continuously enhanced and help professionals achieve the characteristics of the profession.

Professional development is the process whereby practitioners improve their competencies, and this is possible through well-defined competencies that the professional strives to enhance (Hoyle, 1982).

Teaching as a profession builds on the claim of expert knowledge base—the knowledge of the domain and the knowledge of how to transact the knowledge. Downie (1990) characterises the teacher as a professional who has a wide knowledge base, can make knowledge relevant to children's context, has a reasonable sense of structuring the knowledge in the classroom context, knows the significance of the teacher's personality and personal attributes and its impact on children. Further, the professional teacher is someone who values continuous learning and develops herself and her practice of teaching within the larger framework of values of the profession.

With this background, it is pertinent to see the Early Childhood Development (ECD) field as a profession and the status of early years teachers as professionals, especially within the Indian context.

Early Childhood Development as a Profession and its Professionalisation

Early Childhood Development as a domain is a well-established field of study with its roots in developmental psychology. The emerging social needs for care of young children in institutionalised settings gave prominence to programmatic approaches for care and development of young children. The primary aim of quality Early Childhood programmes is to provide children access to opportunities for appropriate and optimum development and learning outcomes. Research has consistently shown that the single most important factor in determining quality of a programme is the early childhood educator.

With this recognition of the critical role of the early childhood educator in providing a quality programme, there are growing expectations from the practitioner. For instance, she must promote holistic development and learning for all children, she must be sensitive and follow inclusive practices. Further, she must understand curriculum development and transaction with a deep understanding of the subject and learning abilities of children. At the same time, we also want her to be a researcher, a reflective practitioner and work with multiple stakeholders. This educator is interchangeably referred to as 'worker', 'caregiver', 'teacher'—indicating the lack of a clear professional identity of the early years teacher. The foremost need of the ECD profession in India is to provide a professional identity to its early years' teachers.

The reasons for this need are apparent, yet understanding it within the idea of 'professional' is critical.

The early years teacher is the most important person in a child's life after parents and family members. Teacher-child interactions are central to the nature of the ECCE programme the teacher offers. The way a teacher interacts with children is possibly influenced by her personal characteristics such as personality, temperament, mental health and contextual variables such as education level, caste and class of teachers and children, classroom and centre characteristics. Research on teaching effectiveness has shown that teachers have implicit beliefs about the subject matter, their students, and their roles and responsibilities that significantly influence how they behave in the classroom (Ball and Cohen, 1996).

Tschannen-Moran et al. (1998) analyse that these beliefs are constructed from the teacher's personal experience of teaching, their expectations or ideals about teaching, their inner state, their knowledge of the subject matter and the reinforcement they receive for their behaviour from others. Teachers' belief about their own efficacy influences other behaviours, such as willingness to work and openness to new ideas, that in turn affects not only children's school achievement, but also social and emotional growth.

Working with young children and transacting a curriculum involves continuous expert decision making and judgement on the part of the teacher-caregiver. This ability to engage with proficiency in handling children's questions, identifying and working on individual needs, thinking about continuous development and creating rich learning environments needs rigorous professional preparation. This preparation is required prior to becoming an early years practitioner, as well as continuous in-service development opportunities and interactions with peers in the professional network (NAEYC, 2009, p. 6)

All of these indicate the vast knowledge base and personal dispositions and attributes that an early years teacher would need to possess. On the other hand, a set of possible reasons underlie the current state of early years profession as a partially or unestablished profession and its semi-professional status.

The knowledge base of understanding children, child development, the process of learning and of working with children is viewed as a general-social-personal knowledge and not as one that stems from the 'study of the discipline'. This reflects in a shorter training period, a lower importance of the role of early years teachers, the resultant lower social acceptance, lack of continuous strengthening of knowledge and skills to engage with children and less autonomy as a teacher (Saracho & Spodek, 1993).

One way to 'professionalise' the early childhood domain is by meeting the first necessary criteria of the profession—providing the requisite knowledge base with longer duration programmes for teachers. The knowledge base does exist. The challenge is to see that it is viewed as necessary, a standard that is required to become an early childhood teacher. The path to professionalism must be such that it sets high but achievable goals and expectations so that it does not discourage those who want to be part of this field (Freeman & Feeney, 2006). Given the nature of the field, and one of the critical roles of the teacher to provide 'care' and a nurturing environment to young children, it demands 'selflessness' from the teacher (Spodek, 1995). This interferes with the identity, social status and perception about the teacher's work and role as a professional. This further makes the notion of ECD as a profession complex and problematic.

The status of early childhood teachers in India is an accurate reflection of the status of (semi)profession that is discussed above. The knowledge base that ECD holds is not widely known in the social milieu. The opportunity to get professionally trained is limited to degree and diploma programmes offered by a few university departments and specific approach-based certificate programmes such as the Montessori training programme. Most teachers are 'trained' in-service without any prerequisite knowledge base of child development. This widespread approach to becoming an early childhood educator in the country has itself resulted in low status and recognition of practitioners as 'workers' or 'caregivers'.

Several national documents such as the National Focus Group Position Paper on Early Childhood Care and Education (NCERT, 2005), National Curriculum Framework for Teacher Education (NCTE, 2009), the Early Childhood Care and Education Policy and Framework for Standards and Quality (MWCD, 2013), the National ECCE Curriculum Framework (MWCD, 2014), Preschool Education Curriculum (NCERT, 2019) highlight the critical need to strengthen the ECD profession, recognise the early years educators as professionals, and provide appropriate professional development inputs. Recently, the National Education

Policy 2020 has provided a clear direction for professionalisation of the ECD domain in India.

The slow yet consistent recognition of the need for quality early childhood programmes, and therefore, qualified and skilled teachers, has seen many interesting initiatives by civil society organisations, university departments and practitioners, to strengthen the early childhood profession in the country. In this context, this edited collection is well placed to highlight the work of academicians, practitioners and researchers working in this domain in India. It brings together ideas and practices suitable for strengthening the early childhood professional development. It hopes to strengthen the ongoing dialogue around the need for professionalisation of the Early Childhood Development field and provide a quality reference source for professionals interested in studying the domain. All charts, figures and tables accompanying the text have been developed by the authors unless otherwise stated.

The volume is divided into four sections.

The first section *History and Policy of Early Years Teacher Preparation* includes chapters that articulate theoretical ideas along with empirical evidence on the need for professionalisation of the domain, the higher education space and scope of Early Childhood Education (ECE), and recommendations for policy provisions for India. The experience of Mobile Creches, Delhi, a forerunner for ensuring care of children of construction workers, lays out the history of teacher and caregiver preparation through the past few decades of work in this area. An analytical paper on the Nai Talim's approach to teacher preparation for providing pre-basic education and its relevance today gives access to a rare resource and a lens to view contemporary practices.

Section two on *Curriculum and Pedagogy for Pre-service Teacher Preparation* includes a set of papers which reflect the various kinds of ECE professional development programmes offered at the higher education level in India. These papers present the curriculum framework for preparing early childhood teachers and teacher educators offered at Azim Premji University, a vocational programme for early childhood personnel by Tata Institute of Social Sciences, and a Distance Education programme offered by IGNOU. The chapter "Early Educator's Professional Development: Insights from Bhutan" suggests the universal nature of early years curriculum and key components of the curriculum and practices recommended in Bhutan. The section further discusses the various cultural tools for literacy and learning, and preparing teachers for inclusive practices in the early years setting. Every child in the early years programme requires individualised attention from the adult in her environment to provide holistic learning and development opportunities. One chapter each on cultural and contextual inputs for language development, and inclusive environment for children present strategies for teacher development, and specific strategies for teacher training for working with hearing impaired children. A paper on 5Ws and 1H of teacher professional development outlines the key aspects that should be considered for enriching teachers' practice in an ongoing manner.

Section three on *In-service Professional Development of Early Childhood Teachers* provides a perspective on in-service programmes offered by the National Council of Education Research and Training (NCERT); capacity development programmes for Anganwadi Teachers of Integrated Child Development Services (ICDS) scheme by Quest, Pune, Akshara Foundation and Prajayatna. Azim Premji Foundation's flagship programme in ECE at Telengana and Prajayatna capture the multimodal strategies that work in the field where quality intervention is a necessity. These papers highlight the practices and models followed by organisations that offer in-service capacity development to strengthen the professional development of Anganwadi Teachers. Evaluation of teachers in a systematic manner is a clear step towards supporting professionals to better their quality of performance and become reflective practitioners. A chapter by Muktangan, Mumbai, on the practices they follow for teacher evaluation outlines the scope and effectiveness of teacher evaluation in their programme. A paper on preparing teacher educators for ECE, an in-service model, based on the experience of Azim Premji Foundation provides a framework for a graded integrated approach to professional development of in-service personnel.

The fourth section, *Resources for Early Childhood Educators*, is specially included to provide practising professionals tools and methods to organise curriculum and plan the programme with children. A description of the Toolkit for Teachers developed by Muktangan and the Teachers Handbook by Azim Premji Foundation outline processes and steps for teachers to organise their early childhood programme, a much-needed practical resource for teachers. The original text of the Syllabus for the Training of the Pre-basic Education teachers by the Hindustani Talimi Sangh, a rare artefact, is included in this volume to give ECCE educators a view into the consistent yet distinct approach of the Gandhian philosophy to preschool education.

The conclusion and recommendation acknowledge the consistent measures being taken by various stakeholders in strengthening the quality of professionals in the ECD domain in India. It further proposes a few necessary steps we must take as a country in order to change the 'semi-profession' to a critical profession that would result in the best of teachers offering a high-quality programme of early childhood development, ensuring lifelong learning and well-being for young citizens.

References

Ball, D. L., & Cohen, D. K. (1999). Developing practice, developing practitioners: Towards a practice based theory of professional education. In G. Sykes and L. Darling-Hammond (Eds.), *Teaching as the learning profession: Handbook of policy and practice*. Jossey Bass.

Downie, R. S. (1990). Professions and professionalism. *Journal of Philosophy of Education, 24*(2), 147–159. https://doi.org/10.1111/j.1467-9752.1990.tb00230.x.

Freeman, N. K., & Feeney, S. (2006, September). The new face of early care and education: Who are we and where are we going? *Young Children*, 10–16.

Hoyle, Eric. (1982). The professionalization of teachers: A paradox. *British Journal of Educational Studies, 30*(2), 161–171. doi:10.2307/3121549.

Ministry of Human Resource Development. (2020). *National education policy 2020*. Delhi.

Ministry of Women and Child Development. (2013). *National early childhood care and education (ECCE) policy, 2013*. Delhi.

Ministry of Women and Child Development. (2013). *National early childhood care and education (ECCE) curriculum framework, 2013*. Delhi.

Ministry of Women and Child Development. (2013). *Framework for standards and quality*. Delhi.

National Council of Educational Research and Training. (2009). *National curriculum framework for teacher education.*

National Council of Educational Research and Training. (2019). *The preschool curriculum (2019)*. https://ncert.nic.in/dee/pdf/Combined_Pre_school_curriculumEng.pdf.

Saracho, O. N., & Spodek, B. (1993). Professionalism and the preparation of early childhood education practitioners. *Early Child Development and Care, 89*(1), 1–17.

Spodek, B. (1995). Professionalism and the early childhood practitioner. *Early Child Development and Care, 114*(1), 65–79. DOI: 10.1080/0300443951140106.

Tschannen-Moran, M., Hoy, A., & Hoy, W. (1998). Teacher efficacy: Its meaning and measure. *Review of Educational Research, 68*(2), 202–248. https://doi.org/10.2307/1170754.

Section 1
History and Policy of Early Years Teacher Preparation

1

Promising Policy Developments and Challenges for Teacher/Caregiver Education in ECCE

Venita Kaul

India has the distinction of being home to the largest community-based integrated programme for children below six years, known as the Integrated Child Development Services (ICDS), with early childhood development centres or anganwadis operating across the country. Consistent with the life cycle and holistic approach for enhancing children's optimum development, ICDS offers six services to children and pregnant women, which cover the domains of health, nutrition and preschool education.

Each of these services, delivered by a minimally trained, multipurpose worker, has its own epistemological foundation and skill base, which should inform the planning and delivery of these services. This requires the service provider to be adequately knowledgeable, multi-skilled and professionally supported to be able to ensure effective transaction or delivery of interventions. While the responsibility for the health services is largely with the health functionaries, overseen by the health departments, the preschool education component is exclusively left to the departments of Women and Child Development who do not necessarily have the required domain knowledge or institutional capacity for this component, which may be in many cases better located with the education departments. As a result, the preschool education offered by this programme, which is the largest provider for preschool education in India in the public domain, is at best minimalist in terms of quality (Kaul & Sankar, 2017).

The other major provider for preschool education is the private sector which employs teachers, but again, in the absence of any institutional mechanisms for registration or regulation or enforcement of standards, there is no premium given to training or academic qualifications in this sector, particularly in the affordable category of preschools. On the contrary, there is a prevailing belief that preschool education can be imparted by anyone, preferably a woman, and does not necessarily require any special qualifications or training. Yet this does not hamper participation of children in preschools, since, as a recent study in three states indicates, almost 80% of four-year-olds were participating, even in the rural areas, in some or the other preschool education programme (Kaul et al, 2017).

The moot question therefore is, are these locally recruited service providers from the community in ICDS or private preschools sufficiently prepared, supported and incentivised to enable them to deliver high quality preschool education to the children in their critical early years, as envisaged in the national policies? And if not, what are some of the areas or aspects that need to be prioritised to meet the expected standards?

In this paper, I attempt to respond to these questions, wherein I argue for the need for professionalisation of the ECE sector of which preschool education is a part, in the context of India. I begin by discussing the rationale and need for professionalisation, given (a) the critical importance of the early years for lifelong learning and development, and (b) the recent emergence of an evidence-based science of early childhood development which offers ECE a credible knowledge base and therefore, demands a more professional treatment. I then move on to examine the policy and programmatic environment that exists in India and discuss the extent to which it is conducive for the required professionalisation. Based on this review, I identify some gaps and issues that need to be addressed to institute a more knowledge-based approach towards ensuring quality standards in preschool education. I conclude with a few recommendations.

Why the ECE Sector Must be Professionalised

What is meant by the term 'professionalisation'? Drury (2011) in the context of education/teaching laments on how the education field is characterised by the absence of professionalisation, as it rests on 'relying on a combination of 'expert judgment', 'best practices', and 'conventional wisdom', which are in turn informed by an ambiguous and inconclusive body of evidence—educators struggle to develop meaningful training, induction, mentoring and professional development programmes and engage in endless debates. Instead, according to Drury, what is required for professionalisation is for the education field to develop a 'coherent, agreed upon knowledge base as in the case of medicine.' (Drury, 2011, p. 1).

As compared to education, the domain of early childhood care and education is relatively in an advantageous situation in this context, as it has benefitted significantly from the last few decades of very significant research from across disciplines, including from neuroscience, child development and economics, which have together yielded credible evidence to build up a science of Early Childhood Development (Shonkoff, 2000). This evidence provides a multi-disciplinary knowledge base that not only allows for a more professional approach to ECCE, but demands it, since it requires from all stakeholders and providers a more complete understanding of the critical importance of the early years for lifelong learning and development and an in-depth understanding of the 'whys and ways' to ensure an enabling environment for every child in these foundational years.

Critical Significance of ECCE: Learning from Neuroscience and Other Disciplines

The most significant evidence offered by research from the field of neurobiology has been the confirmation of the fact that the brain grows at its most rapid pace in the first six years of life, reaching almost 80% of its adult size by age 5–6 years. Further, the development of the neural architecture of the brain is significantly influenced not only by the genetic predisposition but also by the quality of environment the child gets within these years in terms of cognitive and social interaction and stimulation. A third significant finding is that within this age span of the first 6 to 7 years are located some 'critical periods' for development of some specific cognitive, language and psychosocial competencies, each of which requires a correspondingly conducive environment within that age span to optimise its development to its maximum potential. Since these competencies lay a holistic foundation in a child's life for later learning in school and beyond, the experiences and environment the child needs for their nurturance and development at this stage need to be ensured. These opportunities and experiences, which may not always be available to the child in the home, especially from more economically or socially marginalised families, may need to be integrated within the Early Childhood Education curriculum.

Research from the fields of Child Development and Education has indicated that the social equity gap in these critical early years can lead to cumulative learning deficits at the school stage due to socioeconomic disparity. Recent research in India has indicated that despite children attending preschool education programmes, their school readiness levels particularly in the cognitive and language domains are very low. The study also indicates, albeit in a small sample, that the learning gap can be narrowed if not closed with good quality early childhood education programme (Kaul, Bhattacharjea et al, 2017).

Spending on good quality early childhood education is increasingly being perceived as an investment and not an expenditure. Three major research studies that have provided the basis for significant cost–benefit analysis of investment in ECE in this context are the Perry Preschool Study in 1962, the Abecedarian study in 1970s and the Chicago Child-Parent Centres study in 1980s. Each of these has helped us estimate both immediate and medium-term returns to investment in good quality ECE. While the first one estimated the total benefit–cost ratio as USD 8.6 to every dollar invested, the second study reported a benefit of 2.5 USD to a dollar and the third study a benefit of 10.8 dollars to every dollar invested (Barnett and Nores, 2017).While there has been recent research too in this context, including a study in India which estimated a benefit of INR 25 to every rupee invested (World Bank, 2015), '[n]one of the researches suggest that programmes of mediocre quality can be expected to have large positive or lasting impacts on children' (Yoshikawa et al, 2013).

Early Childhood Education in India: Policies and Provisions

Ensuring good quality ECCE, especially for the disadvantaged communities, requires a supportive policy and programme framework, which is something India can certainly boast of. The Indian Constitution at the time of Independence committed through Article 45 to education of all children up to the age of 14 years, thus including the under-sixes. Although subsequently children under six years were not included within the RTE Act (RTE, 2009) which made education up to 14 years a justiciable right, it has been retained as Section 11 of the Act as an encouragement to states to endeavour to provide for preschool education for three- to six-year-olds as a preparation for formal education. The decision to not include it as a fundamental right was revisited by a subcommittee of the Central Advisory Board of Education to re-examine the feasibility of its inclusion but it failed to recommend its inclusion.[1]

However, there have been two very significant policy initiatives favouring ECCE in the last decade:

    a. the National Policy on ECCE (2013) from the Ministry of Women and Child Development which was followed up with a National Curriculum Framework and Quality Standards for ECCE. While this was at the national level, states have also taken the initiative to develop contextualised state curricula and, in a few cases, even state policies on ECCE.

b. The second is the most recent National Education Policy (NEP 2020), brought out by the Ministry of Education, Government of India, which has made a few positive recommendations for ECCE. These include (i) incorporation of ECCE for children from three to six years within the academic domain of the Ministry of Education. (ii) Carving out of a foundational stage by combining education of children from three to eight years as the first stage of the education structure to ensure a sound foundation for children and a seamless learning continuum from pre-primary to grades 1 and 2.

In terms of provisions for ECCE, as mentioned earlier, the coverage is fairly satisfactory. The ICDS offers six services for children below six years and pregnant and lactating women. These include non-formal preschool education for three- to six-year-olds. Preschool education is offered through 1.3 million Anganwadi Centres across the country which are run by a locally recruited multipurpose worker known as the Anganwadi Worker, and a helper. This programme caters to the poorest households through a process of self-selection. The other major provider is the private sector as mentioned earlier, which is expanding exponentially across the country, including across rural India, with offer of low budget options to parents, especially as composite preschool and primary schools. The NEP 2020 now proposes four different models of ECCE including independent Anganwadi Centres as well as school-based models to allow for contextual variations, but with emphasis on curricular linkages and continuity with primary schools/grades. Challenges of multisectoral convergence across MWCD and MOE will require to be addressed to allow for these multiple models to be successful.

Recent longitudinal research in India, known as the Indian Early Childhood Education Impact Study (IECEI), followed up 14,000 four-year-olds till the age of eight years in rural segments of three states in different regions of the country. The study indicated that as many as 80 per cent of the children were in a preschool, either in an anganwadi or in a private preschool, or sitting as underage children in a government primary school. While the overall participation status was a positive finding, the concern as mentioned earlier was that despite attending preschool programmes the children's school-readiness levels at age 5+ on school entry were very low, especially in cognitive and language domains. This raised the issue of the quality of the preschool provisions, which the study comprehensively assessed and found it to be on the whole developmentally inappropriate. This explains the poor outcomes. The study also provided strong evidence of a positive association between school readiness levels at age five and learning levels in language and mathematics at the early primary stage consistently till the age of eight years. This finding provides credible evidence of the fact that the early learning crisis in elementary schools today is to a considerable extent due to the poor-quality preschool education available to the children across sectors, in these critical foundational years.

The quality assessment of the preschools across public and private sectors revealed a predominance of formal teaching of the 3 R's and a significant neglect of what is known as play-based developmentally appropriate curriculum, which the National Curriculum Framework (2013) professes (Kaul, Bhattacharjea et al, 2017). The study recommended the development of a progressive but integrated foundational curriculum for children from three to eight years, which should address the foundational academic and developmental needs of children, while being flexible enough to allow for individually paced learning. This recommendation is gradually receiving acknowledgement and accceptance at the policy level.

The study also identified some significant factors related to quality of the preschool programme that positively impact school readiness levels at age five. These included classroom planning, organisation and management (which is essential for ensuring age/developmentally and contextually appropriate activities), a planned schedule followed by the teacher, classroom arrangements with a balanced mix of group and individual activities, an interactive teaching–learning process which includes opportunities for creative activities, individual/group activities, free choice play and activities for pre-numeracy and pre-reading skills and concepts. A worrisome finding was that formal teaching of the 3 R's, which was seen as a common practice across programmes, emerged as having a negative association with school readiness of children, thus reflecting that this can well be counterproductive.

Most importantly, a key factor that characterised good quality programmes was the teacher's profile and disposition, which, if democratic and interactive, added value to the quality of the preschool programme. Teacher quality, and the need for a professionally trained teacher, significantly contributed to the quality score related to classroom planning and management, thus confirming that competent and capable preschool teachers who are appropriately and professionally trained, prepared and supported are an imperative.

Teacher Development in ECCE in India

While there is a policy framework in place in India to support ECCE, which is informed by the scientific knowledge base confirming the nature and significance of this domain, the implementation arrangements, or provisions especially for teacher recruitment and development need much greater attention. Some case studies of good practices in ECCE conducted as part of the IECEI study indicate that effective teacher development requires a comprehensive approach with a balance of induction training, recurrent training and regular onsite mentoring by experienced teachers and a supportive supervision system. In addition, for a professional system to thrive there is need for effective career mobility, professional networking and opportunities to upgrade knowledge and skills to meet with emerging priorities. The issue is to what extent are these enabling factors provided for? Some major issues that emerge are as follows:

Teacher Positions for ECCE and Eligibility for Recruitment

Despite the ECE sector having expanded over the last decade with a significant number of children participating in preschool education, there is limited demand for trained preschool teachers. This is largely because the ICDS is the main channel for delivery of preschool education and it does not recruit 'teachers'. Instead, it recruits multipurpose anganwadi 'workers' locally, who are considered to be honorary workers, pays them a fixed honorarium and provides a multi-sectoral induction training of one month, which includes only four days for preschool education. This training is conducted by Anganwadi Training Centres (AWTCs) which are largely in the NGO sector and are often of uneven professional quality. While this training is limited, the expectation is that the workers will conduct a good quality preschool education programme for children at par with trained teachers. ICDS also has provision for refresher training for five days for all six services, which again translates into one day for preschool education, and that too is not always available to all workers, due to the large numbers involved. The NEP 2020 while committing to universalisation of quality ECCE by 2030, commits in the longer term to preparing professional ECCE teachers through a B.Ed. teacher education programme of four years' duration (at par with that proposed for elementary education). But in the more immediate and possibly medium-term time frame, it expects the anganwadi model to be the major delivery mode, with some strengthening in terms of quality, and the existing Anganwadi Workers as the main service providers as teachers. The strengthening is proposed in terms of a six months online training in preschool education for Anganwadi Workers if they possess academic qualifications at the level of secondary and above and of a one-year duration for those below the secondary stage. The policy also does not comment on the workload of the workers due to their multiple responsibilities in other domains such as health, nutrition, and community education.

In the case of the other major provider, the private sector, there is a *laissez faire* situation with full freedom for anyone to set up a nursery school or preschool programme, without adherence to any standards. This situation is largely because of the absence of any system of quality assurance or regulation in place, despite this being a recommendation of the National Policy on ECCE (2013). The NEP 2020 does commit to a process of regulation and accreditation which it is expected would cover the early childhood or foundational stage as well.

Access to Professional Teacher Education Programmes in ECCE

Although there is no specific regulation for ECCE services, in terms of teacher preparation, a Diploma in Preschool Education has been included in the basket of teacher education programmes that are officially notified by National Council of Teacher Education (NCTE), the regulatory authority for teacher education programmes for all stages of education in the country. The notification specifies the eligibility criteria and curriculum framework for each programme. This Diploma, of two years' duration, has grade 12 completion as its eligibility. To that extent it corresponds to the Diploma in Elementary Education for grades 1–8. The Diploma in Preschool Education was revised and its scope expanded in terms of the curriculum to include not only the preschool stage but also the transition from preschool to early primary grades. This revised version was notified in January 2015 along with the revised specifications of other programmes.

Although this notified programme should technically be considered the officially prescribed programme for preschool teacher preparation, the demand for this programme is very scarce due to the reasons discussed above. With preschool education not being officially a part of school education in the public sector, except in a few exceptional cases, the presence of this programme especially in District Institutes of Education and Training (DIETs) is negligible. Most institutions that offer teacher preparation programmes in ECCE, including the notified programme, are in the private sector and some of these have also sought and received recognition from NCTE.

Inequitable Distribution of Teacher Education Programmes across the Country

A recent study (2014) by the Centre for Early Childhood Education and Development (CECED), Ambedkar University, Delhi, on teacher education in ECCE indicates that there is an inequitable geographical distribution of teacher education institutions in ECCE, with the majority of institutions concentrated in Delhi and the NCR region, and in Andhra Pradesh and Telangana. There are very few institutions in the Northeastern part of the country, in Haryana, Himachal Pradesh and Punjab. In Gujarat and Maharashtra, which have pioneering institutions in the area of ECCE, the numbers are declining due to low demand as aspiring teachers do not want to pay the opportunity cost of a two-year Diploma if they can get jobs through shorter duration programmes, or without training.

Issues of quality and parity in teacher education

The above study also reports on the wide diversity in programmes that are being offered. On the one hand, the notified and approved duration of the ECCE Teacher Education programmes is two years; on the other, the private institutions, which are in the majority—including both recognised and unrecognised programmes—offer Diploma and Certificate programmes of varying duration, ranging from one month to two years, thus reflecting issues of disparity in certification and quality of training and a clear violation of NCTE regulations. Some other issues that the study identified include a lack of a clear and coherent vision among heads of teacher education institutions regarding ECCE, an absence often of any theoretical or philosophical framework guiding the programmes, dated curricula and conventional teaching/training pedagogy based largely on blackboard teaching and lectures. A major constraint reported in updating curricula was the lack of available reference materials on new theories and pedagogies which need to be incorporated in any update and the tendency therefore to fall back on the conventional. The teacher educators too in most cases lacked teaching experience which was a severe limitation. The study clearly indicated the need for stricter regulatory mechanisms to enforce the desired specifications.

Some Recommendations

Since the prevailing policy climate is moving in a favourable direction for ECCE and for preschool education in particular, with ECCE being considered for inclusion as a fundamental right, the issue of quality and professionalism of this sector becomes even more crucial. It is in this context that this paper makes a few suggestions and recommendations:

(a) *Institute positions of regular early years teachers in the system:* The early childhood years are the foundation stage in upward continuity with early primary grades in the NEP 2020. There is, therefore, an imperative need to move away from the existing concept of a multipurpose, minimally trained worker as service provider for preschool education, towards instituting regular positions in the system of teachers or educators equivalent to at least primary teachers for the foundational stage, with provisions of regular professional teacher development. The graduate degree proposed in the NEP 2020 would be a welcome reform in this area.

(b) *Set up regulatory and accreditation systems to ensure standards:* The National Curriculum Framework for ECCE (2013) was accompanied by Quality Standards for ECCE. These need to be expanded or adapted to address the early learning continuum from age three to eight years and used as reference for the regulatory process. These should be applicable across sectors and should include teacher eligibility and professional development aspects as also enabling conditions to support effective delivery of education in these foundational years. The recommendation in the NEP 2020 to institute a regulatory-cum-accreditation framework and mechanisms in the system holds promise in this regard.

(c) *Develop and support a comprehensive teacher education/ development strategy:* For both pre-service and in-service teacher development include initial training, need-based refresher programmes, on-site mentoring and supportive supervision systems and career progression pathways to incentivise quality and ensure teacher motivation as committed in the NEP 2020 for all stages of education.

(d) *Teacher development curriculum to be guided by vision for early years education and role of teacher:* The training of teachers should flow from a clear understanding and articulation of what is the desired vision and expectation from teachers at this early stage. Sahlberg (1997) makes an interesting comparison in this context between developing teachers as a professional and/or a skilled technician, with England at that stage focusing largely on teaching skills and assessment methods while Finland emphasised teacher autonomy and creativity. Developmentally appropriate curriculum in early childhood years requires more of the latter, whereas the current practice in India (as discussed earlier) is to resort to formal teaching of the 3 R's through rote memorisation. The need therefore is for a better balance of theory and practice with the intent of enabling deeper understanding among teachers of how children learn and ways to adapt the given curriculum to respond to individual differences and support-paced learning. This may involve moving teacher development into the higher learning institutional structures, as recommended by the Justice Verma Committee (2012) that was constituted by the Supreme Court of India.[2] The proposed reform by NCTE in teacher education of developing four years' integrated programmes leading to B.A., B.Ed. may be explored for an integrated approach to pre-primary and primary teacher education to address the transition in a more seamless and effective manner as the foundation stage.

(e) *Development of targeted programmes for preparation of teacher educators*: This is a key area of reform. When most teacher educators are not trained or experienced in the pedagogy of the early stage, the quality and efficacy of training and mentoring is significantly compromised. There is also a need to develop and make available texts for teacher educators on a regular basis to keep them updated in terms of new curricular thrusts and pedagogies. Involving teacher educators in curriculum development and supporting professional networks and opportunities could also be some significant steps forward.

Notes

1. Unfortunately, the recently approved New Education Policy (2020) has also skirted the issue of extension of RTE (2009), although it was mentioned in the first draft of the policy, and has failed to even discuss it.
2. Refer: Vision of Teacher Education in India: Quality and Regulatory Perspective. Report of the High Powered Commission on Teacher Education Constituted by Hon'ble Supreme Court of India; August 2012.

References

Barnett, S. B. & Nores, M. (2017). Costs and benefits of early childhood education and care. In Miller, et al (Eds.). *The Sage handbook of early childhood policy* UK: Sage.

Centre for Early Childhood Education and Development. (2011). Preparing teachers for early childhood care and education. Delhi: Ambedkar University.

Drury, D. (2011). The professionalization of teaching. *Education Week*, 30(36), USA.

Kaul, V., Bhattacharjea, S., Chaudhary, A. B., Ramanujan, P., Banerji, M., & Nanda, M. (2017). The India early childhood education impact study. New Delhi: UNICEF.

Kaul, V., & Sankar, D. (2017). Early childhood care and education in India. In R. Govinda, & M. Sedwal. *India Education Report*. India: Oxford University Press.

Karoly, L. A., Greenwood, P. W., Everingham S. S., Hoube J., Kilburn M. R., Rydell, C. P., Sanders, M., and Chiesa, J. (1998). *Investing in our children: What we know and don't know about the costs and benefits of early childhood interventions*. Santa Monica, CA: RAND.

Ministry of Human Resource Development. (2009). Right of children to free and compulsory education act. Government of India. Retrieved from- https://mhrd.gov.in/sites/upload_files/mhrd/files/upload_document/rte.pdf.

Ministry of Women and Child Development. (2013). National policy on early childhood care and education. Government of India. Retrieved from https://wcd.nic.in/sites/default/files/National%20Early%20Childhood%20Care%20and%20Education-Resolution.pdf.

Ministry of Human Resource Development. (2012). Report of Justice Verma commission on teacher education. Government of India. Retrieved from https://mhrd.gov.in/sites/upload_files/mhrd/files/document-reports/JVC%20Vol%201.pdf.

Ministry of Education. (2020). National education policy. Government of India. https://www.mhrd.gov.in/sites/upload_files/mhrd/files/NEP_Final_English_0.pdf.

Shonkoff, J., & Phillips, D. (2000). From neurons to Neighborhoods: The science of early childhood development. Washington DC: National Academy Press.

The World Bank and Boston Consultancy Group. (2016). Early childhood education in India: An economic argument. Paper presented at CECED Conference. New Delhi.

2

Higher Education in the Development of Early Childhood Professionals

Prerana Mohite

Early childhood programmes reflect a society's values and beliefs concerning children, families, and education. Embedded in communities, nations and cultures, preschools both reflect and affect social change (Tobin, Wu & Davidson, 1989). There is an underlying belief that the care and development of very young children was always considered the family's responsibility until the changing social setting (women in the work force, smaller families, emphasis on early entry to preschool, formal learning at a young age) demanded that formal institutions for care and education of young children be developed outside the family.

There is an intrinsic cultural belief and understanding that women are caring and loving and are gentle with children so they are best suited to become teachers/caretakers of children. Despite subsequent theoretical advances and research evidence related to fathers'/men's role and capabilities in caring for children, currently the profession of Early Childhood Care and Education (ECCE) is gendered in favour of females. Hence higher education programmes of ECCE are mostly restricted to women from the onset.

The early twentieth century was witness to the rise of the child study movement, the scientific study of the psychology of the child as well as the educational ideas of Maria Montessori. Both ideas have had an enormous impact on education of young children throughout this century.

In India organised education of the child below primary school age did not receive the attention it deserved until very recently. During the pre-independence period all these efforts were confined to the voluntary sector and ECCE received no support from the government. It was in 1944 that a government document, popularly known as the Sergeant Committee Report, emphasised, for the first time, the importance of pre-primary education and linked it with the child's educational performance in primary school. The report viewed pre-primary education as a necessary adjunct to primary education.

ECCE in the Contemporary Context

During the post-independence period, the movement for the education of young children drew great support from the private and voluntary sectors. Apart from its educational values, the welfare dimension also gained recognition. The country's Five-Year National Plans, while paying lip service to the need and importance of early childhood education, suggested no definite plan or policy in this behalf nor did they make substantial allocations for promoting this field. Many committees and commissions were appointed both in the education and social welfare sectors, but no systematic efforts were made for the implementation of the recommendations of these committees. The Fifth Five Year Plan was a noteworthy initiative with a provision for an integrated package of essential services to young children and pregnant and lactating mothers and the Integrated Child Development Scheme (ICDS) was launched in 1975 with 66 pilot projects. ICDS was broadly conceived as an integrated intervention strategy for the holistic development of the young child in the wider context of the family and the larger social group in which the child lives. The integrated package of services, of which non-formal pre-school education is one component, is delivered through the anganwadi (courtyard school) by an Anganwadi Worker who is picked from the community and given training for three months. ICDS is currently the world's largest community-based programme of early childhood development.

It has demonstrated that even a modest investment in child development goes a long way in developing human resources.

The importance of early care and education for children's lifelong learning has now been widely established and acknowledged. Evidence from research on critical brain development during early years and its long-lasting impact on further learning and development have made a clear case for providing quality early childhood programmes to children.

In addition to these research evidences, there are significant contextual factors and changing current social conditions which have challenged traditional views of childhood and children. These are:

- Smaller families
- Changing socioeconomic role of women (more women in the workforce)
- Growing ethnic diversity of developing countries
- Changing views on early education and the purpose of early education, with emphasis on early learning
- The need and demand for organised care of young children outside the family

In the context of child rights, holistic development of children across diverse situations and settings has been emphasised in all ECCE programmes and schemes. All these add up to a growing demand for ECCE and important consequences for what is expected of those who work with young children. Thus, the relatively new field of ECCE seems to have developed in a haphazard manner and has evolved with more of the welfare and later, developmental perspective.

Changes in the Field of ECCE in Response to Social Conditions

In a way, ECCE services have increased and expanded with numerous ECCE programmes that have mushroomed.

As demonstrated through scientific surveys and reports, these programmes do not have a unified approach and there are variations in terms of the content, pedagogy, age group, titles, teacher qualifications, eligibility requirement, age group of children and other parameters. Most programmes have developed their own in-service or on-the-job training. This situation has resulted in lack of minimum quality standards of ECCE. There are good quality programmes but these are few and isolated and cater to a small segment of the population.

The main concern for the country and all stakeholders is how to provide quality education to children? Several standards of quality have been worked out by reputed national institutions and international ones (such as UNICEF). All these quality standards have singled out 'a good teacher' as the cornerstone and key factor of a quality ECCE programme.

Given this situation, the key and primary task is to prepare a well-trained work force for ECCE at different levels. The challenge is why and how and who. What is the path ahead to address these critical issues? One critical factor with immense potential to augment the situation is the provision of higher education for the preparation of ECCE professionals of all cadres.

ECCE Programmes in Higher Education

Currently, there is an unprecedented demand for and a great diversification in higher education, as well as increased awareness of its vital importance for human, sociocultural and economic development, and for building the future. ECCE undoubtedly can be considered as the critical base across all parameters of national development.

At this juncture the key question that merits attention is, whether we have adequate number of quality education programmes in our system of higher education to prepare teachers who have the appropriate expertise and skills to work with young children.

Universities are considered the most effective institutions to implement programmes of ECCE, to provide a sound knowledge base and relevant practical, field-based experiences to students. The Maharaja Sayajirao University of Baroda is one good example. It runs several courses on ECCE at different levels. Other examples include School of Vocational Education, Tata Institute of Social Science (TISS); Ambedkar University, New Delhi; and Distance Education Course on ECCE run by Indira Gandhi National Open University (IGNOU).

Due to the absence of uniform qualifications and certification across the age span, programmes have adopted different approaches. Multiple programmes operate depending on the state polices related to teacher education, certification standards and requirements. To further complicate the situation, the titles of the degree/diplomas/certificate programmes often do not carry a clear indication of their content and purpose. Programmes bearing the same nomenclature may not share the same goal and may have different duration. There exists a network of public and private institutions of higher education that offer a complex array of early childhood programmes of degrees, diplomas and certificate courses of varying duration, content, and eligibility levels. Higher education institutes are not able to provide adequate number of trained teachers. There are no effective regulatory bodies or set of regulations to accredit and monitor such courses. This has led to the entry of private institutions to fill this gap by offering an array of ECCE programmes. Thus, multiple factors have contributed to lack of clarity and quality in many ECCE programmes operating across states.

There is an urgent need to explore the potential of higher education for ECCE programmes to build a clear vision and plan to provide good quality ECCE programmes across the age span of zero to eight years.

Thus, on the one hand, there is growing demand and expansion of different types of ECCE programmes, and on the other a lack of well-trained ECCE professionals. The call therefore, is for higher education institutes to initiate sound certificate, diploma, and degree programmes which can prepare good ECCE educators of different cadres.

ECCE as a Profession/Career

Most positions of ECCE workforce (day care workers, preschool teachers, supervisors, administrators, heads) do not prescribe well-defined requirements. Preschool teachers with postgraduate diplomas, or a certificate course (of varied duration) are not differentiated in terms of salaries, roles, and responsibilities. 'If I get a job with short term qualifications in ECCE, why should I do a degree or diploma course?' Such questions are often raised by potential candidates.

If students are not attracted to graduate or postgraduate ECCE courses, what is the motivation and viability for higher education institutions to introduce and run such courses? Also, there is an underlying sociocultural belief and view that 'working with young children does not require special knowledge or skills' and that anyone (particularly women) with limited education and training can deal with preschool children.

Such a scenario has a serious impact on the status of ECCE programmes in higher education for both the candidates seeking admission as well as for the higher education authorities. This situation is one of the most important reasons contributing to the weak status of ECCE programmes in higher education.

This is a broad perspective of the overall situation. An even more serious challenge is related to the existing courses, their content and pedagogy; there is a need to revisit and revise these to match them with the needs and requirements of a wide range of ECCE programmes, and most importantly, to upgrade the ongoing programmes and develop new ones that are in line with the holistic development of children.

We are all familiar with the manifold charges that are leveled against higher education training courses by different stakeholders and not infrequently by the very teachers who have had the benefit of this training. An analysis of these will help and guide in further directives. One common complaint is that the training provided in these colleges is not related closely enough to the actual work conditions of schoolwork. When the trained teachers pass out of their programmes, they are not able to translate their educational theories and principles into practice. Their knowledge of theory and of schoolroom practice remains confined in watertight compartments instead of mutually enriching and inter-penetrating each other. Inevitably, soon after being caught up in the treadmill of the school routine they fall into the traditional, often uninspiring methods of teaching and fail to bring fresh life and vitality into their class. Very often the teachers themselves complain that their knowledge of theory, laboriously imparted in college, has been useless because they cannot implement and translate these in the field in the existing preschool setup.

This leads to certain important questions: what have the institutions of training contributed to the improvement of preschool/ECCE education? Have they succeeded in creating among students a proper attitude towards their profession? In addition to the content and skills, have the pre-service programmes equipped them to be change agents? Who will infuse desired quality in ECCE programmes at the field level? Doesn't the professional education of a large majority of teachers stop as soon as they leave the college? What justification can one then offer for these training colleges and courses?

As one attempts to carve out a path forward, it may help to review recent research evidence and social changes that have important consequences for what is expected of those who work with young children; it may also be useful in working out future directions. A few highlights are collated and summarised below:

- Research has shown that the behaviour of the ECCE practitioners plays a key role and that it is linked with their education and training. This highlights the need for a system-level investment and intervention to build a comprehensive, holistic teacher development and capacity enhancement programme, thus fulfilling the essential requirement of high-quality teaching outcomes (OECED, 2005). Consequently, the qualifications, education and capacity building of the ECCE practitioners also form an important policy-level issue to be acknowledged and addressed at priority.

- Although the importance of well-qualified and well-trained staff has not only been advocated, but also agreed upon, there is a frequent resistance observed on the part of the government to raise the staff qualifications, because of the subsequent increase in remuneration and the overall cost of service.
- However, one must also take into consideration that research examining the perception—whether higher qualifications lead to better pedagogical practices—has revealed mixed results. While it is generally true, few studies have also shown that workers with bachelor's degrees were more effective practitioners. For example, the study by Siraj-Blatchford (2010) on effective provisions of pre-school education, England (EPPE), has also shown that the key contributing factors to high quality ECCE were related to staff with higher education qualifications, leadership skills and long service; support and handholding by the staff members with more experience and training to the less qualified staff with a focus on establishing good understanding of child development and learning.

It finds that the observed behaviour of less-qualified staff turned out to be positively influenced by working alongside highly trained staff (Sammons, 2010). The same has also been reiterated by some other studies and thus it refutes the general conclusion that universally stresses upon a proportionate relationship between higher education of

ECCE staff to higher pedagogical quality and subsequently to better learning outcome for the child.

As Early et al. (2007) aptly put it, teacher quality is a very complex issue. The relationship between the education level of the staff and the quality of classroom learning or outcome is not so simple. They in fact, studied the relationship between the two and found no association or contradictory association between them. They argue that an effort to increase effectiveness of early education will likely require a wide range of capacity building activities and support mechanisms while interacting with the children.

Sheridan et al. (2009) also specify supporting communication and interaction of the staff with children as an essential component to improve ECE pedagogical practices.

- Another important step towards addressing the quagmire of qualifications and their relationship with quality ECE education, could be to set standards not only for teachers but also for assistant teachers and directors in the ECCE programme accreditation system used in higher education.
- States continue to expand programmes for young children and their mothers; alongside, there is a need to ensure the professional development and accountability of the ECCE workforce.
- In almost all ECCE programmes in higher education, there is widespread agreement that field-based experiences are critically important for teachers working with children of all ages, to develop new teaching skills or improve existing ones. There is no broad standard of field experience, such as student teaching, for the preparation of teachers working with young children.
- In most states, examining bachelor's and master's degree programmes that are linked to state teacher certification standards, are more likely to require students to complete a student teaching experience than those programmes that

are not linked to certification. Across several programmes of ECCE in higher education, there are inconsistencies about the nature, timing, and number of practicum requirements for students' course of study. In order for early childhood practitioners to build an applied understanding of development and learning across the age spectrum, it is critically important that they engage in a variety of field-based learning opportunities. Most field-based experiences across teaching programmes do not have a focus on infants and toddlers; most focus on preschool or school-age children.

These highlights, neuroscience research on critical brain development during early years, the prevalent situation of the field of ECCE and its status in higher education as well as present sociocultural settings across India, all together will have to be taken into consideration in working out further directives to provide good quality ECCE programmes to all children across diverse settings.

In summing up the status of ECCE in India, it is evident that the discipline of ECCE has developed in a largely ad hoc manner as per the demands and needs of a particular social and educational context. Consequently, the higher education system has not been able to organise systematic programmes of ECCE. It is equally evident that ECCE programmes and centres are in much demand. The task ahead consists of myriad challenges requiring holistic and practical measures. Some reflections on the path ahead are presented in the next section.

The Path Forward: Some Reflections

Undertaking and planning the way forward is a major challenge and will require transforming policies and practices in multiple arenas, with the engagement and collaboration of diverse players and stakeholders. After three decades, the National Education Policy (NEP 2020) has outlined a new roadmap to overhaul

India's education system. It is heartening to note that among other aspects, the policy has recognised the significance of early childhood years as the foundation of individual development and learning path. It also promises to bring transformational changes to higher education. This will have important implications for the scope of early childhood education and may lead to expansion of this field. The need to initiate and engage in this task cannot be over emphasised as it will be an investment in children's development and learning, and in turn will lead to a better future for the nation.

It is time that higher education institutes understand and reflect upon the situation and begin planning in this direction. A threefold path is proposed in this direction.

1. To initiate and develop courses that can prepare a trained workforce of ECCE teachers, supervisors and administrators.
2. States need to develop adequate certification, regulatory mechanism and standards for initiating new programmes as well as for monitoring ongoing programmes.
3. Revisiting existing teacher education programmes and upgrading these by creating a unified approach to the preparation of educators working with children from birth through age eight.

More specifically,

- States can intentionally redesign their certification systems for early educators, so that the higher education system will adjust and make changes in the required course content, age group focus and field-based experiences (for example, the curriculum developed by GCERT (Gujarat Council of Educational Research and Training)).
- Till now emphasis was placed mainly on preschool age children in private settings, which affected only a limited segment of the ECCE workforce. There is a need to create a unified approach to the preparation of educators working

with children from birth through age eight for diverse ECCE settings.
- Revising the current system of teacher and administrator certification could erase disparities in professional expectations and preparation among age groups birth-to-age-eight spectrum and lead to clarification of purpose of ECCE higher education degree/diploma programmes.
- This will ensure clearer roadmaps for students who enroll in different programmes, helping them identify whether a course of study will prepare them for the demands of their chosen careers.
- Aligning content with evidence to strengthen content for infants and field-based learning experiences are equally significant. Many ECCE stakeholders emphasise relying on research evidence to guide ECCE policies, programmes and practices yet there is uneven application of such evidence across multiple domains of early learning and development of children, from infancy to eight years.
- Strengthening required content to align with research evidence on child development and teacher preparation, and equalising required content for all age group spectra will require us to define well-articulated expectations for ECCE higher education programme improvement and to support faculty to engage in appropriate programme improvement activities and professional development.
- Identifying leadership and committing resources to strengthen early childhood higher education will involve negotiating with the states, federal and philanthropic sources. Additionally, the resources may have to be relocated for quality improvement, for example, monitoring.
- It is very important to define and recognise required formal qualifications and professional development standards for ECCE workforce at different levels. ECCE qualifications indicate the recognised level and types of knowledge, skills and competencies that ECCE staff have

received. Formal education in ECCE refers to the level and type of education that ECCE staff pursue to acquire such knowledge, skills and competencies to work in that sector.
- Providing professional development opportunities to staff who are already working in the ECCE sector to update or enhance their practices, that is, in-service training, continuous education or professional training.

Undertaking and planning the way forward is a major challenge and will require transforming policies and practices in multiple arenas, with the engagement and collaboration of diverse stakeholders. The need to initiate and engage in this task cannot be overemphasised as it will be an investment in children's development and learning, leading to a better future for the nation.

To quote M.K. Gandhi, 'If we want to reach real peace in the world, we should start educating our children. Basic education links children, whether of the cities or the villages, to all that is best and lasting in India.'

References

Early, D. M., Maxwell K. L., Burchinal M., Alva S., Bender R. H., Bryant D., Cai K., Clifford R. M., & Zil, N. (2007). Teachers' education, classroom quality, and young children's academic skills: Results from seven studies of preschool programmes. *Child Development, 78*(2), 558–580.

OECD. (2005). Teachers matter: Attracting, developing and retaining effective teachers. Paris: OECD.

Sammons, P. (2010). The EPPE research design: An educational effectiveness focus. In Sylva et al. (Eds.), *Early childhood matters: Evidence from the effective pre-school and primary education project.* London: Routledge.

Sheridan, S. (2009). Discerning pedagogical quality in preschool. *Scandinavian Journal of Educational Research, 53*(3), 245–261.

Siraj-Blachford, Eram. (2010). Learning in the home and at school: How working class children succeed against the odds. *British Educational Research Journal, 36,* 436–482.

Sylva, K., Siraj-Blatchford, I., Taggart, B., Sammons, P., Melhuish, E., Elliot, K., & Totsika, V. (2006). Capturing quality in early childhood through environmental rating scales. *Early Childhood Research Quarterly*, *21*, 76–92.

Tobin, J. Joseph, Wu, Y. David, & Davidson, H. Dana. (1989). *Preschool in three cultures: Japan, China and the United States.* New Haven, Connecticut: Yale University Press.

3

The Role of NGOs in Developing ECCE Professionals in India

Experiences of Mobile Crèches

MRIDULA BAJAJ

The status of children in a society is indicative of the value it assigns to promoting and protecting their rights as citizens of that country. A just, democratic, and equitable society would, it is assumed, value the rights of children as human beings eligible for dignity and respect.

As mentioned in the National Family Health Survey 4 (NFHS) (2014–15), the current situation of young children in India where 36% are undernourished, 58% anaemic, 38% not fully immunised and 27% not enrolled in any preschool does not augur well for children as they fail to reach their full potential. This is possibly the result of the inadequate care and lack of early stimulation and preschool education that they would have been exposed to because of their parents' poverty and struggle for survival. Lack of adequate basic infrastructure, social security and poor early childcare services have contributed in large measure to the existing status of young children (Kaul & Sankar, 2009; UHDR, 1948).

Despite the increasing research evidence from developmental neurosciences which suggests that foundational competencies as a result of intense brain circuitry is constructed very early in life, the state has not taken advantage of the latest knowledge (Breur, 2000; Shonkoff & Phillips, 2000). Deprivation during this critical period of development in early childhood can have a lasting impact on the growth and development of individuals in later years (Centre on the Developing Child, 2007). As pointed out by Kaul & Shankar (2009), the economic benefits of investing in young children have demonstrated returns in the range of 7% to 17%. And yet India has failed to make the necessary investment to reap the benefits of this simple economically wise option.

If India is to take advantage of its demographic dividend, it is critical that every child gets an opportunity to develop to her full potential. Early investments in the foundational years have been found to cut down the cost of poverty alleviation programmes. It therefore makes sound economic sense for a country to make investments during the early years of childhood when the foundations for cognitive, physical, socio-emotional development and language are synergistically laid (NEP 2020).

It is important to bear in mind that optimum development takes place in a loving and supportive environment where physical and emotional care is provided together with adequate nutrition, health and opportunities for learning (Anandalakshmy, 1998). In most societies, the family is assumed to be the best option, but the state has an obligation to support the family to provide the necessary environment for childcare and development. As the child grows, the state needs to supplement the family's efforts with additional institutional support which should ideally be run and managed by ECCE professionals. In the light of the above, it is important to understand the state's role and responsibilities towards its youngest constituency and assess whether it is making adequate investments to develop ECCE professionals in India.

Commitments by the State

The constitutional framework of India provides every citizen of this country equality and a life of dignity. The Directive Principle 39(e) commits that 'the tender age of children are not abused'; and (f) 'children are given opportunities and facilities to develop in a healthy manner' with 'freedom and dignity' and are not exploited and abused. Article 47 directs the state to enhance the nutritional and living standards of the people. Article 45 of the Directive Principles lays down that 'the State shall provide ECCE for all children until they complete the age of six years'. *It was a promise, not an obligation.* In 2002, the 86th Constitutional Amendment made Education a fundamental right, but it left out ECCE from its ambit with a recommendation that a new Article 24A be inserted in the section on fundamental rights, providing the *right to care and protection and assistance in basic needs and protection from all forms of neglect, harm and exploitation* (Bajpai, 2006; Pratham, n.d.).

In response to the above constitutional commitments the Government has from time to time formulated different policies and laws to ensure that these can be fulfilled as promised. Whilst various articles apply universally, special laws and policies specifically catering to the needs of young children have been formulated and accorded legislative approval.

The right to food has specific articles focusing on the provisions for different age groups and the young child finds special space in terms of maternity rights, crèches and hot cooked meals in the now universalised ICDS programme (Sinha, 2016, p. 93).

The right of children to free and compulsory education (RTE 2009) addresses ECE under Section 11 of the Act. It states: 'With a view to prepare children above the age of three years for elementary education and to provide Early Childhood Care and Education for all children until they complete the age of six years, the appropriate Government shall make necessary arrangement for providing free preschool education for such children.' RTE (2009) while acknowledging the need for preschool programmes for children in the age group of 3–6 years does not include the age group of birth to three years in its ambit, nor does it commit to including education for the young child as a justiciable right for the under-six.

In 2013, a National Policy on ECCE was adopted which spelt out its holistic and synergistic nature, and laid down priorities and steps for its implementation. It clearly and unambiguously emphasised the need to provide for free, universal, inclusive, equitable and contextualised learning opportunities for laying the foundations to attain the child's full potential (p. 8). It further commits to universal access to quality Early Childhood Education by enhancing human resource capacities with systems for effective governance. However, without adequate provisioning for budgets and concrete plans this policy has failed to provide the impetus that ECCE clearly needed.

The importance of the holistic nature of interventions during the early years has also been recognised in the National Education Policy announced recently in July 2020. The policy proposes a bold departure in designing a new curricular and pedagogical structure, with a 5+3+3+4 design covering children from 3 years to 18 years. One of the major criticisms of this policy is the lack of clarity in working out the details or strategies for implementing and universalising the foundational phase of three years of preschool and two years of primary by 2030. The policy is also silent on the age-appropriate learning for the under-threes including the interventions required to build awareness and capacity among parents and other caregivers.

One of the most important elements of achieving universalisation and retaining the holistic spirit of interventions is the critical component of appropriately trained teachers and Anganwadi Workers. Here too, there are promises of professionalising the ECCE cadre, but the differentiation in the approach for preschools attached to schools and those being run in Anganwadi Centres merits serious reconsideration.

The ambitious Integrated Child Development Scheme (ICDS) launched in 1975, was a comprehensive programme designed in response to global research promoting integrated interventions for the very young. It has over the years spread to the far corners of the country reaching out to about 54% of mothers and young children (NFHS, 2014–15). It faltered in its implementation and failed to show the desired impact because of the limitations of an ill-equipped human resource which narrowed it down to a feeding programme. With multiple evaluations and efforts to revive the sagging scheme, the investment required to train the 14 lakh Anganwadi Workers (AWW) and helpers was not made. The failure to appoint a specially trained AWW for preschool education is another major reason for the abysmal quality of preschool education in the anganwadis. The ICDS also fails to address the comprehensive need of the under-threes, a period when maximum brain development takes place. It had during its restructuring almost eight years ago, planned for anganwadis-cum-crèches. Some states like Delhi, Rajasthan and Madhya Pradesh attempted to take this on. Unfortunately, due to withdrawal of support by the central government after a few years, it did not take off. In a situation therefore, where there are no arrangements for crèches, young babies, and often toddlers, by force of circumstances, accompany their mothers to farms and worksites or are left uncared for to the vagaries of the community and environment (Shonkoff & Phillips, 2000; UNICEF, 2016).

Other interventions planned for crèches through the National Crèche Scheme or through the sectoral labour laws like the Plantation Act, Factories Act and most recently the Building and other Construction Workers Act have also failed to have the desired impact. Most of the above could not be enforced as the provisioning had inadequate budgets, a faulty design which was dependent on the number of women workers employed and did not provide for a holistic approach, reducing the services to providing just custodial care (Pratham, n.d.).

Private ECCE Services in India

The private sector, in response to the increasing demand for preschools and day care entered the fray since it seemed a profitable venture. The nursery and kindergarten play schools provided services that were not only questionable but sometimes detrimental to the child's developmental needs. The sector is largely unregulated though attempts are being made by some states and regulatory bodies like the National Commission for the Protection of Child Rights (NCPCR) to issue quality guidelines. However, most parents are keen to give their children an early start and wish them to acquire reading and writing skills without realising the negative consequences this can have on them.

Addressing Issues of Diversity and Inequality

Issues of diversity, migration and vast inequalities across social groups continue to exist, leaving large sections of the under-six population bereft of any provisions during these critical stages when the foundations for health and learning should have been laid. The yawning gaps in the provisioning for young children affected by migration, displacement due to natural or human-made disasters and those with special needs throws up challenges for planning and managing programmes for the most marginalised sections of society.

In fact, the current policy framework, budget allocations and programmes are a patchy attempt to address their fundamental rights to survival, development, protection and participation. Within the above limitations, what emerges as one of the most significant determinants affecting adequacy and quality of services is that of adequate and appropriate human resource capacities to provide ECCE services to the most vulnerable and marginalised sections of society. Khullar (1991) identifies gaps in training as one of the most important factors responsible for the shortcomings in existing day care services. Bajaj (2001) reiterates that it is vital that the issue of training receives high priority as that alone can change the focus from providing custodial care to developmental care. Without a cadre of professionals in this area, the goals of enhancing quality cannot be accomplished.

Whilst the four-year degree course recommended for preparing Early Childcare Professionals in the NEP 2020 is laudable, the strategy and the necessary budgets required to achieve this are important. Whilst planning this exercise, it is important to bear in mind that some of the highly qualified workforce refuse to work in rural and tribal areas and it may be prudent to design courses that provide the necessary qualifications but also focus on enhancing capacities to engage meaningfully with young children who need concrete experiences to explore, innovate and create. The foundations for learning can be nurtured and facilitated by persons who have a genuine interest in channelising the interests of children through play activities. A more pragmatic approach would be to design modular courses which provide opportunities for upgrading qualifications over a period of time after workers have assimilated the importance of early childcare and development, are aware of what the age-appropriate needs of children are and have picked up the skills to provide the necessary opportunities for development of young children.

Given the growing demands for ECCE services, it is important to conceptualise and draw up a perspective plan to develop professionals to address the growing demand for a universal and quality ECCE programme for all children. It is also important to examine the kind of professional programmes that already exist for preparing professionals to work with young children and pick key strategies developed by other ECCE organisations.

Strategies and Methodologies for Capacity Enhancement in ECCE

Concerted and sustained investments to build capacities across all levels are required if one is to achieve universal quality ECCE programmes given the scale and complexity of the public delivery system. Extensive investments will be required to improve the delivery mechanisms, the management skills and training practices, if one is to address the human resource requirements comprehensively and train the different levels of personnel required to improve the quality of ECCE

- Service providers: for under-three and for 3–6-year-olds
- Supervisors, field trainers: for oversight and support for field services

- Administrators and managers: for planning, analysis, strategic oversight, facilitating governance
- Trainers: for designing and conducting capacity enhancement programmes for different levels of professionals
- Technical experts and academics: for curriculum design, research, policy, and strategic planning

The preparation for different cadres would need different inputs and training, including varied qualifications. All of them would require professional customised training which should be designed in a way that it prepares them to take on their responsibilities and roles to deliver what is expected from them.

The critical components required for training ECCE service providers are:

- Basic knowledge and understanding of the principles of child development, health and hygiene and the basics of teaching pedagogy
- Skills to interact with and play with children of different age groups, plan and organise activities, provide for their physical and medical needs, and maintain excellent community relations
- A positive attitude and high energy which reflects love and respect for children, creativity, problem-solving skills and a yearning for learning and self-improvement

The expectation from a person who is expected to provide comprehensive services for a child under the age of three would be different from a person expected to look after 3-6-year-olds.

Similarly, the content would need to be modified based on where the services are expected to be provided as the situation and context of an urban settlement would be very different from a tribal region. It would therefore be best if the service providers belong to the same community as far as possible and the training is designed in a way as to be 70% practical, and that gives them hands-on-experience, as they are the lynchpins around which the entire quality of delivery rests.

Training needs to take into account the background and literacy levels of the trainees and must incorporate experiential and participatory methodologies comprising role play, actual preparation of teaching materials, exposure visits and reflective discussions. On-site supportive supervision, collective sharing and problem solving are useful strategies that have shown appreciable results. The training design and content should necessarily incorporate the comprehensive nature of the programme and should therefore, integrate the necessary inputs of health, nutritional, cognitive and socio-emotional needs of young children as part of its curriculum. Since they are expected to work closely with the parents and community members, community communication would need to be integrated in the basic course design. This will enable them to respect the traditional practices and use them to bring about sustainable changes in the childcare practices of the family and the community.

Beyond the strategies employed to enhance the skills and knowledge of the personnel working directly with children, efforts need to be made to keep their morale and motivation levels high. As the quality of services rests largely with the service providers, it is necessary that they are provided with regular hands-on support and mentoring from their supervisory cadre. Clarity on roles, guidelines, protocols, and system support are other contributing factors which support the discharge of quality services in a regulated manner. Last but not the least, regular inputs and feedback should be sought to review and improve the quality of the services as their learnings from the hands-on engagement with children and community members in the field would be very useful.

The same would be true for the supervisory cadre: they too should ideally come with some field experience and the ability to link up with the local resources and stakeholders. Their training inputs would necessarily move beyond just understanding child development to having an in-depth knowledge of community dynamics, administrative systems, protocols, guidelines, and the ability to find solutions to problems. The expectation from them would be that they increasingly take on the role of a mentor and be the first port for solving problems especially for the 14 lakh Anganwadi Workers.

The managers, planners, and others, after postgraduate studies (advanced diploma, MA/MSc) in the core subject would have the option to move on to the specific field they would like to pursue, based on their abilities and interest. Apart from hands-on learning, they should have opportunities to hone and further refine their skills through specialised courses in policy and advocacy, research methodologies, curriculum development, etc. based on their specific interests. Modular courses in the field of ECCE can be designed leading up from certificate level courses to degrees and post-graduation and would allow a progressive pathway to upgrade their qualifications in the discipline.

It is increasingly recognised that ECCE professionals at all levels should be fully trained, adequately paid and supported with appropriate working conditions, equipment, materials, and guidance. A perspective plan for this discipline requires a detailed plan with clear time frames and involvement of multiple institutions including NGOs, universities, and other academic bodies to respond to the growing needs of ECCE.

Mobile Crèches

Capacity Enhancement Experiences

Programmes for preparation of ECCE professionals have been historically ignored and marginalised within the higher education landscape in India and are virtually non-existent and non-regulated even today. At another level, the voluntary and private sectors have taken initiatives to develop human resource capacities to enhance the quality of their ECCE programmes. Whilst these have the benefit of being culturally rooted and have provided evidence of increasing impact on the young child, these initiatives reach out to very limited numbers. However, important principles and learnings can be derived from the innovative capacity enhancement initiatives for scale-up by the government.

Some pioneering initiatives have been taken by some organisations to address the lack of availability of trained personnel and important lessons can be gleaned from their experiences. Different organisations have employed different strategies but most of them focus on 3–6 years age group whilst others only focus on the health aspects for the under-three. Mobile Creches over the last fifty years have undertaken customised trainings for a comprehensive ECCE programme for a diverse spectrum of children living in slums, construction sites, rural and tribal regions and for specific vulnerable groups like women living in prisons, working in tea plantations, etc.

A brief reflection of where and how Mobile Creches, an NGO that is a pioneer in the movement for ECCE, has contributed to building capacities, initially for the workers and teachers in direct contact with the children, then to the supervisory cadre and gradually to decision-makers both in the government and voluntary sector. They demonstrate the evolving and increasing maturity of their training capacities. The quality of the training can be gauged by the fact that the women who have been trained are willing to work in difficult conditions and display high levels of motivation, energy and a determination to carry on working despite the constraints of low and delayed remuneration and weak supporting systems.

Developing a Comprehensive Programme in ECCE and Seeding of Training Initiatives

At a time when there was limited understanding of ECCE and very few models with a comprehensive approach to provide services for the under-six, Mobile Creches (MC) was convinced of the need to provide an integrated programme which would address all the domains of physical, mental and socio-emotional development. Experts from the field of public health, paediatrics, nutrition, child development and Early Childhood pedagogy were consulted to develop a core programme which has stood the test of time. This has been refined at periodic intervals to keep abreast of the latest scientific advances and knowledge emanating from each discipline.

The foundations for training were established when the need for preparing more childcare workers for the organisation was felt and there were no recognised organisations offering such training. Secondly, it was important to continuously upgrade the skills and abilities of the existing staff. Experienced staff who had mastered the nuances of running crèches and had specific abilities of communication and facilitation, were selected to be further groomed in the techniques of training without labelling it as teacher training. As news of MC's programme spread and the need for quality ECCE programmes was felt by other organisations working with disadvantaged communities, a Training Department was formally instituted in 1989 with the sole objective of training staff of other organisations as also building a cadre of trained ECCE staff through a comprehensive two-year Bal Palika Training Programme. Keeping in mind the context, ground realities and formal evaluations, the duration was gradually condensed to nine months. Slowly, the demand for this too declined with low demand in ECCE and increasing opportunities from other disciplines like beauty parlours, computer operators and the services industry, till it was closed down permanently. Another group comprising experienced staff was identified to mentor and coach internal staff to ensure that internal capacities stayed in tune with successful practices and relevant researches in the field of educational pedagogy, public health and nutrition.

Developing Capacities of Other NGOs

MC evolved as it began to build capacities of other voluntary organisations like SEWA, Urmul, World Vision, SIDH and others to initiate programmes for the under-six for their own constituencies. In many of the organisations cited above, Early Childcare Education programmes were initiated after an in-depth needs assessment process. For each client, different issues and concerns emerged, based on which a training intervention was suggested.

With SEWA, where the focus was on encouraging and supporting women financially, the need for childcare emerged as a critical need. Mobile Creches with its long experience of setting up and running crèches in urban slums were ideally suited to replicate their model. However, the context was slightly different as SEWA insisted that the crèches should be self-sustaining to some degree. The parents would be required to pay a fee as the crèches enabled them to earn a livelihood. SEWA believed in the inherent capacity of women to organise themselves as *sangathans*, and left the decision making to them to ensure quality oversight and financial sustainability. This was a significant departure from the kind of training that MC had been doing till now. Community participation assumed significance in this engagement and was reflected in the amount and direction of training that took place at SEWA.

With Urmul, situated in the tribal belts of Rajasthan, the focus was on community development and empowerment so early child care education centres were planned as an essential component of community development. In this context, training was imparted to semi- and non-literate girls from remote villages where the training focused on hands-on learning, building skills, using local materials for play with the young children and ensuring that the interventions were holistic in nature. These were prolonged interventions stretching over 1–2 years during which organisational leadership in ECCE was developed to sustain the quality of the programme. On the flip side, the relationships ended as soon as financial support for the training came to an end. However, because of the long relationship, the organisational understanding on the importance of ECCE had been developed and they were able to sustain the programmes over a long period of time.

MC's engagement through training about 12 well-known organisations in the development sector revealed that organisations were unwilling to commit to initiating programmes for the under-three or for migrants because of the specific challenges that were inherent in working with this target group despite the fact that MC excelled in providing services for both these target groups.

Partnerships to Initiate Crèches at Construction Sites

This was a strategic attempt to expand crèches at construction sites as the need from builders emerged from other metropolitan cities and tier 1 towns. A few NGOs had responded with educational interventions for the older children only, as they had no internal capacities or inclination to initiate a comprehensive programme for the under-sixes. MC sourced funds to transfer financial support together with 'transferring the business' of running crèches to enable the organisations make the initiatives sustainable. The financial and technical support extending over 2–3 years made them ready to source funds independently on an ongoing basis, have a dialogue with builders, hire and train workers and provide the backend systemic support to enable them to provide quality services for the young children of migrant workers at construction sites.

Through this initiative, Mobile Creches was able to get organisations in Ahmedabad, Chandigarh, Bengaluru, Noida, and other cities to run creches at building sites with the active cooperation and collaboration of the builders there. In the absence of anganwadi and other services, this has enabled the expansion of the necessary support services for children of migrant workers and is a win-win situation for all the stakeholders.

Capacity Building of Government Functionaries for Running Crèches through the ICDS

The AWC was visualised as part of the restructuring exercise in 2008 to respond to the emerging need for day care especially for the under-three. The crèche would be an integral part of the existing AW centre and had the flexibility to accommodate 15 children for eight hours if required. MC with its vast experience had been instrumental in designing the scheme and felt equipped to undertake training of all levels of government functionaries. It also felt that through a process of setting up a few model AWCs and then building capacities of some key organisational representatives as well as strengthening existing systems, it would be able to demonstrate the systems required as also the impact before it withdrew after some time.

Initiating a dialogue with the state functionaries to sensitise and motivate them to agree and move forward in conceptualising a design was the first step in the process and was the biggest challenge! What followed was a collective process of planning for logistics, undertaking field visits to build familiarity with the geographical and cultural context. The next logical step of providing technical support to hire and train workers, provide support in the designing of space and procurement of essential supplies and materials was a logistical challenge as it transgressed into the state territory of hiring and procurement. Help to set up the crèches together with sustained support to get the community on board was followed by strengthening the supervisory and monitoring mechanisms. Regular meetings were conducted with the senior officials to facilitate convergence and strengthen governance systems.

MC was able to set up 23 AWC in Delhi, 57 in Rajasthan and 91 in Madhya Pradesh. These were huge successes and ran for a few years considering that there was a complete absence of the understanding of a crèche, its needs or benefits. The fact that they ran for 2–3 years and the childcare providers were willing to carry on working despite the fact that they did not get salaries for extended periods, stands testimony to the need for a crèche as also the quality of training imparted by Mobile Creches. Withdrawal and lack of government support for the AWC component in the ICDS programme ultimately led to the closure of this initiative.

The learnings from the above initiatives reinforced that skills and knowledge transfer can be undertaken even with semi-literate women but the real challenge lies in building motivation and positive attitude among the child care providers to deliver quality services in difficult circumstances for the marginalised sections of our society. Institutional support systems, and adequate and regular remuneration are required to nurture the childcare providers, for which commitment from the top leadership is essential.

The Way Forward

The setting up of the ECCE Council at central and state levels together with the Task Force for convergence, envisaged in the New Education Policy 2020 will go a long way in translating the strategies outlined for the Foundation Phase into a reality. The Plan of Action together with the Budgeting Exercise and preparation of the Human Resource required for universalising and transforming the ECCE landscape are critical steps that need immediate attention.

It would be advisable to glean important learnings from the capacity enhancement initiatives undertaken by Mobile Creches. Its five decades of leadership in the field of ECCE manifests a fine amalgam of training local semi-literate women for providing quality services with the backing of professionally run systems of supervision, monitoring, capacity enhancement and periodic evaluations. If the goal is to achieve universalisation of quality ECCE, then this strategy may be a sustainable possibility in the immediate term as developing and preparing courses with a four-year degree specialisation in ECCE may take time especially for the rural and tribal areas.

Capacity building and decentralisation are essential but not sufficient conditions for improved governance. There needs to be a central mechanism at the level of an ECCE Council that sets standards, maintains quality, safeguards equity concerns, redresses uneven development and allocates (and accounts for) resources in a transparent and equitable manner. This would require improved institutional frameworks, improved workforce management policies and professionalisation of management. Accountability at senior levels of administration and governance needs to be measured through appropriate mechanisms, subjected to public scrutiny and linked to flow of funds.

The multi-sectoral nature of early childhood development allows it to be anchored in different development goals of the different ministries including, but not limited to health, nutrition, education, labour, and social justice and empowerment. Major initiatives undertaken for poverty reduction, environmental sustainability, disaster reduction and communal harmony should have services for young children integrated within them. The Task Force envisioned in the New Education Policy 2020, comprising Early Childhood professionals, advocates and policy-makers from the different ministries, needs to work together in identifying ways and means to make sure holistic early childhood development becomes part of the national agenda. The stakes are high. They call for joint effort and commitment. Sustained advocacy through all possible channels is essential, including, and particularly, the national, regional and global consultations on capacity building to support quality ECCE services for the 157.6 million young children in India.

There is an urgent need to create a social and political will to invest in the children as it is time that India moves to planning for the ideal rather than adopting the minimalistic approach. The young child of India deserves uncompromised, unconditional access to universal, free, quality care, health and education. These children are citizens of today and adults of tomorrow: they will carry the India we build for them. India can only progress and prosper if sound investments are made for its human resource during their period of childhood.

References

Alliance for Right to Early Childhood Development. (2016). *Rights to the youngest: Towards a legal framework for early childhood development*. Books for Change.

Anandalakshmy, S. (1998). The cultural context. In M. Swaminathan (Ed.). *The first five years: A critical perspective on early childhood care and education in India.* (pp. 272–284). Sage.

Bajpai, A. (2006). Rights of the child: An overview. In *Child Rights in India: Law, Policy, and Practice.* Oxford University Press.

Bruer, J. (2000). *The myth of the first three years: A new understanding of early brain and lifelong learning.* The Free Press.

Center on the Developing Child, Harvard University. (n.d.). Brain architecture. http://developingchild.harvard.edu/science/key-concepts/brain-architecture/.

Centre for Budget and Governance Analysis. (2018). *Of hits and misses: An analysis of Union Budget 2018–2019.* www.cbgaindia.org.

Centre for Learning Resources. www.clrindia.net.

Datta, V., & Konantambigi, R. M. (Eds.). (2007). *Day care for young children in India: Issues and prospects.* Concept Publishing Company.

HAQ Centre for Child Rights. (2018–19). Budget for Children in #NewIndia. haqcrc.org.

International Food Policy Research Institute. (2016). The new challenge: End all forms of malnutrition by 2030. In *Global nutrition report 2016: From promise to impact: Ending malnutrition by 2030* (pp. 1–13). International Food Policy Research Institute (IFPRI).

Kaul, V., & Sankar, D. (2009). *Early childhood care and education in India.* World Bank. http://www.educationforallinindia.com/early-childhood-care-and-education-in-india.pdf.

Khullar, M. (1990). In search of relevant education: Occasional paper No. 17. *Sociological Bulletin, 39 (1 and 2).* Centre for Women's Development Studies.

Law Commission of India. (2016). *Early childhood development and legal entitlements, Report–259.* lawcommissionofindia.nic.in/reports/Report259.

McCain M. N., Mustard J. F., & Shanker S. (2007). *Early Years study 2: Putting science into action.* Council for Early Child Development.

Ministry of Women and Child Development. (2013(a)). *The national policy for children.* http:india.gov.in/national-policy-children 2013.

Ministry of Women and Child Development. (2013(b)). *National early childhood care and education policy.*

Ministry of Women and Child Development. (2016). *National plan of action for children 2016: Safe children happy childhood.* wcd.nic.in/acts/national-plan-action-children.

Ministry of Women and Child Development. (2017). *National programme for creche and day care facilities.*

Ministry of Human Resource and Development. (2020). *National education policy 2020.*

National Family Health Survey. (2014–15). *india.rehiips.org/NFHS?4shtmlindia.gov.in.* Pratham. https://www.pratham.org/.

Shonkoff, J. P., & Phillips, D. A. (Eds.). (2000). *From neurons to neighborhoods: The science of early childhood development.* National Academy Press.

Swaminathan, M. (1985). *Who cares? A study of childcare facilities for low income working women in India.* Centre for Women's Development Studies.

The Global Hunger Index. (2016, May). http://reliefweb.int/sites/reliefweb.int/files/resources/130918.pdf.

UNICEF. (n.d.). *Convention on the rights of the child.* www.unicef.org/crc.

United Nations. (1948). *Universal declaration of human rights.* www.un.org/en/universal_declaration_of_human_rights.

UNICEF. (2009). *Who cares for the child? Gender and the care regime in India.*

UNICEF. (2016). *The state of the world's children 2016: Fair chance for every child.* http://www.unicef.org/publications/files/UNICEF SOWC 2016.pdf.

World Health Organization, United Nations Children's Fund, World Bank Group. (2018). *Nurturing care for early childhood development: A framework for helping children survive and thrive to transform health and human potential.* Geneva: World Health Organization.

4

Continued Relevance of Nai Talim's Pre-basic Teacher Education Curriculum

Varadarajan Narayanan and Rajashree Srinivasan

In the 1930s, Mahatma Gandhi launched a comprehensive rural reconstruction programme, comprising work in the areas of health, sanitation, village industries, reorganisation and revitalisation of village institutions and education. The vision envisaged for work in the domain of education came to be called *Nai Talim*, an experiment that remained very active in the Indian educational scenario till the late 1970s. This essay explores a lesser discussed theme within this experiment: pre-basic education. This essay has two objectives: one, to provide a more expansive picture of the Nai Talim experiment beyond the programme for seven years of schooling that is widely known so that one recognises the place this experiment had for pre-basic education; two, aligning with the focus of this volume, to describe briefly the nature of the pre-basic education segment within Nai Talim and the teacher education programme that was developed to support this segment. Accordingly, this essay is divided into three parts. In the first two parts, we discuss the place of pre-basic education within the overall scheme and outline some of it features. The third part of the essay focusses on the features of the teacher education programme for those who would be involved in pre-basic education. The essay ends with the lessons these offer for the contemporary practice of early childhood education.

The Scope of Nai Talim

Heretofore, the 'story' of Nai Talim has been narrated focussing on three aspects:

(a) Gandhi's experiments in educating his own children and the children of members of the two communes he helped establish in South Africa, and the reflections on these that found concentrated expression in his writings from 1937 onwards as an educational programme for rural India

(b) the educational conference that was held at Wardha in October 1937, which led to the formulation of an elaborate and radically different programme for seven years of Basic Education, laid out in the report of the Zakir Hussain Committee titled *Basic National Education*

(c) following the adoption of this programme by the Indian National Congress and the formation of the Hindustani Talimi Sangh, the spread of Basic Education to several states and provinces, and their subsequent, but gradual decline after about two decades

While these aspects of Nai Talim are undoubtedly significant and cannot be ignored, exclusive focus on these have led to ignoring several other dimensions along which Nai Talim was sought to be developed.[1] Based on the experience of running Basic Schools in several parts of the country, in the early 1940s, the programme was extended to eight years (from age seven to fifteen). However, by the mid-1940s, the Nai Talim programme underwent three other very important changes. First, the eight years of school education began to be considered as only one segment or stage in the overall educational programme. Accordingly, work began to develop four more stages such that Nai Talim could now be seen as 'education of everybody for every stage of life': adult education, pre-basic education (for children under the age of seven), post-basic education (for those who have completed basic education and for a period of another three years) and a rural university (Aryanayakam, 1949). It was also argued that adult education would remain the most central component for Nai Talim, because the overall scheme as such depended on the participation and contributions of two institutions, namely, the family and the community at large.

Second, parallel to the development of curricula for these four stages (apart from Basic Education), efforts were made to strengthen the training of teachers who would be part of Basic Schools. The Zakir Hussain Committee had already developed a rudimentary programme for the training of teachers (Hindustani Talimi Sangh, 1938). However, in the wake of this expansion of scope of Nai Talim, efforts were made to develop separate teacher training programmes for each of these stages. In addition, the Hindustani Talimi Sangh also developed a community worker programme (*gramsevak karyakram*) such that its graduates could complement the work of teachers in working closely with the members of the communities and villages within which these schools were located.

Third, from its early formulations, Nai Talim required that the 'process of education throughout ... should centre in some form of manual and productive work, and that all the other abilities to be developed or training to be given should, as far as possible, be integrally related to the central handicraft chosen with due regard to the environment of the child'.[2] Whether this was indeed achievable for all subjects and for all grades and stages of education was a challenge that proponents of Nai Talim came to call the problem of correlation and this was something they consistently sought to resolve. In no way an easy task, especially given the abstraction that certain parts of some subjects inevitably contain, this led to the emergence of a large body of literature on this issue.[3]

Unfortunately, these three aspects have received very little attention from educationists apart from proponents of Nai Talim. In this article, therefore, we attempt to draw the attention of practitioners of early childhood education to the programmes of pre-basic education and teacher education for the same that were developed within the framework of Nai Talim. In the next section, we discuss some of the central motivations for the development of the pre-basic education programme and how these motivations shaped its very nature.

An Overview of Pre-Basic Education

Within the five-segment division of Nai Talim, the education of very young children was expected to cover the entire span from the moment of conception to the age of seven,[4] when the child would enter first grade of Basic Education. However, there were two other reasons for the development of an elaborate pre-basic education programme and, correspondingly, for the training of teachers who would work with children of this age group: one, that children of this age group were largely neglected by the existing system of education and, two, the recently introduced Kindergarten and Montessori scheme were largely urban phenomena, expensive and, for both these reasons, inaccessible to the rural population (Narulekar, 1950).

The pre-basic education in Nai Talim is organised around the principle of considering the school and the family as a seamless continuum. This continuum is not merely confined to the care and affection that the child would receive at school as she did at home. It is also expected that teachers and gramsevaks would be involved in ensuring the well-being of the family, especially the mother, and also that parents' involvement with the school would be no less significant. These expectations are vivified in the way pre-basic education is divided into four distinct stages and what is prescribed for each:

I. Conception to birth: focus is on the health of the mother, ensuring good diet and required activities, cleanliness at home and surroundings.
II. Birth to two-and-a-half years: the focus continues to be on health of the mother and child, their diet, helping mothers to learn to look after the child well and ensuring proper physical growth of the child.

III. Two-and-a-half years to four years: this is the stage when the child is slowly introduced to the environment of the pre-basic school and builds a relationship with the teacher. It is not expected that the child would spend long hours at the school. Rather, the child spends only as much time as she likes to, because the objective is to help the child become familiar with the environment of the school. For the child, this is also the period of sense-training and getting involved in a few purposeful activities.

IV. Four years to seven years: the child is expected to spend more time at the school, with involvement in directed activities and play; the focus is also on self-expression, habit formation, obeying commands; recognising objects around the school. This stage is characterised by the growth of the child into someone who can take care of a large number of things more or less by herself; this is also the stage when the child is slowly getting ready to be a part of the Basic School.

The syllabus for pre-basic education was envisaged as comprising five subjects: health and sanitation, water, food, creative activity and gardening (Narulekar, 1950, p. 27). Table 4.1 provides the list of activities in these five subjects that pre-basic education would focus on and what each of these activities are expected to result in, in terms of the child's learning. This table is also indicative of correlated teaching and learning. The activities mentioned in this table are based on the programme that was adopted at Sevagram. Programmes in pre-basic education carried out at other places may or may not be identical to what is provided here.

Table 4.1: *Child education at pre-Basic stage*

Activity	Material	Knowledge of Subject
Body cleanliness. Cleaning of teeth, hands and legs	Pot of water, bowl, soap, tooth powder, margosa stick, etc.	How to clean his teeth, nose, mouth and ears; how to wipe the body, gargle; consequences of dirty habits, diseases

(Contd.)

Table 4.1: (*Contd.*)

Activity	Material	Knowledge of Subject
Combing hair, cutting nails	Oil, comb, mirror, medicines for destroying lice, scissors, knife	How to clean and comb hair; how to keep nails clean
Washing clothes	Soap, soda, *rita* (soapnut), ash, bucket, basin, string	How to wash clothes clean, to dry, and to fold them. The knowledge of the material and how to use it
Cleaning the school: sweeping and dusting	Broom, basket and spade	Co-operative work; the importance of staying in a clean place; the effects of clean surroundings on health
Cleaning grain; removing husk and stones	*Sup*, basket, measure, and scales	Knowledge of different grains, measuring and weighing; some knowledge of farming
Storing and filtering of drinking water	Pot, lid, rope, and bucket; material for cleaning vessels, cloth for filtering water; tumbler	How to keep water clean; dirty water is the cause of diseases; names of diseases
Spinning, cleaning of raw cotton; ginning and sliver making	Mat, raw cotton, small rod, wooden plank, ginning machine, *takli*, basket, weighing scales, *dhanush takli*	General knowledge: arithmetic, language, knowledge of social behaviour
Creative play	Pieces of tile, coloured stones, wreaths; shells, mud vessels, pieces of wood, toy wooden cart; bamboo beads, flowers and leaves; bamboo scales, grinding machine and bags	Arranging playthings, takli-making, weighing, making clay pots, dividing things, grinding, filling, and bead-threading

(*Contd.*)

Table 4.1: (*Contd.*)

Activity	Material	Knowledge of Subject
Gardening	Spade, watering can, rope	Sowing seeds; digging, weeding, watering, knowledge of seeds, measuring ground, making water-runnels
Music	*Dholak, khanjari, kartal, ektar,* and gong	Songs, bhajans, acting, dancing and *tipri*
Drawing and painting	Wooden plank, mud bowls, colour, bamboo brush, earthen plate, coloured thread, paper, cotton, etc.	Painting, making designs with powder, handicrafts

The brief discussion on the scope of pre-basic education—working with mothers, children, the community at large and spanning aspects such as health and nutrition, hygiene, engaging with children on a range of activities to ensure their all-round growth—indicates that the demands placed on those, especially teachers at the pre-basic schools, are enormous. For the Hindustani Talimi Sangh, it was an imperative, therefore, to develop a specialised programme for teachers who would be working at pre-basic schools. The Sangh published an elaborate syllabus for this programme in 1945 and then a revised version of the same in 1953.

In this essay, we use the 1953 edition to discuss the syllabus for the preparation of pre-basic education teachers. The next section provides an overview of this programme, highlighting its central characteristics. It also identifies certain aspects that are still relevant for the practice and for thinking about early childhood education today. The entire text of the syllabus for this pre-basic teacher education programme is provided in the section four of this volume.

An Analysis of the Pre-Basic Teacher Education Programme

The pre-basic teacher education syllabus is titled *Pre-Basic Education: A Syllabus for the Training of Teachers* (TPbT) (Hindustani Talimi Sangh, 1953). The syllabus is divided into six parts. Part one outlines the principles and scope of Nai Talim. Part two deals with the scope of pre-basic education. Part three titled The Training Course for Pre-basic Teachers (TPbT), describes how the institution should be organised. Part four refers to the staffing and equipment requirements. Part five sketches the necessary qualifications for admission. Finally, part six details the programme of work and studies.

Institutional Arrangements

The teacher education institution, referred to as the 'training centre' or 'training institute' must be located at the centre of the village and serve as the village community centre. In alignment with the vision of pre-basic education that positioned the developing child as integral to the community, the institution was planned in ways that included various dimensions and actors of the community life, who could potentially influence the child's development and learning. It is to include a pre-basic school, a basic school, a child welfare centre, a child clinic and a crèche. The staff of the institution must include a psychologist, a specialist in adult education, staff of the welfare centre, clinic, school teachers and a principal of the institute. The building and educational equipment were to reflect local material and craftsmanship. Thus, the institutional arrangements of this teacher preparation programme were a comprehensive and contextual response that aligned with the aims of establishing the linkages between pre-basic education and adult education.

The concept of pre-basic education as proposed in Nai Talim makes severe demands on the teacher. The curriculum is established on the premise that the relationship between home, school and community is central to children's development and learning of co-operative values. The syllabus states, 'This educational programme includes the education of the entire village in happy, healthy and clean community life; education of the parents in wise parenthood, and of the children from the time of preparation before their birth until they reach the seventh year, when they enter the next period of their development' (Hindustani Talimi Sangh, 1953, p. 3). To realise the vision of this educative process, the syllabus sketches the capabilities to be developed through pre-service education. It explicates two dimensions: qualities and qualifications of the teacher. The former is emphasised based on the assumption that the teacher's personality is the 'greatest educational factor' for the child's development. Interest in the life of nature, making friends easily with parents, a calm and equable temperament, a gift for storytelling, music and artistic capabilities and 'sanitary conscience' were identified as some inclinations that the teacher may need to possess. In essence, 'he must be a real lover of children and must have a clear vision of the new social order, which is the goal of his work' (Narulekar, 1950, p. 38). The minimum qualification required was primary education and it stated a preference for those with two years of post-basic education or a course of gramsevak. Against this backdrop of the role of the teacher, the syllabus has been analysed along the following categories: i) values and the goals of the curriculum; ii) assumptions about knowledge and learning; iii) curriculum organisation; and iv) pedagogic approaches.

Values and Goals of the Curriculum

The pre-basic teacher education syllabus does not articulate explicitly the goals and values of the curriculum. It unfolds across various sections of the syllabus. The introductory message portrays *Nai Talim* as a system that challenges the conventional schooling system and aims to establish a 'new social order based on co-operative work for the good of all.' Aligning with these expectations, the syllabus (Hindustani Talimi Sangh, 1953) outlines the possible outcomes of the two-year programme as giving the student: 'A complete picture of the scope and goal of national development; he will experience for himself the meaning and the joy of education through work, and he will learn to understand and to identify himself with the new social objectives of Nai Talim' (p. 5).

Some broad principles that form the basis of this curriculum may be identified:

    (a) education should function as an instrument of social transformation, egalitarian order and national development

    (b) the educational processes of curriculum are to align with the chosen ideals and accepted principles of Nai Talim

    (c) developing sensitivity to the needs and interests of the child was critical

    (d) building a co-operative self-sufficient community as the basis of a democratic society and citizenship ideal was a central aim of teacher preparation

    (e) focus is on transforming experience into knowledge through 'work'

    (f) nurturing an identity shaped and influenced by the core values of Nai Talim

Assumptions of Knowledge and Learning

In the background of such a conceptualisation of human life, values and aims of teacher education, the TPbT recognised that knowledge and understanding of the student teachers were the outcomes of learning through 'work' in which the student-teacher is engaged. Knowledge is broadly conceived as patterns of activity or 'work' combined with thought and contributing to acting in the world. Developing a repertoire of ways of thinking, feeling, and doing things would allow the student-teacher to make an integrative understanding of his/her environment and identity therein, in order to prepare oneself for the 'new' social order. The TPbT, thus, sought to develop a repertoire of knowledge, skills, values, habits and dispositions through a carefully crafted syllabus that integrated theoretical knowledge across multiple areas with the student-teachers' own experiential realities and through such a process prepared teachers to achieve the goals of social reconstruction.

Curriculum Organisation

The section on 'Programme of Work and Studies' describes the architecture of the curriculum by outlining the design, approach and the relationship across different areas of study. The syllabus is divided into 12 sections. These could be referred to as areas of learning or study for a pre-service teacher.

1. Organisation of community life
2. Social training
3. Child study
4. History of child education
5. Basic principles and objectives of pre-basic education
6. Content of pre-basic education
7. Organisation of work
8. Cleanliness and health
9. Nature study (including gardening and care of pets)
10. Language and literature, including speech training
11. Music and rhythm
12. Art and crafts: creative activities and crafts suitable to children under seven

Although twelve distinct areas are recommended in organising curricular inputs for teacher education, it emphasises the interconnections between different areas. Similarly, it recognises that the sources of knowing and understanding exist in and outside the premises of the 'training centre'. It, therefore, devoted considerable space to discuss in concrete terms how the student-teacher would engage in the 'establishment of friendship with parents and the community' (Hindustani Talimi Sangh, 1953,

p. 8). While there is no clear 'stated' structure to the curricular areas, there are references to a sequence to be followed. For example, it states, 'the first practical programme before the training centre will be the organisation of community life: First, the small compact community of the students and staff of the training centre. Secondly, the wider community of the children, parents, and neighbours' (Hindustani Talimi Sangh, 1953, p. 6). The principle of correlation as an integration of productive activity with the academic subjects, which is envisaged in the pre-basic education curriculum is also set out as an expectation in the teacher preparation programme. For example, the work being done at the training centre is sought to be correlated with the larger community life. It is this principle of correlation that seems to also lend coherence to the curriculum emphasising that only when the interconnections between the pre-basic school, home, and the village and the training centre have been worked out that the new social order envisaged by Nai Talim can be achieved.

Pedagogy

Educational action is central to defining the TPbT syllabus. It recognises that education is action-oriented and 'the technique for the training of teachers for Nai Talim is work-centred' (Hindustani Talimi Sangh, 1953, p. 5). Education of teachers is attempted through a direct study of processes of education as they occur in the teaching-learning situations. At the same time, the syllabus clearly recognises that the pedagogical knowledge required to work with pre-basic children is expansive and hints at the need for conceptual inputs from various domains of study. A deeper understanding of the content and pedagogical processes of working with pre-basic children is sought where 'theoretical studies must evolve out of the problems of actual work' done by the student teacher. The pedagogic approach in the TPbT hints at employing tools and methods of the various curricular areas to help synthesise the conceptual inputs and action-orientedness in order to help the prospective teachers understand the continuum of pre-basic education to adult education.

Relevance of the Curriculum in Contemporary Contexts

The pre-basic education proposed by Hindustani Talimi Sangh encompasses a broad vision that sought to bring alignment between the parents, community and teachers in the care and development of their young ones. As outlined in the preceding analysis, the central focus in the curriculum was on developing capabilities among student teachers to work with parents and community. It is critical in today's context too for two reasons. First, anganwadis and balwadis are attended by young children of the poorest of our nation, whose development and learning requires close attention and whose parents too require education in health, sanitation and care. Therefore, teacher education programmes need to emphasise the continuum of adult and children's education. Second, the synergy across the triad (home–school–community) gains prominence in the light of the National Education Policy (Government of India, 2020), which recommends the beginning of schooling at three years of age.

Transitioning to regular school life as early as three years certainly demands that schools work towards a congruent relationship between parents, teachers and the community. These dimensions need to be engaged in great depth and detail in teacher preparation today. The TPbT syllabus, developed over seventy years ago, offers significant pointers to early years teachers, teacher educators, curriculum designers and policy makers on the centrality of parental involvement and community engagement in the education of teachers and children.

Notes

1. This is the case with almost every historical account of Nai Talim, including those written by people were closely associated with running basic schools. Consider, for instance, Marjorie Sykes, *The Story of Nai Talim: Fifty Years of Education at Sevagram (1937–1987)*. Wardha: Gandhi Seva Sangh, 1988. Sykes does mention efforts made towards

the four new segments and also teacher education mentioned in this paragraph. However, what Sykes writes about these hardly helps understand the details of these programmes, especially their curricular aspects. Other accounts follow Sykes without exception. See also the more recent Ramesh Pense. *Nai Talim: Gandhi's Experiment with Truth in the Realm of Education.* Sevagram: Nai Talim Samiti, 2012.
2. The finest account of the problem of correlation and ways to resolve it. See Ramanathan (1962), Chapter 15 and 16.
3. This excerpt is from the text of the resolution passed at the Wardha Educational Conference, October 1937. See Hindustani Talimi Sangh (1938).
4. This indirectly reiterates the emphasis on adult education because given that a child at this stage of her life would spend more time at home than at a pre-basic school, it was important that parents and the family at large were both well-informed about and involved in bringing up the child.

References

Aryanayakam, E. W. (1949). *The story of twelve years.* Hindustani Talimi Sangh.

Hindustani Talimi Sangh. (1953). *Pre-Basic Education: A syllabus for the training of teachers.* Hindustani Talimi Sangh.

Hindustani Talimi Sangh. (1938). *Basic National Education: Report of the Zakir Hussain Committee and the Detailed Syllabus with a Foreword by Mahatma Gandhi.* Hindustani Talimi Sangh.

Ministry of Human Resource Development. (2020). National education policy. https://www.mhrd.gov.in/sites/upload_files/mhrd/files/NEP_Final_English_0.pdf.

Narulekar, S. (1950). *Plan and practice.* Hindustani Talimi Sangh.

Ramanathan, G. (1962). *Education from Dewey to Gandhi: The theory of basic education.* Asia Publishing House.

Section 2

Curriculum and Programmes for Pre-service Teacher Preparation

5
Curriculum and Pedagogy for Early Childhood Professional Development

Kinnari Pandya

'Teaching is a complex process' is a notion that is well argued and widely accepted. However, this notion differs based on 'grade levels' a teacher is expected to teach. For instance, it is a belief that complexity involved in teaching increases from lower grades to higher grades. It is important to rearticulate this and recognise that each stage or grade has its own unique complexity and challenge, and that the teacher needs to respond to this complexity.

It is widely believed that in order to work with children below eight years, a person only need enjoy working with children, should have worked with children, be mothers themselves, and know some singing and theatre. If one has prior experience of being a teacher or knowledge about child development, and has basic English proficiency, it works to one's advantage at the time of recruitment as an ECE teacher. We often see that teachers who work with young children have qualifications ranging from high-school to graduation with child development degrees or trained in a specific philosophy of ECE with a teaching certification.

Most teachers with characteristics described above undergo in-service training for the duration of four days to a month, or six months, depending on the sector they have joined as early years teachers. Such beliefs about the non-significant prior knowledge base that early years teachers require, the intensity and duration of their training, the attributes of the teachers, and the responsibility they hold for developing young children's capabilities is a reflection of the overall ECE profession, and is seen as second to the mainstream school teaching both as a profession and in terms of status.

Recognising the increasing need for quality early childhood teachers and professionals working in the space in our country, the Azim Premji University launched a specialisation (a set of courses) in Early Childhood Education (ECE) in 2015 within its Master of Arts in Education programme. This curriculum was developed by a group of experts in ECE, faculty teaching child development and learning courses, and with several years of experience as practitioners themselves. The Master's programme aims to prepare professionals for a wide-ranging work profile such as curriculum developers, teacher educators, policy planners and analysts, and researchers to contribute to improving the status and quality of education in the country. This paper presents a curriculum for preparing ECE professionals to work across the spectrum and elucidates the core theoretical considerations for a curriculum for early years educators, illustrating the ECE specialisation offered at Azim Premji University.

Curricular Framework for Early Childhood Professional Development

Imagine the role of an early years teacher at her ECE centre.

On a Day-to-day Basis

She needs to prepare her class environment, organise materials, welcome children, draw up the activities based on the existing curriculum, engage with children, all in a calm, patient manner and seeing her role as a facilitator documenting children's work, plan for the next day's task, work with her assistant teacher as a team, and so on.

On a Periodic Basis—Weekly or Monthly

The teacher needs to spell out in detail the curriculum activities that she wishes to engage children in, plan for organising the activities and materials, assess children's development and learning, share children's progress and concerns in parent-teacher meetings, organise health check-ups, field trips and nature walks, planning and reflection sessions with her colleagues.

On an Annual Basis

Consolidate the progress of each individual child and the whole class through the year, plan and revisit the curriculum (what went well, what needs change), new ideas to be incorporated, organise annual day/mela where parents and community can come together, in-service workshops for self-development, and so on.

Further, several teachers, as practising professionals themselves, document their everyday experience in the form of a reflective journal that would be a compilation of their work done through the years.

In order for a teacher to perform her role in an effective manner, it would be useful to understand the pre-requisite knowledge, skills and disposition she would need before she begins her journey as a teacher. A teacher educator would need to understand and should be able to do everything that a teacher is required to do as a part of her role in a school set-up. Further, the teacher educator must have advanced level of conceptual knowledge to enable her to guide the process of curriculum development, mentor the teacher on-site with demonstration and reflection, be able to conduct studies and document the journey of a teacher. A teacher educator in the role of an educator would need to actively engage with theories and practice of teaching, and explain the complex interplay of theory and practice in a meaningful manner to the student teachers. An informed teacher educator would further be able to ask meta-questions, engage in research, generate new knowledge with the insights from her experiences as a teacher, teacher educator and her experiences with teacher students.

Figure 5.1 suggests the overlap in preparation required for teacher and teacher educators to perform their roles effectively.

The figure below indicates the common core of a teacher's and teacher educator's knowledge, skills and dispositions.

Figure 5.1: *The overlaps and distinctions in knowledge, skills and disposition of a teacher and teacher educator*

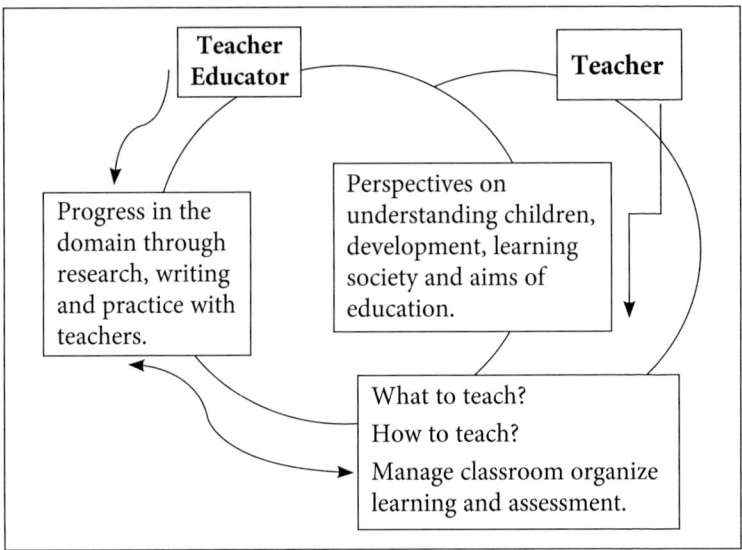

For instance, the knowledge in terms of perspectives on child development, learning and societal structures and aims of education are central to the process of teaching learning and therefore form the core knowledge base for teacher educators and teachers. A second key element of the common core is what to teach and how to teach. The tools to make the judgement on curricular and pedagogic decisions ought to be available to both teachers and teacher educators through their understanding of the role of teacher's practice inside the classroom. Similarly, the dispositions required for organising learning, managing the classroom, ways of assessment based on purpose of assessment form the common core for teachers and teacher educators. Perhaps the only key distinction between the teacher educator's knowledge base may be the extended engagement with research outside of the teaching-learning process. Professionally trained teachers interested in self-growth and furthering the quality of their practice would also engage with research questions and advanced literature pertinent to enriching the classroom practice. However, the contribution of such research work is often not available to wider stakeholders to further the practice or the understanding of education domain.

What happens inside every classroom with children is unique to the experience of a teacher and the children therein. However, when you look at the same experience through a lens of psychological, sociological and philosophical perspective, then the theory in practice provides an enriched view of the theory itself. Similarly, when a teacher educator works with to-be-teachers in the teaching-learning process, the experience of building practical skills through already used pedagogic ideas often provides a new insight to the practice itself.

The above idea is aptly captured in this statement 'Education as an area of interdisciplinary knowledge is not merely an application of a few core disciplines, but a praxis and a context where theories and practical wisdom are generated continuously.' (NCFTE, 2009).

It highlights that the practice of teaching is central to the process of education where existing knowledge from core disciplines is applied, relevance of theoretical ideas and practical insight is continuously discovered, and newer wisdom generated. While the core disciplinary knowledge for teachers and teacher educators may be similar, in their respective practices as teachers and teacher educators, this knowledge has a meaning associated particular to that context.

FRAMEWORK FOR TEACHING–LEARNING AND CURRICULUM FOR EARLY YEARS EDUCATORS

The next section of the paper discusses the Framework for Teaching-Learning by Linda Darling-Hammond (2005) that is relevant to all education programmes. Further, this framework is mapped to the Early Childhood Education specialisation offered at Azim Premji University.

The Framework for Teaching–Learning can be understood in the context of formal preparation of teachers for the practice of teaching. This framework suggests three key components that are central to a programme in education visualised for professional practice of teaching, where learning for children and systems of education are laid in a democratic socio-political sphere.

Knowledge of learners and their development in a social context: it includes understanding of learning, human development and language of learners

Knowledge of subject matter and curriculum goals: educational goals, purposes of skills and understanding subject matter.

Knowledge of teaching: questions on the how of teaching, teaching subject matter, teaching diverse learners, assessment and classroom management

Each of these components intersect and guide the professional practice of a teacher. Learning is assumed within a democratic societal framework that would overlay a range of principles for understanding learners, subject matter knowledge and the idea of teaching.

An illustrative curriculum model of pre-service professional development of teachers for early years educators followed at the Azim Premji University between 2014 and 2021 is discussed below. Most curricula for professional development of practitioner will and should look at each of these components.

Early Childhood Education Specialisation

The Masters in Education programme is *not* a teacher preparation programme; however, our alumni often choose to become teachers for different grade levels and experience the praxis of theory and practice discussed above.

The first year of the two-year programme in education focuses on building core foundational knowledge through different disciplinary perspectives: understanding questions on the nature and purpose of education, child development and learning, understanding the sociological aspects of educational processes, schools and the schooling system in India, curriculum studies, history and political economy of education. As one can see, the programme is primarily for non-teachers, and therefore has several conceptual courses that will help students to locate education in a broad human-social-political-historical-economic spectrum.

In the second year of the programme, learners have to choose an area of interest, wherein they extensively study a specific subject area such as language pedagogy, science education, mathematics education, teacher professional development, early childhood education, school leadership and management—all of which broadly focus on the school years. This one-year specialisation in Early Childhood Education aims to help learners:

- Develop a comprehensive understanding of the development of early child education as a field; the historical and contemporary relevance and significance of ECE
- Gain an overview of various policies, programmes and schemes pertaining to early childhood education in India and critically analyse them
- Plan and implement curriculum and pedagogic practices that are developmentally and culturally appropriate
- Develop capacities of the learner to work with children, families and communities through direct engagement with the field
- Forge linkages between curriculum and pedagogy in pre-primary and early primary education

Source: MA Education, Early Childhood Education specialisation document, Azim Premji University, 2014.

Knowledge of Learners and Development in Context

Knowledge about learning, human development and language is central to understanding the role of an educator in the domain.

Child Development and Learning is among the core courses that develop theoretical ideas such as understanding growth and development of children, domains of development, process of learning in children, factors influencing children, theories of child development for all domains of development (social, emotional, cognitive and moral development), role of play in child learning and development, and other psychological processes such as motivation, intelligence, memory and conceptual development.

The ECE Specialisation: The courses in the ECE specialisation build on this overall understanding of child development and focus on learning and development for children below 8 years of age. The courses focus on characteristics of young children, significance of early years, nutrition, health and social wellbeing in young children's development, the developmental processes that each domain encompasses, the role of development in learning and of learning in development, development of language and the role of a multilingual environment in early years, atypical developmental pathways for each domain, the role of early identification of disabilities, and so on.

Knowledge of Subject Matter and Curriculum Goals

The second key component for developing professional knowledge among educators is knowledge of subject matter and curriculum goals, and consists of educational goals, purpose of skills and expertise in content and subject matter.

The core foundational courses in the MA programme develop an overall understanding of the nature and purpose of education, forms of knowledge, various sources of curricula, assessment and the cycle of planning educational content and skills for each stage of development.

The ECE Specialisation: The ECE specialisation draws upon the ideas in the core courses on philosophy and curriculum studies and extends the understanding to the domain of early years. The various philosophical ideas on the notion of child, childhood, role of caregivers, different approaches to Early Childhood Education, principles of educating young children that emerge from these, implication of these ideas and positions on care and education of young children on various national and international policies and programmes, form the thrust of the specific courses in the specialisation.

An extensive course on curriculum and pedagogy for early years education delves deeper into the notion of curriculum for young children, the sources of curricula that are informed by developmental theory, context and culture, the child and the others in the child's environment. The understanding of a curriculum for providing optimal development opportunities to children as against preparing children for schooling is the thrust of the early years curricula. Play- and activity-based pedagogic approaches to enhance development in each domain are enumerated, and activities planned and tried in the context of Anganwadi Centres. The core of preparation for teaching learning 'experiencing being with children, planning and implementing a teaching plan, reflection on the plan, and oneself' for teaching is the highlight of this component. The nuances of early years curricula and perspective is further enhanced through looking at various key approaches to ECE that have emerged and evolved across the globe—curriculum models for early childhood development such as High Scope, Reggio Emilia, Project Approach, Montessori model, and so on. Visits to schools that follow these philosophies enable students to see the practical application of these models, and their strengths and limitations, and scope to adapt these to other contexts. Preparation of some key skills and interlinkages with children's engagement in music, movement and creativity is also emphasised through this component. Separate courses on children's literature, conceptual development in young children and arts in early years offer in-depth insight into critical aspects of early years curriculum, pedagogy and learning. One of the critical aspects is to see the continuum between early years education and early primary grades teaching-learning. Aspects of transition and ideas of 'readiness'—ready children or ready schools or both—need attention in a curriculum for early years and therefore, preparation of teachers and teacher educators for working on these aspects.

Knowledge of Teaching

The third key component of a professional development programme for educators is the knowledge of teaching. Knowing about teaching (meta understanding), and teaching (practice) are interlinked aspects for teacher educator preparation. The MA programme in its design to prepare a range of professionals provides choices to students to engage with specific courses and field-based experiences on teachers, teaching, assessment and inclusion at the school level.

Given the nature of knowledge required for early years professionals, and the overarching relevance of teaching experience for teachers and teacher educators, one of the key and unique features of the specialisation is direct teaching experience for all students. Students are required to engage with direct teaching experiences in Anganwadi Centres, which provides exposure in preschool classrooms and encourages reflective practice through journal writing and discussions that establish the connect between theory and practice of teaching.

The practical experience of teaching would allow for students to plan and implement curricular content first-hand. Nuances of classroom management that require planning, preparation for transacting curricular content, development of teaching learning material that is low-cost, contextual and age-appropriate, and assessing if the teaching efforts have led to children learning or experiencing the curricular content, are all brought to the fore. It also provides an insight into creating an unbiased environment for all children in the classroom, and promoting sensitivity to issues relating to gender and special needs, among others. This teaching experience is supported by preparation that runs through the semester and courses offered; it also informs students about theoretical models and concepts that exist for each: for instance, the anti-bias curriculum, ideas on inclusion, introduction to special needs, working with diverse learners, play and activity-based pedagogy, curricular frameworks, and so on.

Further, as teachers and teacher educators, research methods such as systematic observation of children so that we can assess their progress in learning and development and reflect on the overall ECE programme itself, are crucial and offer critical knowledge base. The curriculum of the specialisation lays specific emphasis on the concept of assessment, the cyclical process of curricular planning starting from aims of the curricula, the content for young children, pedagogy and assessing young children. Through the component of understanding assessment for young children, students actively explore topics such as documenting young children's experiences, preparing anecdotal records, observing children, using and creating developmental checklists, other forms of continuous assessment, documenting children's learning through portfolios, and so on.

Further, a yearlong experience of engaging with the field through systematic research orientation is available through a 'field internship' that involves writing a proposal, developing tools and plans, implementing the plan or collecting data, analysis and reflection, followed by writing and presentation of the study.

Through this component learners can explore a range of topics such as play- and activity-based teaching, action research on experiencing teaching, developing a curriculum and trying it out, comparative study of preschools that follow different philosophical models, ethnographic experience of work in an Anganwadi Centre and reflections on the life of Anganwadi Teachers and challenges faced by them, best practices by organisations in the ICDS system, studying the various ECE models of Islamic preschools, and so on, through to exploring their own interests, or working on specific topics suggested by the organisations where they intern. This experience provides an opportunity to systematically plan, implement and reflect on several aspects related to early years education in the country. This engagement on a specific topic, brings the praxis of theory and practice to life for several to-be professionals, helping them generate new knowledge, as well as reflect on existing theory. Through the courses on research methods, curriculum and pedagogy for early years education, ethics when working with young children is deliberated upon, preparing students to work as responsible adults and caregivers in any context as a professional. The understanding of ethics is further strengthened through the practical experiences the students engage in through their two years of the programme.

Darling-Hammond's (2007) Framework for teaching-learning elucidates the various curricular components that define the key features of a programme for education professionals. It further reaffirms the scope to formalise the domain and to view professional development and professional practice of early years professionals as equal to upper-grade teachers, if not higher.

Pedagogy for Adult Learners

A central principle that influences the pedagogy for adult learners is the 'practical personal knowledge' that they bring with them. In order to help adult learners reflect on their own beliefs and experiences, it is critical to build on the prior knowledge of the adult learners. Students enrolled in the programme are usually of age 25 years or more. This group of learners would have themselves experienced a certain kind of early years programme, perhaps several years ago, or would have been parents, teachers, or have known others who had enrolled in some kind of ECE programme.

It therefore became critical for us as faculty members to ensure that our pedagogy involved ongoing reflection—both on new theoretical ideas, and fresh practical experiences provided through the programme. To 'hear' adult learners, and provide validation to their prior knowledge, by listening to their narratives about self as teacher/practitioner, is a practice that faculty members saw as valuable. It reaffirmed the idea that adult learners are 'co-teachers', and their own sharing is also a reflective exercise for them as well as a learning moment for peers.

Another feature that ensures adult learning is to provide fresh experiences. We often come across adult learners who are comfortable with their world view or space—schools, people, environments they have already worked in, and would want to go back to the same space over and over again. In order to ensure that students come out of their comfort zones, and explore newer ideas and spaces, some tasks are are designed that require students to explore a range of unfamiliar settings. This helps learners' introspect on their understanding of a concept or philosophy. For instance, a student who has prior experience of working in a Montessori setup may prefer to work on assignments and field experiences on the same method. Such students would be consistently encouraged to explore other models and spaces where ECE is offered and reflect on their prior experience with a fresh insight.

Along with encouraging a variety in experiences to broaden students' perspective and scope of the domain, the option of going deeper into an idea or question of interest is available to students. For instance, the field practice experience is a platform for a student who wants to understand how organizations run large scale programmes for early years, or how one can work with diverse learners, especially children from lower socioeconomic backgrounds, and so on.

Due to one's own experience most adults have some idea, right or wrong, about what an early years curriculum should be like. However, it is only through experiencing the process of developing curricula and trying out activities through planning and teaching that one realises the complexity involved in this process of teaching-learning, guided by theory that makes the movement from naïve to expert professional possible.

This element of professional preparation for educators is an important part of the programme pedagogy. Students who have been through the specialisation have often shared that the pedagogic practices followed have helped them understand themselves better, and their own biases while working with children. Ongoing reflection through classroom sharing and journal writing provide the opportunity for reflective practice—a critical attribute for developing professionals with an attitude for life-long learning.

Adult learners, especially in a master's programme, come with a certain idea of what professional role they would like to take up after graduating from the programme. Since the vision of the programme is to prepare a range of professionals who could contribute to education as a domain, the assessments within the courses and pedagogy, especially in the specialisation, are planned considering the future roles the students may play as professionals. For instance, in order to prepare students to be curriculum developers, an exercise in curriculum development that is guided through close supervision is given. Similarly, preparation of a short in-service training module, or peer-teaching to prepare students to work with adult learners, independent teaching, research and documentation, are some of the specific techniques used in class as assessed or non-assessed components.

'Group work' and interpersonal skills are essential professional dispositions required among adult learners. Several experiences are planned to enable students to work in teams, and opportunity provided for reflection on group dynamics and working with people of different temperaments. For instance, an art fair/mela is organised by students each year as a part of their coursework wherein they must engage with kindergarten children and teachers of a local school in art activities through the day. The event is a culmination of theories of development, play and art-based pedagogy, and involves several days of planning and preparation to work with school children.

Mentoring and supportive supervision is critical for continuous development of an individual. Ethics of care, considerations for student's interest and strengths, planning and support for placements, continuous in-depth guidance by faculty members who supervise the internship projects are seamlessly interwoven through the student-teacher relationship developed during the specialisation and MA programme.

These pedagogic practices for working with adult learners need to be contextualised based on the target group's prior knowledge, and the objectives of the professional development programme.

The students who have completed the programme perform a range of roles in the ECCE sector. It has reaffirmed the idea that the core conceptual aspects of the curriculum and pedagogic practices would remain the same for early years teachers and teacher educators' professional development programmes. The extent and depth of the engagement will vary depending on the context.

Signficance for Implementation of National Education Policy, 2020

The specialisation in Early Childhood Education offered within the Masters of Arts in Education since 2015 at Azim Premji University brought early years into the realm of overall educational and schooling spectrum, considering the critical need to view education in a continuum from kindergarten onwards; this aligns with the vision the National Education Policy 2020 has laid out for school education in India.

The policy focuses on providing quality Early Childhood Care and Education for all children of India. This indicates a need for prepared teachers and teacher educators who are equipped to provide quality ECCE programmes. The curricular framework and specific components discussed in the paper provide a framework for development of all ECCE professionals. While the programme illustrated here is a full-time degree programme, similar curricular structure and principles can be followed for short-term programmes for in-service professional development or shorter duration pre-service preparation programmes. Systematic and rigorous preparation of early years teachers and teacher educators will ensure high-quality programmes for young children on the ground, resulting in better learning and development outcomes, also changing the identity of early educators and teachers, and improving the status of the profession in general.

The policy further recommends that professional development programmes should be offered by university departments; currently there are only a handful of pre-service degree programmes in ECE offered by universities. A framework such as the above could be further adapted and strengthened by university departments and recognised to certify students as teachers, thereby changing the current status of the early years profession in India.

REFERENCES

Azim Premji University. (2014). *Specialisation in early childhood education— A proposal.* Unpublished

Azim Premji University. (2017). *Specialisation in early childhood education— Concept and structure.* Unpublished.

Darling-Hammond, Linda & Baratz-Snowden J. (Eds.). (2007). Introduction. *A good teacher in every classroom: Preparing the highly qualified teachers our children deserve.* Jossey-Bass.

Ministry of Human Resource Development. (2020). *National education policy 2020.* https://www.education.gov.in/sites/upload_files/mhrd/files/NEP_Final_English_0.pdf Accessed August 8, 2020.

National Council of Educational Research. (2009). *National curriculum framework for teacher education.* New Delhi. https://ncte.gov.in/website/PDF/NCFTE_2009.pdf Accessed December 20, 2020.

6
An Early Educator's Professional Development
Insights from Bhutan

Karma Gayleg

The early childhood period, spanning from prenatal to eight years is the most critical and sensitive period in life as it coincides with phenomenal brain development. As a result of growing evidence from brain research on the importance of the early years in shaping the human brain, behaviour and competencies, there is increasing recognition of and demand for early childhood interventions. Even as a myriad of early childhood programmes focusing on different age groups of the early childhood period emerge all over the world, the need to design contextually appropriate interventions and services is key to achieving quality and relevance in such programmes. There are home-based interventions as well as group interventions based in early childhood centres, schools and community platforms such as health, adult literacy and parent group programmes. Children's exposure to quality experience in the early years of life is critical to their development and learning. In the context of centre-based group interventions, quality constitutes the learning environment, safety, materials, developmental appropriateness of the learning activities and the facilitator or educator managing these aspects and interacting with children. Amongst all the components of quality, early educators and caregivers are pivotal in determining the quality of experiences and the trajectory of developmental outcomes. Therefore, investment in the professional development of early educators and caregivers is central to realising quality experiences and achieving optimum development outcomes for children.

The early childhood programme in Bhutan is relatively young but is rapidly growing and expanding. Within the definition of quality interventions and minimum standards for centre-based programmes, the capacity and quality of educators stand out as one of the key pillars of quality programmes, the others being the quality of learning environment and structures; standards and curriculum; and interactions and activities. Therefore, there is considerable emphasis on the quality and professional capacity of educators. It is not enough that early educators are academically qualified; they should also be committed human beings with qualities and dispositions such as compassion, empathy, creativity and leadership.

The Importance of Professional Development of Early Childhood Educators

Professional capacity includes educational qualifications as well as training specific to child development and to the age-group of children the educator will work with. As with any profession, early educators need to be trained, motivated, and supported to be effective. Their professional development should include preparation before they get into the profession as well as consistent ongoing interventions to ensure that they keep their knowledge and skills up to date and continue learning as a lifelong process. Professional development programmes must also be based on the needs of their day-to-day functions, structured to connect research and practice and responsive to their background, experiences, and the current context in which they work. Even though there are numerous challenges to structuring professional development strategies, considering that the enormity of the work of the early childhood workforce is often unacknowledged and underestimated, the effort towards professionalising the early childhood workforce is critical, given the wealth of evidence supporting it. Yet, policymakers and society have high expectations for the early childhood field and for the children who are cared for in such settings. Early educators are often expected to promote high levels of achievement among all children, respond sensitively and appropriately to a wide range of needs, implement complex pedagogy, have a deep understanding of subject matter, engage in serious reflection about their practices, and work collaboratively with colleagues and families.

Early childhood educators have immense responsibility in providing quality care and education for young children. There is also overwhelming agreement from the science of development that the relationship a child has with a teacher or caregiver including the degree to which the child experiences care that is sensitive and responsive, is the central and most critical component of child care quality (Shonkoff & Phillips, 2000). Hence, there is little doubt regarding the centrality of the role that early educators play in children's holistic development, for which the professional capacity and efforts toward professional development are critical to realizing quality and effectiveness in early childhood settings.

The Goals of Professional Development of Early Childhood Educators

The primary goal of professional development programmes for early childhood educators is to develop knowledge, skills and attitudes required to be facilitators of learning for young children. Professional development programmes should therefore seek to expand the understanding of children's growth and development, how children learn best and what children need to learn. Professional development programmes should also help educators to develop skills to apply their knowledge and understanding of children's development and learning into practice, so as to be able to assist children to learn in the most meaningful and stimulating way. There are also expectations specific to different contexts, of competencies and knowledge that educators must be equipped with. In the context of Bhutan, the aim of any professional development programme is to develop competency in the following areas.

1. Child Growth and Development

The understanding of the universal science and theories of how children develop is fundamental to an early educator being able to provide the care, stimulation and support necessary for children to progress on a positive developmental trajectory. Within this, the understanding of the different stages of development from conception to birth to infancy to toddler-hood to the preschool years is equally imperative for early educators to be able to clearly comprehend the developmental needs of each of the stages and provide developmentally appropriate interventions and support. Another area of understanding that is integral to the understanding of children's development is the domain of development. As both parents and teachers tend to sometimes focus on the development of children's cognitive abilities, the importance of other areas of development such as emotional, social, language and physical abilities are underestimated and neglected. It is therefore important that early educators acquire clear understanding of the importance of each of these areas, how they are inextricably intertwined and the need for balanced holistic development in order for children to realise their full development potential.

Early educators also need to recognise the importance of the cultural context within which children are born and raised, and be able to relate the universal child development principles to local cultural practices, traditions, languages and values. This would enable educators to design and provide learning programmes and activities that are grounded in the local cultural context.

2. Programme Planning and Development

The most important task of an early educator on a daily basis is to plan and design learning programmes that are stimulating and meaningful for children. The importance of play, as universally acknowledged, should underpin all learning activities and early childhood education programmes, considering the impact of play-based activities on the effectiveness of learning for young children.

In the aspiration for interactive play-based learning activities, the importance of relationships between educators and children as well as among children needs to be recognised as being central to the effectiveness and productivity of any interaction. Typically, relationships in our society are based on respect for each other and elders, love, compassion, support and tolerance. The same principles need to be applied in the education of young children for them to be able to learn, practice and perpetuate these values.

In play-based activities, there is a need for variety and creativity in learning activities. Early educators need to be able to plan and prepare activities that are varied, stimulating and meaningful, encouraging learning through experiential interactions, songs, arts and crafts, the local environment, folklores, projects, pretend play, group activities and free play.

Hence, a professional development programme for early educators should address these needs and help educators with knowledge, skills and attitude in not just planning and preparing day-to-day programmes and activities but also in organising and conducting them effectively.

3. *Health, Nutrition and Safety*

Apart from facilitating and mediating children's learning, the early childhood educator also has the responsibility of ensuring children's safety and promoting health and nutrition for optimum development. The safety of children while in the care of educators includes protection from physical harm such as those posed by punishment, accidents and natural calamities. The educator has the role of creating an environment that is free from imminent threats and reducing vulnerability by explaining to children potential risks and helping them learn behaviour that reduces vulnerability to physical harm. Another aspect of safety is ensuring that children are free from psycho-social threats such as abuse and trauma caused through punishments and inappropriate social interactions. In addition, educators also have the role of educating parents on safety and protection.

Teaching healthy habits such as proper management of wastes, hand washing and proper toileting, and creating an environment that is healthy and free from hazards is also part of the work of educators. In addition, early educators also promote healthy diets and discourage unhealthy foods both at the centre and at home.

Therefore, there is a need to develop the capacity of educators in health, nutrition and safety. Any professional development programme for early educators would need to consider capacity building in this area.

4. Curriculum and Learning Environment

The universal principles of early childhood curriculum support a curriculum that is child-centred, play-based, flexible and developmentally appropriate. The curriculum in Bhutan is guided by a national framework of learning and development benchmarks, supplemented by a curriculum implementation guide. As such, while the Early Learning and Development Standards serve as the curriculum and learning outcomes framework for early childhood curriculum, the actual curriculum is designed locally at the early childhood centre, based on the relevance and need of different contexts, which is also integral to emphasising place-based learning and culturally grounded learning programme. This contributes to orienting children in the local language, lifestyle, customs and tradition while at the same time preparing them with skills and attitude for a fulfilling lifelong learning journey and a productive life with strong social and cultural foundations.

5. Socio-emotional Learning (SEL)

SEL is another key learning area for young children, which helps to build strong emotional and social competencies. Within the definition of SEL (Elias et al., 1997) the process of integrating thinking, feeling, and behaving in order to become aware of the self and of others, make responsible decisions, and manage one's own behaviours and those of others, the development of the following key competencies is critical for a child to develop holistically:

(a) Self-awareness: being able to assess one's feelings, interests, values, and strengths and maintaining self-confidence
(b) Self-management: being able to regulate one's emotions to handle stress, control impulses, and persevere in overcoming obstacles
(c) Social awareness: being able to take the perspective of and empathise with others
(d) Relationship management: being able to establish, maintain and manage healthy and harmonious relationships
(e) Responsible decision making: being able to make decisions based on moral, ethical and social norms

The curriculum also includes basic learning in early literacy and math and acquiring of foundational skill in these areas. The specific skills expected to be developed in each of the areas are as follows:

Early literacy skills

- Children's ability to understand and use language through listening, speaking and acquiring of new vocabulary
- Children's understanding and knowledge of the functions of printed symbols, such as letters, words, and pictures and of printed text, and how it relates to meaning
- Children's understanding of what a book is, and how it is to be used and read
- Children's ability to identify the names and shapes of letters in an alphabet. This skill paves the way for phonological awareness
- Children's ability to identify and manipulate sounds and the understanding that sounds (and letters) are combined to make words. A child with phonological awareness is able to recognise and create rhymes and alliterate

Early Mathematics Skills

- Children's understanding of numbers, quantity, order, ways of representing numbers, one-to-one correspondence, and counting
- Children's ability to understand patterns, which are things that repeat
- Children's ability to distinguish between alike and different objects and to sort them according to one or more attributes
- Children's ability to describe and compare measurable attributes, as well as to classify objects by certain attributes
- This knowledge area refers to a child's ability to understand ideas about shape, size and position

Learning With and From the Environment

Learning through the environment and using environment friendly materials and practices to develop children's awareness, understanding and appreciation of the environment is an important aspect of the process of learning in early childhood settings. The aim of learning with and from the environment implemented through activities such as planting and growing a tree, nature walks and using nature as learning spaces and theme, is to help children understand, appreciate, respect and care for nature. Furthermore, preparation of learning materials from locally available resources and waste materials is encouraged to inculcate conservation ethics and behaviours for sustainable use of resources.

Learning about Cultural and Traditional Values

Learning about tradition and culture is an important task for children in Bhutan. With modernisation, there is apprehension that most children, especially those brought up in cities in small families may not learn and understand the values and customs.

So, parent involvement in story-telling, songs and dances, arts and crafts, etc. are encouraged. Even as part of regular activities such as dramatisation and pretend play, folk culture and traditions are promoted. Children are also encouraged to participate in community events and local festivals.

Another important area of learning is life skills. Daily chores such as washing, cooking, cleaning, etc., are important life skills that all children must be taught. Earlier, they were passed down through generations but as lifestyles and family dynamics change, these essentials are brushed aside. These values and skills have to be taught in early childhood education through play-based pedagogy.

Meditation and Mindfulness

Meditation education as a regular part of the early education programme provides children the opportunity to develop mindfulness and the development of the ability to reflect on their own speech, thought and behaviour. It also contributes to developing focus and concentration and increasing the attention span, ultimately contributing to increasing the pleasure and effectiveness of learning.

Besides, the early childhood education curriculum also emphasises learning in art, science and technology that are expected to be promoted through play-based learning.

Gross National Happiness as the overarching goal of all efforts in every field is succinctly infused in the early childhood curriculum. Through the simple day-to-day activities that are carried out in Early Childhood Care and Education Centres, by ensuring that children's learning experiences are meaningful and fun-filled, it is believed that the foundations of happiness are laid. When there is a goal such as gross national happiness, provided it is not pursued with compulsive obsession, the early childhood programmes have a direction that enables them to support children in a way that balances their present wellbeing and future success. GNH as a guiding light is therefore an immensely enriching element in the early childhood curriculum.

Family and Community Partnerships

Many studies confirm that family involvement in early education strongly influences children's behaviour, learning and health outcomes. Bronfenbrenner (1974) has also said that the family is the most effective and economical system for fostering and sustaining the child's development, without which intervention is likely to be unsuccessful, and what few effects are achieved are likely to disappear in a few years. Family and community involvement contributes to embedding educational programmes in the local culture, traditions and values. On the other hand, the educational programme contributes to improving care and parenting practices in children's homes. The following strategies are emphasised to enhance parent and community involvement:

i. Parenting education for improvement of care and parenting practices
ii. Parent involvement in centre programmes to enrich learning by infusing local culture and values
iii. Participation in management of the centre as centre management committee members
iv. Participation in sustainable learning material development and centre maintenance works

Considering the importance of the ability of educators to engage families and communities, any professional development programme should consider the professional development needs of early educators in this area.

Interaction and Relationship

The early educator has an important part to play in helping children interact with others and in enhancing children's motivation to learn, which can only be achieved through respectful, responsive and supportive relationships with children. At the same time, the educator is also expected to be able to help children behave and conduct themselves appropriately in group settings. Given this responsibility, early educators need to have knowledge and skills to engage children meaningfully and manage them when needed. Professional development programmes for early educators should be able to address this aspect of the educator's capacity in order for her/him to be able to provide meaningfull and stimulating learning experiences for young children.

Observation and Measurement of Children's Progress

Observe and assess what children know and can do, in order to plan and provide a curriculum that meets their developmental and learning needs.

Types of Professional Development Programmes for Early Childhood Educators in Bhutan

In keeping with theories of professional development, the professional development of early educators has been envisioned, designed and strategised to meet the growing demand for quality early childhood education and the professional need of early educators. There are both short, intensive programmes addressing the practical needs of early education programmes as well as long-term programmes aimed at addressing the academic needs of educators. A Diploma in Early Childhood education, amongst other types of short-term training, is aligned with the core competencies and designed to address the professional development needs of ECCD Facilitators. The three-year mixed mode Diploma Programme which has 20 modules covering key learning areas, is designed to suit the working pattern of ECCD Facilitators, where educators attend residential school for six weeks during winter vacation and carry out their academic projects as they carry out their regular work in their centres. Other courses conducted as refresher training contribute to constantly refreshing and updating the knowledge and skills of early educators.

REFERENCES

Brackett, Marc A. & Susan, E. R. (2014). *Transforming students' lives with social and emotional learning*, Yale Centre for Emotional Intelligence. Yale University. http://ei.yale.edu/wp-content/uploads/2013/09/Transforming-Students%E2%80%99-Lives-with-Social-and-Emotional-Learning.pdf.

DeMeulenaere, M. (2015). Promoting social and emotional learning in preschool. *Creating a nature-inspired outdoor learning environment for urban spaces*. https://eric.ed.gov/?id=EJ1060261.

Dinnebeil, L. A., Boat, M., & Bae, Y. (2013). Integrating principles of universal design into the early childhood curriculum. *Dimensions of Early Childhood, 41*(1), 3–1.

Durlak, J. A., Weissberg, R. P., Dymnicki, A. B., Taylor, R. D., & Schellinger, K. B. (2011). The impact of enhancing students' social and emotional learning: A meta-analysis of school-based universal interventions. *Child Development, 82*(1), 405–432.

Edwards, S. & Nutall, J. (2009). *Professional learning in early childhood settings*. Sense Publishers. Monash University. https://www.sensepublishers.com/media/801-professional-learning-in-early-childhood-settings.pdf.

Elias, M. J., Zins, J. E., & Weissberg, R. P. (1997). *Promoting social and emotional learning: Guidelines for educators*. ASCD.

Harvard Graduate School of Education. (2006). Family involvement makes a difference. *Harvard Family Research Project- Series 1A*. Harvard University.

Morrison, J. W., Storey, P., & Zhang, C. (2015). Accessible family involvement in early childhood programmes. *Creating a Nature-Inspired outdoor learning environment for urban spaces*.

Ministry of Education. (2011). *Draft ECCD policy*. Royal Government of Bhutan.

Ministry of Education. (2012). *ECCD curriculum implementation guide*. Royal Government of Bhutan. 17–13.

Ministry of Education. (2014). *Bhutan early learning and development standards*. Royal Government of Bhutan. 23–46.

Ministry of Social & Family Development. (2011). *Achieving excellence through continuing professional development: A CPD framework for early childhood educators*. https://www.childcarelink.gov.sg/ccls/uploads/CPD_Guide_5_FA.pdf.

NAEYC, (2008). *Promoting excellence in early childhood education*. USA.

Rao, N., & Li, H. (2009). Quality matters: Early childhood education policy in Hong Kong. *Early Child Development and Care, 179*(3), 233–245.

Samuelsson, I. P. & Kaga, Y. (2008). *The contribution of early childhood education to a sustainable society.* UNESCO.

Shonkoff, J. P., & Phillips, D. A. (2000). *From neurons to neighborhoods: The science of early childhood development.* National Academy Press.

Timperley, H., Wilson, A., Barrar, H., & Fung, I. (2007). *Teacher professional learning and development: Best evidence synthesis iteration (BES).* Wellington: Ministry of Education.

World Forum Foundation. (2014). *Universal curriculum principles.* Nebraska: World Forum Foundation. USA. https://worldforumfoundation.org/workinggroups/curriculum/.

Zaslow, M., Tout, K., Halle, T., Whittaker, J. V., & Lavelle, B. (2010). Toward the identification of features of effective professional development for early childhood educators. Literature Review. Office of Planning, Evaluation and Policy Development, Department of Education.

7

Cultural Tools for Children's Literacy and Learning

Asha Singh

In all professions there is the possibility of interactions becoming routinised with rituals ignoring the presence of the persons. You may recall a time when a sales person treated you indifferently or when you were in great pain the doctor examined you casually. Familiarity and conformity to everyday-ness leads to fatigue and boredom in transactions that need to be people-centred. Professional encounters with diffused empathy and absence of person-oriented curiosity lead to discomfort. What would such interactions do to children? Teachers, especially those dealing with young children, need to be cautious in not slipping into customary actions.

As a teacher of young children, it seems imperative to review, reflect and reassure yourself that children's responses are sources of inquiry. For an involved teacher deriving joy from watching and listening to children becomes a natural process. Children need attention, opportunity, encouragement and recognition, and learn best with opportunity, freedom, and love.

How will children react to indifference and absence of awe and joy in their environments? Scholars interested in how children learn insist that children learn by appropriate stimuli and experiences from their environment (Holt, 1967; Burgemeester, 2017). John Holt (1967) declared that for small children learning is as natural as breathing. Children need opportunities to experience, explore and experiment. Many schools fill their classrooms with attractive objects, abundance of materials and schedules for activities. Keeping children meaningfully engaged could be a positive driving force for early childhood learning and socialisation. In fact, formal settings for young children bereft of personalised, engaging and energetic interactions restrain children's sense of curiosity and wonder. Nature of social relationships and attitudes to learning are embedded in childhood exchange of dialogue, ideas and how the more experienced pay attention to multiple perspectives.

Everyday Rhythms: Variety, Familiarity and Surprise

Imagine children's reaction if as a teacher of 3-4-year-olds, you went into the class wearing a turban singing '*Sabziwala, sabzi lelo, taazi taazi khet se aayi sabzi, sabzi waala...*'. The classroom would transform into an imagined play space with pretend elements to grab children's immediate attention. The question *What is in my basket?* would make children recall the names of vegetables *aloo, gobi, matar, bhindi*, etc.

The flow of the chatter could take many routes as individual contexts bring in the child's social world. Children may recall and share family talk on vegetables and bring in comments adults may not be ready for. Teacher's questions such as *Where do you get vegetables from?* or *Who cooks dinner?* will signal interest and children will learn to model asking questions and teacher will gain information about what children know. Teachers engaging in conversation by asking question as well as listening to children signals an interest in allowing children to express their thoughts, views and feelings. Children develop self-confidence and also the value of curiosity.

Using local and familiar figures in a dramatic way makes for classroom appeal, engagement and comprehension. Such sociocultural tools demystify the school setting, making curricular transaction less monotonous, resonating with Dewey's concept of experience as a source of learning. Everyday figures such as the postman, the vegetable vendor, the milk delivery person can all become points for discussion and exchange of communication. The discussion around the postman could examine some of the following: what are letters, why do people write letters, how are letters transported, etc. Of course, the discussion on letters can then be converted into a paper and pencil activity, such as creative ways of preparing and sending letters, etc. In using presentation of identifiable persons in the sociocultural contexts, learning becomes a collaborative exercise linking the classroom to the world beyond. Learning takes a new meaning as school connects to everyday experiences and is not seen as a distinct, separate space.

Such activities can be further extended by involving children in classroom processes, quiz or role-play; for example, 'Tell me what role I should play tomorrow' enthuses children to be innovative contributors. Planning for the classroom fills children with enthusiasm to probe, look around and identify roles and situations for classroom reflection.

Materials and Methods: Diversity and Inclusion

It is quite common to see children mimic adults in their environment such as wearing grandfather's spectacles or pretending to check notebooks (like a teacher), carrying a purse (like a mother or aunt) or walking behind the mother at a construction site pretending to carry a basket of pebbles. Objects like scarf, *dupatta*, old shoes/sandals, broom, duster, bags and small baskets will transform the class to a mini-community of residents exchanging dialogues. The exploring of roles, searching for words, experimenting with objects from a familiar social, physical environment will create self-directed experiences to recall imagery, act like others in the neighbourhood experiencing physical movement and coordination. Diversity of objects helps familiarise them with many kinds of labour. When a child plays with a broom, sweeping the floor, while another child picks up a bag and pretends to go to school, we are dealing with a diversity of roles. Use of different objects as play tools legitimises their presence and addresses possible stigma associated with societal roles. Children's responses can be many, and the teacher's role is crucial to admonish and reaffirm perceptions 'Oh! He has a dirty broom' turning it to 'Yes, when he cleans, the broom becomes dirty.'

Close classroom links with community life and sociocultural realities offer a sense of identity and emotional comfort. For very young children, school is the first space outside of home where efforts to create familiarity and security enable children to express and absorb classroom exchanges with ease; they offer an emotional buffer space. A playful milieu, where children's natural behaviour patterns emerge and their urge for active participation and the need to touch, feel and explore are encouraged, is essential to their development.

Often in the classroom we resort to fixed ways of dealing with children. Our belief is that the children have to be taught and adults know what to teach. For instance, we forget that while we are playing a vegetable seller, we are also helping them learn to classify vegetables (green leafy vegetables, part of the plant they grow on, root vegetables, etc.) or differentiate them from fruits ('I don't have mango, guava or banana as they are fruits'). Flash cards with pictures and words can then help them to relate seamlessly with print. Over zealousness on 'sit down' learning and emphasis on reading and writing often 'makes us lose out on fun with children' (ECCE teacher in a workshop). This paper appeals to and urges early childhood teachers to retain and create playfulness, cultural familiarity and laughter in the classroom. Charlie Chaplin is believed to have said, 'I wasted my day, I did not laugh even once'. As teachers, instead of thinking that during formal interactions 'we lose all the fun' we could make fun organic to curriculum transaction.

Appealing Tasks: Engagement and Comprehension

Frequently proposed in early childhood educators training is the popular notion of learning by doing. This idea was formulated by the educationist John Dewey in his book *Experience and*

Education (1938). It is commonly noted that a great deal of learning comes from outside the classroom. Informal learning is shaped by language use and opportunities for observation, absorbing concepts and ideas. In the midst of a natural setting with fields, trees or birds, a child may run behind birds, watch trees changing their form or colour, or watch the insects and fishes in the fields. The idea of seasons can be woven around observations related to trees:

> When does the red cotton tree flower?
>
> When does the *neem* tree bear fruits? What colour are the fruits? How many birds did you see on your way to school? Do you know their names?
>
> What were the colours of flowers you saw on the way to school?
>
> When does the gulmohar flower?
>
> What happens after the rains?

Children exercising agency of their own watchfulness are collaborators in the learning process and truly develop skills of observation, inference and analysis. Children are often fascinated by vehicles and question their parents about models of vehicles. They can often identify and differentiate the sound of a bus from that of a car or a truck. Curricular content will be enriched by inclusion of child-generated subject matter. Rhymes on modes of transport make excellent classroom content. The child's own experience makes the printed word or textual material more meaningful.

The Curious Child: Physical and Emotional Comfort

Children often see the school and home as two separate worlds. The boundaries of the two settings are separate as well as overlapping. Children will learn that their needs have to be balanced by caring and sharing. Children need to accept that unlike home, the class has many children and each needs to have a turn. Children also need to feel comfortable to share the excitement of an event, discovery encountered outside of the school setting. One father with a five-year-old daughter regaled family and her friends with humourous poems on environment, animals etc. When told by another adult, 'You should narrate these poems in class,' the child promptly replied, 'Poems in school are from *Posy of Poems* (textbook).' The school-home gap is a factor impacted by ignorance of the value of cultural literacy. Family knowledge, community treasures like stories, songs or dance are not seen as learning resources.

On a visit to a small school in a tribal area, it was a little disconcerting to see bright faces sitting in a row and chant in unison '*Namaste* Madam'. Greeting and being silent is customary welcome in schools. The team moved around looking at the classroom display while the children patiently controlled all their limbs in cross-legged position. However, the young male teacher of the class, not obsessed with classroom order, requested the team to interact with the children. The meaningless question posed by the guest to the class was, 'Do you like school?' The teacher eager to put the children at ease as well as with pride in children's potential continued and urged the children to show the guests the local *dimsha* dance. The class rose with amazing agility and soon the room was alive with action and rhythmic steps. The experience conveyed the teacher's confidence and pride in his work with commitment to children. Classroom processes need not exclude children from moving about or participating in sociocultural processes. Social realities of the community define the context of the school and provide the comfort needed to build a social identity. It is refreshing to find special focus on local and folk arts in the National Education Policy (NEP 2020).

Children like using all their limbs as it gives them a chance to be active. Children thrive best when allowed to engage in movement tasks. Movement and learning are inseparable and we deny children the use of the many limbs of our body by stressing on excessive use of sit-down tasks.

While physical order and safety are important the teacher should create opportunities for children to feel free to express, share or seek new information. Children retreat into a shell if ridiculed or checked too often. Piaget's research showed that children are not miniature adults. Being in close proximity to children helps in knowing that children's expressions are windows to their worldview. What adults may call mistakes may often reflect the child's understanding of an event, object or experience. Children may be immersed in a fantasy world through role-play or pretend play at one moment and yet may completely refrain from participation at another. This is a typical developmental behaviour of young children.

Common to classroom processes is the emphasis on letting children talk, talking with them, listening to them and responding to them. It is the response that helps children to feel emotionally gratified to pick up cues often referred to as *guided mediation*, a term coined by Vygotsky. Verbal and participatory interactions provide glimpses of the multiple ways in which children think, feel and make meaning of their experiences. Children have their own ways of expressing and their own understanding of language. They feel comfortable in the language they hear often (MHRD, 2020). Their understanding of multiple meanings of words or interpretation of events is limited, as the following examples show.

Example 1

> The teacher told the child to sit here for the *present*. The child patiently waited till her mother came to pick her up. Quite puzzled the child tugged her mother's dress and whispered, 'She promised me a *present*, wait for her to get it.' Both the mother and teacher were clueless about why the child expected a gift on the first day of school. The tearful four-year-old mumbled, looking accusingly at the teacher, 'You asked me to sit here for the present'.
>
> (Donaldson, 1978)

Example 2

The preschool was in a festive mode preparing to showcase three- to three-and-a-half year old children in a cultural bonanza of movement, music and performance for parents. One child sat watching pensively. She was unhappy at being a bird in the story. She refused to participate. Her mother held her and asked what was troubling her. Promptly the girl confided and holding her mother tight, said 'If I become a bird I will have to live in a nest and fly and I don't want to leave you.'[1]

The unpredictability of children's reactions is an outcome of their specific ways to make meaning of their own reality. The individual child's experience needs attention in the collective context of the classroom. Teachers of young children will testify to children's joy in being patted encouragingly or when spoken to with warmth. Adult descriptions of early schooling often provide nostalgic accounts of childhood schooling; others recall with regret of growing up at a time when schools thought of children as little pails to be filled, not as minds that need to be ignited.

Totto-chan is an account by a creative successful television personality who provides engaging descriptions of her schooling that combined learning with fun, freedom and love. She conveys her gratitude to a tolerant principal and an understanding mother who responded to her search for meaning-making.

Children's Agency: Meaning-Making, Not Fact-Collecting

In many preschool settings in India and other countries, children often have time allotted for 'show and tell', that allows children to develop skills of narration. Through sharing stories about their favourite object children are enabled in small ways to connect their life at home to the classroom, using communication and expression. It also encourages emotional development in a child, as he or she shares their interests, home lives, and joys and struggles with peers. As the narrator (the child) tells the story there is building of sequence as the child attempts to convey the meaning. There may be some search for words which is when some prodding helps. The exercise with the child's own narrative, apart from impacting language, is immensely supportive in enriching self-confidence and self-worth which the teacher needs to be aware of. The important focus in such a practice is to let children describe with gentle prompts rather than rush them, to connect it to curricular goal. The connection to learning goals has to be woven in seamlessly.

There are several ways to augment narrative opportunity to build links to curricular learning:

- Help the child select an item and have them explain to you how it fits with the weekly curriculum theme. For example if the theme is season/s, a child can bring an object of the season such as an umbrella or raincoat, or a fruit specific to the season.
- Help the child practice describing the object and explaining why they want to share it with the class.
- Reinforce effective speaking habits, such as looking at the audience and speaking clearly.
- Ask questions about the item so that the child will be ready to answer when friends and teachers have questions.

There is evidence that early language experiences play an important role in the child's social and emotional development. 'Show and tell' is an interesting way to help children to understand diversity as each child will choose something different. Talking about oneself teaches important communication skills that will serve as a solid foundation for future learning.

Finally, the role of stories is undisputed in connecting children to different communities. Song, dance and stories define cultures and children pick up the nuances of their culture from early years.

Children also are capable storytellers, especially if they have been read to frequently.

One of the most effective ways help children learn about children and different communities is to share stories with them that come from those cultures. They learn about plurality by seeing a culture through its narratives. It also introduces them to narrative styles as well as lifestyles of other children in the classroom. Children should be encouraged to tell stories they hear at home with storytelling values of their family and community. It can be limiting for a child when she is forced to conform to one style or language. To express herself in an unfamiliar language is often stressful and is dismissive of social identity. Instead of correcting the way a child tells a story, or what they put into their story, the class should be encouraged to listen, respond and assume their style is a worthwhile one.

Stories need not only come in the form of books. Many communities are grounded in a rich tradition of oral stories. One of the most important lessons is that stories can be emotionally gratifying as they are highly dependent on everyday spoken conversation. Exposure to a variety of storytelling styles enables children to develop their own powerful style, one that presents their personal affiliations.

A two-year-old child exposed to a multitude of reading materials took a book and attempted to read to the visiting guest. Holding the book to display the pictures to the audience she began 'once upon a time there was a king', turns a page or two, shuts the book and announces 'THE END.' Everyone is amused and there is much laughter.

Several studies (Engels, 1997; Wells, 1986) have indicated the significance of stories in the lives of children and their ability to learn. Gordon Wells' study of Bristol children is evidence for the benefits children had in relating in easy ways to reading and learning at school if they had heard stories at home when they were less than four years old (Wells, 1986).

Conclusion: Promoting Study of Meaning Not Transmission of Facts

The work and research of CECED summarised in their annual reports states some important points and conveys evocative facts for the community of early childhood professionals. These are concerns for limiting the young child's propensity for play and discovery.

- There is an assumption that English is the first step for upward mobility. The supremacy of one language leads to an abundance of private preschools that are sought for teaching of English, a language that renders the first education setting as unfamiliar and alien.
- Schools are driven by goals of literacy and readiness for school. The young child's curriculum needs to enable children to find experiences through exploration, experimentation to experience joys of discovery.
- Children are observed to be sitting adhering to norms of maintaining silence. There are teachers few and far between who are not discipline obsessed, allowing children to break into the local folk dance which they know and enjoy (also personal observation on a field visit). Cultural tools contribute to social and emotional comfort influencing positively children's relation to literacy-driven curricular content.
- There is scant attention to recognising children's need for play or ideas of thinkers such as Montessori who described the inseparable connection between movement and learning almost 100 years ago at the beginning of the 20th century.

In fact, by acts like 'Quiet, finger on your lips!', we are often legitimising disobeying instructions as every child finds ways of whispering despite the finger on the lips. Do we think of the consequences of hidden messages?

Teachers need to move away from formal silence-oriented classroom dynamics and infuse humour and playfulness into the classroom, actively involving the children. Static classroom images need to be replaced with meaningful and fruitful experiences illuminated by cultural contexts. Social familiarity infuses an emotional security as children relate to stories, local songs and games. An experiential continuity of social experiences and curricular goals helps children to become emotionally comfortable to ask questions, and to be actively engaged. In the early years the quality of experiences will help children to build positive lifelong relationship in developing curiosity to learn.

State Support: National Education Policy 2020

The new policy could bring in welcome changes:

(a) it highlights the role of art integrated learning in the fourth chapter with special focus on the first five years.

(b) In chapter 22 local crafts, arts and indigenous play materials find a significant mention. In the minds of the policymakers the idea of familiarity and stepping forward to face challenges seems to take precedence. There is also mention of the educative potential of folk arts. Sections 22.1, 22.2 and 22.3 extensively describe the role of the cultural forms of sociality as tools for pedagogy. Play with simple indigenous toys for young children is both joyful and motivating to innovate and invent. The New Education Policy is positively inclined in promoting the folk arts for self-esteem of the individual child as well as in nurturing cultural pride. The use of familiar social forms is also enriching for the teacher.

In conclusion, it is clear that a teacher probing, asking questions or addressing the individual child in the collective is role modelling curiosity and the need to centrestage the specialness of each child that are basic, invisible tools for literacy and learning. An understanding of child-initiated classroom processes will enliven and energise early childhood classrooms.

Note

1. Taken from an interaction during a theatre workshop for teachers

References

Burgemeester, A. (2017). Jean Piaget's theory of play. Retrieved from https://www.psychologized.org/jeanpiagets-theory-of-play/. Accessed on 27 July 2018.

Centre for Early Childhood Education and Development. (2012–2013). *Annual Report.* http://ceced.net/wpcontent/uploads/2015/03/CECED_Annual_Report_2012_13_6th_Proof.

Dewey, John. (1938). *Experience and education.* Kappa Delta Pi.

Donaldson, M. (1978). *Children's minds.* Fontana/Collins.

Engel, S. (1997). Storytelling in the first three years. (Ed.). *Zero to three, Dec 1996–Jan 1997.* Retrieved from https://www.zerotothree.org/resources/1057-storytelling-in-the-first-three-years on 29 July 2018.

Holt, J. (1967) *How children learn?* Penguin Education.

Kuroyanagi, T. (1982). *Totto-chan, the little girl at the window.* Kodansha International.

Ministry of Human Resource and Development. (2020). *National Education Policy.* Government of India. (2020). https://www.mhrd.gov.in/sites/upload_files/mhrd/files/NEP_Final_English_0.pdf.

Postman, N. & Weingartner, C. (1969). *Teaching as a subversive activity.* Delacorte Press.

Wells, G. (1986). *The meaning makers.* Heinemann.

8
Role of Vocational Education in the Development of Early Childhood Professionals

NEELA DABIR

The need for trained workers in different capacities in the field of early childhood development (ECD) is well established by different reports by academicians as well as government agencies. However, there is wide variety in terms of the duration and content of the training provided by different agencies to train the ECD workers. It varies from a few months to two years and the eligibility for the training too can range from SSC to graduate degree. So far no one offers an undergraduate degree programme for training ECD professionals thereby providing a holistic training in all aspects of managing an ECD programme. Since July 2014, TISS has conducted one such programme through its School of Vocational Education, and it is unique in many ways. Before going into the features of this graduate programme, it would be useful to understand the background and status of the Vocational Education project of TISS.

TISS–SCHOOL OF VOCATIONAL EDUCATION (TISS-SVE)

TISS set up the School of Vocational Education (SVE) in December 2011 to create vocational educational opportunities in different sectors for those who could not complete their education through the mainstream education and are working or willing to work in manufacturing or service sector industries. We entered into an MoU with All India Council for Technical Education (AICTE) in March 2012 and received a seed grant to incubate the National

Vocational University. At that time there was no model available for a Vocational University and we were expected to develop a scalable and cost-effective model for offering vocational education that would have high employment potential. We started the process of developing the vocational education syllabi for different sectors up to the Advanced Diploma level as per the norm prescribed by AICTE for community colleges. Around the same time the UGC announced a scheme for universities and educational institutes to offer a Bachelor's Degree in Vocational Education (B.Voc.) for vocational training programmes in various sectors. Therefore, we also upgraded the programmes by one more year and B.Voc. degree programmes were designed in 19 different sectors. While most of these are largely from the manufacturing and service sector industries, we also included two social sectors in the project: Healthcare and Child Care. The Navajbai Ratan Tata Trust (NRTT) sanctioned a grant for offering vocational courses in Child Care and Geriatric Care at a subsidised cost. As of now we offer two B.Voc. programmes in Child Care and one Diploma programme in Geriatric Care with the support from NRTT. In the child care sector we introduced B.Voc. in Child Protection and B.Voc. in Early Child Development.

TISS B.Voc programmes are based on the model of Work Integrated Training Programme (WITP). The main feature of WITP is to provide trainees an opportunity for learning vocational skills through on the job training at related industry/company/organisations along with the classroom training to understand the theoretical aspects. WITP focusses on job-specific knowledge and skills rather than a broad and varied education. Students spend more time on the job and less time in classroom learning.

TISS-SVE has developed a unique model of offering vocational training courses with the help of hub and industry partners. This model aims at offering the vocational courses in a different way as compared to the traditional way of offering all the theory and practical training in the institution/college where the students are enrolled. The TISS-SVE model on the other hand is based on the

Role of Vocational Education 111

dual system of vocational education practised in Germany. In this system the theory is taught in the classrooms and the skill training happens in the industry, company or places where the students learn the skills in a real-life situation. In order to bring in the scalability and to improve the employability of the students after completion of the course, the model engages multiple partners for theory training (hub partners) and also for skill training (skill knowledge providers) across the country. This is a demand-driven model and therefore if there is no opportunity for on the job training for a course in a particular location, the course is not initiated. The courses offered in different locations therefore differ based on the market demand for those type of skills in that location. Figure 8.1 explains the role of different partners in implementation of vocational education.

Figure 8.1: *TISS -SVE model of Vocational Education*

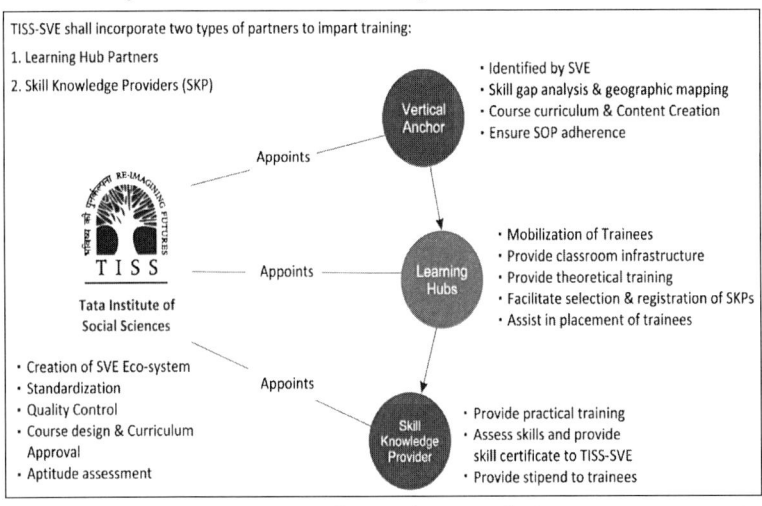

Source: Neela Dabir, 2017. Incubation of National Vocational University 2012–2017. Project Report, Tata Institute of Social Science.

In the case of ECD courses, TISS-SVE is the vertical anchor and the courses are designed by TISS. It will also be pertinent to understand the UGC guidelines for B.Voc. before moving on to the details specific to the B.Voc. in ECD. As per the UGC guidelines for B.Voc., the three-year course should be divided into six semesters and each semester will have a combination of general education courses (12 credits), vocational theory courses (6 credits) and vocational practicals (12 credits). This means that the classroom teaching of 270 hours and skill training of 360 hours should be included in the syllabus for each semester. Another unique feature of the B.Voc. programme is the possibility of multiple exit and entry. Each year is independent in terms of certification and therefore the students who discontinue at the end of first or second year still have certificate for a job. The students completing the first year get a Diploma certificate, at the end of second year they get an Advanced Diploma and those completing the third year get the Bachelor of Vocation Degree. It is also possible to join the programme at the appropriate level after a gap as and when the student wishes to complete the degree programme.

The B.Voc. programme for Early Child Development is a three-year work-integrated programme that helps students acquire all the requisite skills to become an effective Early Childhood educator. The syllabus ensures that the students gain sound knowledge about the theories of early child development. The work integration provides the opportunity to do the practical work in real-life situations and ensures that the students can apply the theories at the field level. The students also gain professional knowledge and skills regarding their roles, responsibilities, work ethics and rights of the children.

Organisation of the Courses Over Six Semesters

As explained earlier the courses included in the programme are a mix of general education and ECD-related courses. The idea is to train them to be at par with students from any other graduation programme like B.A., B.Sc. or B.Com. So, inputs in general education are equally important along with the vocation-specific inputs. It is important to note that in a recent circular from the UGC it is mentioned that students with a B.Voc. Degree are eligible to appear for competitive exams like graduates from other streams.

The list of courses included in the syllabus are listed below:

Table 8.1: *List of Courses in B.Voc Syllabus*

S. No.	General Education courses	ECD-related courses
1.	English	Child Growth and Development
2.	Personal Grooming	Teaching Learning Strategies
3.	Computing Skills	Personal and Professional Growth
4.	Communication Skills	Rights of Children
5.	Digital Literacy	Children in Indian Context
6.	Financial Literacy	ECCE programmes in India and global perspective
7.	Basics of Accounts	Health, Hygiene and Safety
8.	Health and Fitness	Diversities in Families and Communities
9.	Basics of Legal and HR Policies	Children with Special Needs
10.	Basics of Economics and Markets	Approaches to ECCD & Assessment
11.	Entrepreneurship	Partnering with Parents and Community
12.	Employment Readiness	Organisation & Management of ECCD centres
13.		Curriculum planning and assessment

This curriculum has been developed by going through an elaborate process of consultation and vetting by experts in the field of ECD before finalisation.

Right now, we have 15 hub partners across India who have started the B.Voc. programme in partnership with TISS. The response was not very good to begin with but slowly things are improving. The current student strength is 182. Till date 224 students have completed the Diploma from 11 hubs and

31 students have completed the Advanced Diploma from five hubs. Since the first batch was initiated in July 2015, only nine students have completed the B.Voc degree till 2023. (The data presented in this paper is based on enrolments in the B.Voc progamme until 2018-19 academic year.) The trend here is to leave after the first year as most of them get a job at that stage and therefore, very few students complete the B.Voc. degree.

Another reason for dropping out after the first year is the fact that many students enroll for the B.Voc. after an undergraduate degree. They are not interested in getting another bachelor's degree. To overcome this issue, we have also developed the Post-Graduate Diploma in Early Child Development and Education (PGDECDE). This is a one-year programme for graduates from any discipline.

One significant development worth mentioning is the partnership with Navy Women's Welfare Association (NWWA). We have started the B.Voc. programmes within the Navy premises in Mumbai, Delhi, Cochin and Vishakhapatnam. These are offered to the wives of the sailors with 50% sponsorship for fees by the NWWA. The idea is to ensure that a woman can continue to be in the programme even if there is a transfer of her husband to another port.

Organisation of Skill Training through Work Integration

The success of the programme will depend upon the involvement of the skill knowledge providers (SKPs)—preschools, nurseries, play schools, crèche, etc., where the students get the opportunity to learn on the job. The learning objectives for each semester are designed in such a way that the students receive training and acquire skills in a sequential manner. They are assigned simple tasks to begin with and mainly assist and observe the teachers in the work place. By the end of the six semesters, they are equipped to work independently. The job roles and expected employment opportunity also match the training received. The

Diploma holders can be employed as assistant teachers, those with Advanced Diploma can be appointed for the job of a teacher and the Degree holders can be assigned additional responsibilities along with being a teacher. We also encourage rotation of placements for work integration and visits to different settings to give adequate exposure to the students about the range of ECD programmes offered by government as well as non-government organisations and the way in which they are managed. Experience of some settings like anganwadis and special schools are covered through exposure visits.

Uniformity of Training Content across Hubs and Quality Control

The model developed by TISS-SVE has the potential to expand at a fast pace. Also, several partners can offer the same course if the methodology is well-defined with training material for the facilitators and students. A facilitator's guide and participant workbook have been developed for each course. The facilitator guide gives detailed lesson plans for the course content and the participant workbook has corresponding exercises for the students to revise whatever is taught in the class. For the practical work, the students must maintain a log book where they keep a weekly record of the work done at the workplace and the supervisors at the workplace are expected to oversee what they do and sign the log book every week. The trainers are carefully selected by the SVE staff in consultation with the hub partners. Since the trainers are expected to follow the facilitator's guide, the standard delivery of courses can be ensured. There are also guidelines for assessment of the practical work. The exam is conducted by TISS and papers are corrected by external examiners. This ensures objectivity in the assessment process. The process of developing the online examination platform is completed and the question banks are also ready for online examinations. This is important because the examinations are conducted in many places, and so generating a number of question papers becomes easy. The paper correction is now online for quick processing of results.

Feedback from Students and Employers

The team SVE obtains periodic feedback from the students, trainers and SKPs through meetings during visits and telephonic interviews. The students are generally happy to learn in the class and at their places for on-the-job training. They feel more confident in many ways. Some of them have joined the course after a gap of few years in their education. This course gives them confidence to work and manage the household duties efficiently. Some feel more confident about raising their own children. Getting a job after the first year itself is good in a way but the flip side is that they lose the motivation to complete the degree.

Students are able to secure employment after completion of the first year of B.Voc. since they receive a diploma in ECD. We have data for fifty-one students who are employed now in play schools and kindergartens. Their salaries range from Rs. 8000 to 25,000 per month. Information on employment is available for only 76 students. Although many more students have secured employment after completion of Diploma in ECD, we do not have the complete data.

The employers have expressed satisfaction with the knowledge and experience of students. The curriculum has been revised recently after feedback from the trainers and SKPs.

Some of the employers are Dnyandeep Pre-school, Badlapur; Panna English School, Badlapur; TGT Kendriya Vidyalaya, Mumbai; TIFR Day Care Centre, Mumbai; Navy Wives Welfare Association Balwadi, Mumbai; Bachpan Play School and Kindergarten, Cochin; Little Angels, Guwahati; Naval KG Karwar, Naval KG Mumbai; Naval KG, Delhi; Army Public School (Primary Section), Mumbai; Earlybirds Playschool, Mumbai; Greenfields Pre-primary School, Delhi; GD Goenka Pre-primary School, Delhi; and Evergreen School, Delhi.

Conclusion

The journey so far has been quite exciting and we are confident that it will help in developing properly trained ECD professionals. We seek feedback and suggestions and are willing to share the syllabus and study material with those who wish to replicate the programme.

The New Education Policy 2020 has placed a major thrust on universal access to high quality ECCE across the country in a phased manner. It includes strengthening the anganwadi infrastructure and training of the Anganwadi Workers for expected changes in the pedagogy. In the light of the NEP 2020, this initiative by TISS-School of Vocational Education can be considered as a model for replication. The work-integrated training model is scalable and has the potential to train existing teachers as well new entrants to the profession. For achieving the goals of NEP 2020 a large-scale initiative of training EC professionals will be needed.

We have a long way to go and continue to identify areas for improvement of the syllabus and the course.

References

Dabir, Neela. (2017). "Incubation of National Vocational University 2012–2017". Project Report, Tata Institute of Social Science, Mumbai.

Ministry of Human Resource Development. (2020). *National Education Policy 2020.* https://www.education.gov.in/sites/upload_files/mhrd/files/NEP_Final_English_0.pdf Accessed on 8 August 2020.

9
Distance Education for Professional Development
IGNOU's Diploma Programme

REKHA SHARMA SEN, PANKAJ KHARE and PRANJALI DEV*

The focus of the present article is a distance education programme offered by the Indira Gandhi National Open University (IGNOU) called the Diploma Programme in Early Childhood Care and Education (DECE) launched in 1995. A 32-credit programme of one year duration, which can be pursued after Class 12, DECE helps to develop the competencies of the learner necessary for working with children during early childhood years and providing early childhood care and education. The DECE has a nearly equal balance between theory and practical in the ratio 18 credits to 14 credits. It is available in Hindi, English and Tamil. There is no restriction on the number of students who may be admitted. The programme aims to reach out to three groups of learners:

i. Professionals engaged in the sector of Early Childhood Care and Education (ECCE) such as in crèches and pre-primary classes or those aspiring to do so
ii. Entrepreneurs desirous of setting-up ECCE centres or those already engaged in managing such centres

---

* The three authors are equal contributors to the study and the writing of the paper.

iii. Parents and anyone who wants to acquire knowledge about children's development (SOCE, IGNOU, 2018)

The present study provides the enrolment trend, demographic profile of the learners and programme completion statistics of the DECE programme.

Method

The detailed student records available with IGNOU were analysed to understand the demographic profile of the learners of the DECE programme. The records of all the learners enrolled since 1995, when the programme was first launched, till July 2018 were accessed making it a total of 42,417 learner records. Microsoft Access and Excel was used to analyse the records. Complete information for all the parameters was not available in the student records. This gap in data has been reported as 'Data not available' (DNA).

Findings and Discussion

Enrolment Trend

Beginning with 170 learners in the first year (1995), the enrolment in the programme has steadily increased over the years. Since the year 2003, the enrolment in the programme had been more than 2,000 learners every year, except during 2007 when the enrolment saw a dip. Since 2014, the enrolment has shown a steady upward trend. Since 2015, more than 200 IGNOU study centres are operational for this programme (Figure 9.1). Till academic year 2014–15, DECE accounted for 0.35% of IGNOU's total enrolment (IGNOU, 2015).

Students came to know about the DECE programme through different sources including the following:

(a) Information disseminated by the University through its

website, prospectus and through advertisements
(b) Recommendation of current or past learners of DECE and other IGNOU programmes
(c) Recommendation of employers with whom students were currently working, such as a preschool chain, an NGO or a private school
(d) Recommendation of educational institutions where learners were pursuing related courses

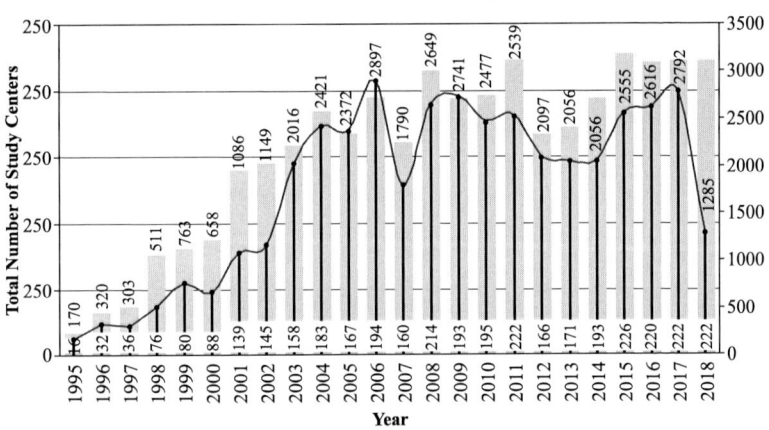

Figure 9.1: Enrolment in and number of study centres activated for DECE (The 2018 data is for first admission cycle only and not for the complete year)

Source: IGNOU 2018

Demographic Profile of Learners

In terms of rural/urban/tribal location, nearly three-fourths (72%) of the learners came from urban areas (Figure 9.2), reflecting that ECCE sector perhaps has a greater employment potential in the urban areas. While there is a boom in ECCE centres in rural areas (Kaul et al., 2017), the data reflects that either the demand for qualified staff is less in rural areas or while the demand exists, the university has not been able to expand its reach to rural and tribal areas. More data and analysis is needed on this aspect. DECE was also offered to international students in ten countries with an enrolment of approximately 500 learners till 2015.

Figure 9.2: *Enrolment by location: urban, rural and tribal*

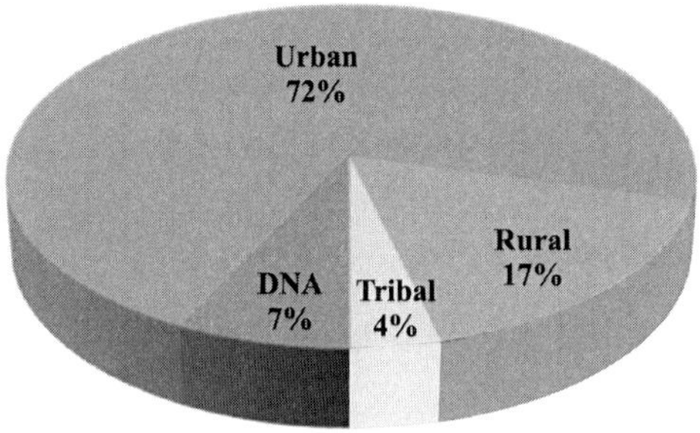

<!-- Pie chart: Urban 72%, Rural 17%, DNA 7%, Tribal 4% -->

Source: IGNOU

In terms of state-wise location of learners, the National Capital Region (NCR) of Delhi had the maximum enrolment (25.6%). The next high enrolment states were Gujarat, Jharkhand and Maharashtra which accounted for 11.3%, 10.5% and 9.5% of the total enrolment, respectively (Figure 9.3).

The densely populated NCR of Delhi has a thriving preschool education sector with need for trained staff, which would explain the high enrolment from this region. Maharashtra and Gujarat have a history of vibrant ECCE services and it is no surprise that the IGNOU's Diploma programme is popular in these states. The high enrolment in Jharkhand could be due to special efforts of the Regional Centre to popularise the programme and the emphasis given to preschool education in the anganwadis of the government-run ICDS programme (Times of India, 2013).

At this juncture it may be appropriate to refer to the data from National Council of Teacher Education (NCTE) which is the regulatory body which notifies the syllabus for teacher education programmes and grants permission to institutions for running teacher education programmes. Data provided by the NCTE regarding the number of recognised pre-primary training courses available in the country shows that nineteen states/UTs,

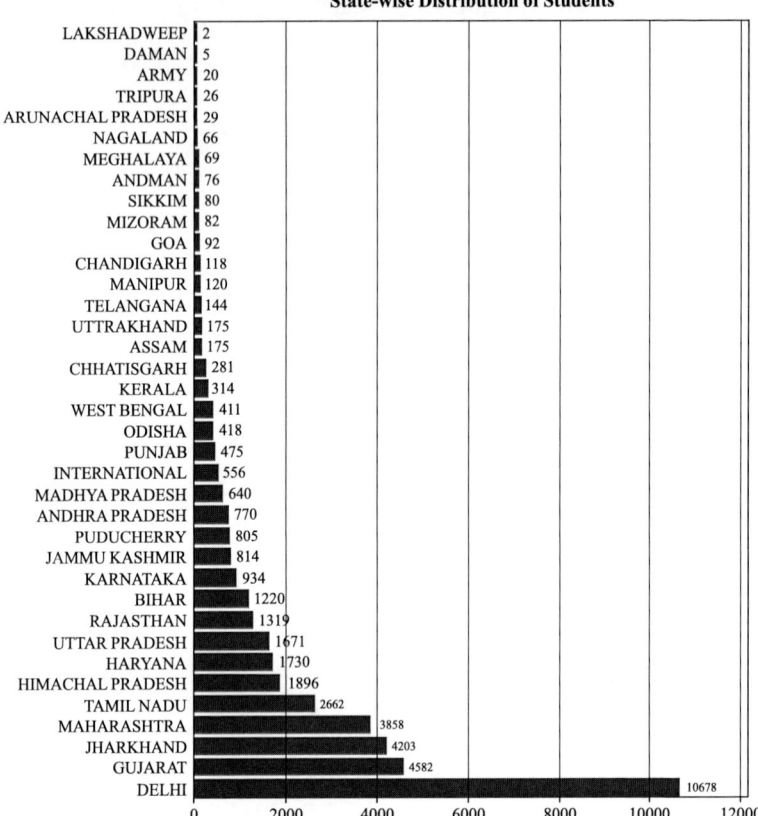

Figure 9.3: *State-wise enrolment*

did not have NCTE-recognised preschool teacher training courses (NCTE, 2020). However, in eighteen of these states/UTs, including in the North-eastern states, learners had enrolled for DECE programme. From inception till 2017, 6726 learners have enrolled in the programme form these states. DECE does not claim to be a pre-service teacher training programme in the sector of ECCE and does not have NCTE recognition for the same. Yet, as enrolment data shows, it is considered to be an acceptable teacher education course in these states and union territories. Furthermore, the states which have NCTE-accredited programmes also see high enrolment in DECE. This could be because of two possible reasons: firstly, that the current number of NCTE accredited programmes are not enough to meet the demand, or secondly, the prospective students want an ECCE qualification through alternative modalities, as their situation may not allow them to undertake regular face-to-face programmes.

The implication of this finding is that distance education needs to be accepted as a legitimate means of acquiring professional qualifications in the sector of ECCE. The NCTE needs to broaden its perspective and work towards developing norms for offering courses in teacher education through the open and distance learning mode. The teacher education study conducted by the Centre for Early Childhood Education and Development (2011), at Ambedkar University, Delhi, also made a recommendation to this effect.

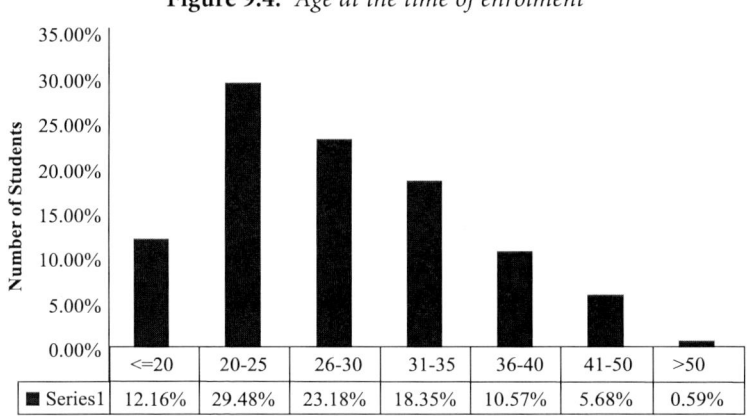

Figure 9.4: *Age at the time of enrolment*

- Analysis of learners' age at the time of enrolment shows about 42% of the learners to be under 25 years of age and 52% in the 26–40 years age range. This points towards the wide-ranging appeal of the programme across varied age groups which is perhaps linked with the varied motivations of enrolment.
- The gender profile reflected a high majority of women

learners (93%); 46% of them were unmarried.
- Regarding educational qualification at time of enrolment, around 71% of the learners had enrolled after completion of schooling; 24.62% learners were graduates and 4.09% learners were postgraduates.
- The social category representation indicated that most of the students belonged to general category (73%) and 10%, 7% and 6% learners belonged to Other Backward Classes, Scheduled Castes and Scheduled Tribes, respectively.
- Till July 2018, the number of persons with disabilities enrolled in DECE was 232. The programme largely attracted unemployed learners (76%).

Programme Completion Statistics

Since the launch of the programme in 1995 a total of 12,533 learners have completed the programme and have been awarded DECE Diploma till the convocation held in 2017. This translated into an average success rate of only 29.55%; however, during the years 2015–16, it was above 55% and indicated that more and more students are completing the programme. Seen in context of the fact that the national pass percentage at the graduate level is less than 40% (MHRD, GOI, 2016), DECE programme completion rate is worthy of appreciation.

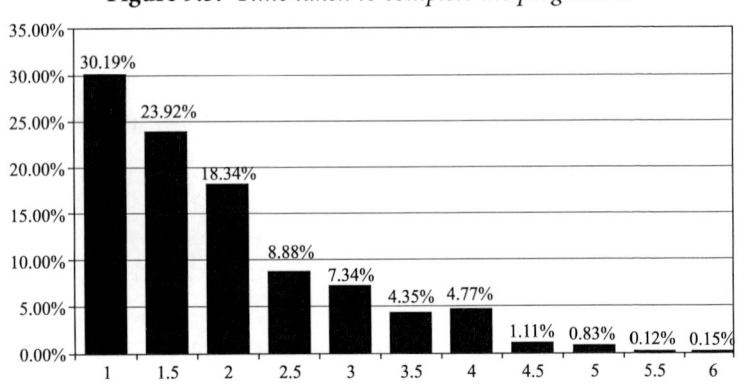

Figure 9.5: *Time taken to complete the programme*

Data for the period 1995 to 2018 shows that the majority of the learners (approximately 75%) complete the programme within two years (Figure 9.5). Around 30% of the learners complete the programme within one year, while another 42.26% of them finish it in a two-year period.

Conclusion

This study, was undertaken to understand the enrolment pattern, profile of the learners who enrol for IGNOU's Diploma in Early Childhood Care and Education, and programme completion statistics. The study assumes special importance in the present-day context where ECCE has captured the nation's attention and has been brought centrestage with the announcement of the National Education Policy 2020. The policy gives due importance to early childhood by recognising it as the foundational stage of learning. The policy considers Open Distance Learning as a source of increased access, equity and inclusion. Specifically, for the training of ECCE teachers, the policy highlights the need for accredited programmes run through digital/distance mode which would allow in-service teachers to acquire ECCE qualification without much disruption to their work (MHRD, GOI, 2020).

That the programme has maintained a steady enrolment rate of more than 2000 since 2003 and that the enrolment has shown a further steady increase since 2014, is an indication that it addresses a felt need in society. The DECE programme has special relevance in 18 states and UTs where, in the absence of any NCTE-recognised ECCE teacher training institution, the learners have had the opportunity of acquiring professional qualification in the sector of ECCE by enrolling in this programme. Since inception till the year 2017, 6726 learners have enrolled in the programme from these states. NCTE has not yet granted recognition for any distance education programme as a pre-service teacher training programme. Given NCTE's own lack of reach in many states and

UTs and the programme's popularity, this has implications for laying down norms for offering programmes through distance education by the NCTE.

An analysis of the learners' profile shows that a large number of learners are unemployed women from urban areas across diverse age groups and from the northern and western states of India. The programme's reach needs to be expanded to rural and tribal populations and southern, eastern and north-eastern states.

By 2030, the minimum qualification for teaching will be a four-year integrated B.Ed degree (MHRD, GOI, 2020). However, in the time period that it takes to operationalise this universally across the country, a multi-layered approach needs to be adopted in order to enable existing in-service teachers, many of whom are untrained, to incrementally enhance their qualifications. Further, many new teachers will also join the workforce before the four-year B.Ed. becomes operational. Given that 19 states do not have recognised teacher education institutions to even offer the present two-year Diploma in Preschool Education after 10+2, it would be challenging to make the four-year B.Ed programme universally available across the country by 2030. With strengthened mechanisms for monitoring the practicum training and internship practice, the ODL, online and blended modes of education can be used for creating modular programmes with multiple entry and exit options at six months, one year and two years. Also, the Foundational Stage articulated in the National Education Policy 2020, comprises sub-stages of preschool years and early primary years. Therefore, two separate programmes for each of these sub-stages, each of two-year duration can be conceptualised, which will give flexible options to aspiring teachers and also lessen the load of immediately devising a full scale four-year B.Ed programme. These programmes can be modular in nature, leaving the choice to the teacher, whether or not she wants to acquire qualifications covering the entire Foundational Stage.

It is in this context that ODL programmes such as IGNOU's Diploma in Early Childhood Care and Education described in this paper assume importance. Norms for offering teacher education programmes for the Foundational Stage must be developed by the National Council for Teacher Education.

References

Centre for Early Childhood Education and Development (CECED). (2011). *Preparing teachers for early childhood care and education.* Ambedkar University.

Ministry of Human Resource Development. (2016). *Educational statistics at a glance.* https://www.education.gov.in/sites/upload_files/mhrd/files/statistics-new/ESG2016.pdf.

Ministry of Human Resource Development. (2020). *National education policy.* https://www.education.gov.in/sites/upload_files/mhrd/files/NEP_Final_English_0.pdf.

Indira Gandhi National Open University (IGNOU). (2015). *Three decades of distance education.* http://www.ignou.ac.in//userfiles/Three%20Decades%20of%20Distance%20Education P_1_5(2).pdf.

School of Continuing Education, Indira Gandhi National Open University. (2018). *Programme guide: Diploma in early childhood care and education.* Indira Gandhi National Open University.

Kaul, V., Bhattacharjea, S., Chaudhary, A. B., Ramanujan, P., Banerji, M., & Nanda, M. (2017). *The India early childhood education impact study.* UNICEF.

National Council for Teacher Education (2020). *NCTE 25th annual report (2019-2020).* Government of India. https://ncte.gov.in/Website/PDF/AnnualReport/English-2019-20.pdf.

Times of India. (2013, February 16). *Dictionaries in 9 languages for tribal children.* https://timesofindia.indiatimes.com/city/ranchi/Dictionaries-in-9-languages-for-tribal-children/articleshow/18534895.cms?referral=PM.

10

The 5Ws and 1H of Teachers' Professional Development

Maya Menon

India has one of the largest education systems in the world, involving, inarguably, the largest numbers of teachers and under-15 children.[1] Children in the age group 0-6 years constitute around 158 million of the population of India (2011 census Untitled Page (icds-wcd.nic.in).

While efforts seem to be underway at the central and state government levels with regard to Early Childhood Care and Education (ECCE), the actual status of education of children in the under-6 years segment is almost unknown (Ohara, 2013). Our learning levels by any international standards are abysmal, and teachers are invariably blamed. The quality of teachers and teaching is of grave concern. One can truly understand this only when one sits in and observes what happens in classes, school after school, across the country.

What is even more worrying is that nobody in a position to drive policy really understands the enormity of the problem and its root causes. Instead, officials and policy-makers take recourse to short-sighted, quick-fix, non-sustainable actions.

So, what can be done? One way is to place rigorous high-quality pre-service teacher education and teachers' Continuing Professional Development (CPD) at the centre of all educational reform.

CPD is a complex domain and not easy to understand. One way to investigate it would be by using the 5W1H approach—Why, What, Who, Where, When and How.

Why is Professional Development of Teachers Critical for India?

We are caught in a culture of contradiction—as a nation we deeply value education, but we do not have a culture of ongoing learning and development. This is particularly noticeable in the teaching profession.

There is indisputable evidence that competent teachers and effective teaching are the most critical factors that improve school systems and ensure learning amongst students. When teacher quality is not satisfactory, there will be and already are deep and long-term repercussions for schools and students.

The vast majority of the teachers teaching our young have themselves had a very mediocre learning experience in school or college or teacher training. Teachers themselves have not grown with a strong sense of personal identity nor have they evolved a professional one. This naturally affects quality of educational experience for young school-goers. Pupils are rarely allowed to think, discuss and question in the classroom. Even dedicated, competent teachers genuinely believe that effective learning happens only if they explain and do all the talking in class. They ask questions more as a token rather than with a concerted plan to engage students in critical thinking. If a visitor sits in on their class, teachers tend to be even more vocal in an attempt to make a *show of effective teaching*. In early years classes there is loud chanting of numbers, words, rhymes, rather than quiet and focused learning of skills.

Without a concerted but thoughtful neutralisation of the insidious negative influences of one's own educational experience, teachers will continue to perpetuate the educational ills done to them. No teacher walks into a classroom wanting to be a bad or mediocre teacher. But many teachers in India are that. To become a country of great schools, we all need to become better teachers, every single one of us.

What Sort of Development Opportunities are Meaningful for Teachers?

One important point to keep in mind is that there is no readymade formula for improving or enabling great teaching. But for any professional development opportunity to be meaningful for teachers, it should be ongoing, sustained and need-based. It could range from something as simple and basic as body language, voice and demeanour, to development of one's personhood, interpersonal skills, teaching methodologies, questioning skills and classroom management approaches, to formative assessment, meaningful use of technology, reflection and documentation. Each of these aspects requires honest review of existing practice, exploring new and more effective teaching approaches recognising these approaches in class and acquiring fluency, with requisite coaching support made available and timely feedback provided.

One model to consider when thinking about professional development (PD) would be to steer teachers from unconscious incompetence to conscious incompetence to conscious competence and finally unconscious competence. It's only thoughtful and focused professional development that helps teachers make the shift. For acquiring unconscious competence in any aspect of effective teaching practice, a teacher needs to practise for at least 50–60 hours.

Students with the best teachers can learn twice as fast as average, and this happens only with effective coaching of teachers and deliberate practice of a range of teaching skills.

What are the Key Obstacles to Professional Development?

There are several depending on the location and context of the teachers concerned.

1. Authentic, self-directed learning is an alien concept to most teachers, because they have never fully participated in their own learning. They have been recipients of a schooling or college experience, but every action they took was with a view to passing or doing well in exams.

2. The vast majority of Education Department officials, school principals, school managements are not able to distinguish between in-service training of teachers and professional development of teachers. These two terms are used synonymously, but they are different. In-service training is training for teachers, without any clear outcome or intent on the part of the stakeholder. Professional development on the other hand is handing over the power to make an improvement in one's practice to the teachers themselves. One doesn't preclude the other. Often effective in-service training is the first step that teachers undertake for their professional development. But both in-service training of teachers and professional development need to emphasise measurable outcomes.
3. Professional development and career growth need to go hand-in-hand. So far, initial teacher education or early childhood care and education, does not have built-in opportunities to think about planning for career growth and/or honing one's craft. The focus continues to be on doing a set of assignments and clearing the exams to get the piece of paper that confers a trained teacher status.
4. Inadequate allocation and ineffective use of funds for teacher development. Professional development at best is a dispensable cost. So, under the guise of PD, schools invite guest speakers or do half-day or one day orientation programmes, that have no clear stated outcomes or follow-up in terms of actions to implement in the classroom. Effective and meaningful professional development doesn't come cheap—but in the long-run it pays to invest for the greater moral imperative of providing rigorous and relevant education to all our children.

Why should One Spend Time and Money on PD when it doesn't Really Change Things Much?

Great teachers are not born—they are made—slowly but surely! As the American writer and philosopher Will Durant said

'We are what we repeatedly do. Excellence is not an act, but a habit.'

However, no professional development or in-service training of teachers goes waste, if there is clarity on the part of the school administrator and the teachers, on the overall objective and expected outcomes after a PD opportunity. Moreover, with if there is effective follow-up and purposeful school-based support, PD definitely brings positive change in the classroom and school as a whole.

Unfortunately, though, often the opportunity of, and money spent on, professional development is squandered, owing to indifference or lack of oversight on the part of decision-makers of the school, be they government officials or private school managements. Sadly, with most school decision-makers, infrastructural improvements tend to take priority and precedence over improving teaching quality—even when there is overwhelming evidence that it's good teachers and great teaching that ensures student learning.

Who should Undertake Professional Development?

All educators teaching at any level—pre-primary, primary, middle, high school, higher secondary and tertiary education need to undertake professional development, through their careers. I recently had a 90-year-old legendary Principal attending a session we were conducting on effective school leadership and she participated like everyone else, raising her hand to ask a question or offer a perspective. That was truly humbling for me!

Educators at all levels need job-embedded assistance as they struggle to adapt new curricula and new instructional practices to their unique classroom contexts (Guskey & Yoon, 2008).

Who should Provide Professional Development?

This depends on what the focus area for professional development is. For example, if a teacher wants to improve her voice modulation or diction (which incidentally is vital for ECCE teachers), a drama professional or voice coach could offer effective PD. Similar specialists could provide support in aspects of music, art, and movement in education. However, if it is pedagogy or classroom routines and processes, and effective assessment practices, the best people to provide professional development are indeed those who have honed their own teaching practices by dint of hard work, reflection, professional development, taking risks and use of imagination.

There is a worrying tendency to get swayed by technology providers' short-term solutions to fix deep-seated problems with regard to educational quality. Technology certainly offers solutions for doctors, architects, artists, lawyers, etc. But professional development for any of these professionals, would not be driven or provided by technology-solution providers. They would be provided by specialist doctors, architects etc. Technology would be a great medium for sharing specialists' ideas and solutions.

When would Teachers be Ready for PD? When should Teachers Undertake PD?

To quote Dylan Wiliam (2012), 'It's important to recognise that 'Every teacher fails on a daily basis. If you are not failing, you are not paying attention. Because we fail all the time' … Our daily experience as a teacher is a failure. Which makes it the best job in the world. Because you never get any good at it. This job (we) do is so hard that one lifetime isn't enough to master it'. So, again as Dylan had said in his speech at SSAT conference, 'every single (teacher) needs to accept the commitment to carry on improving our practice until we retire or die. That's the deal'.[2]

If the teacher education they go through was well-designed and purposeful, all new teachers would know that their professional learning and expertise has only just begun with their initial teaching qualification. There is a lifetime of learning to truly become expert in their chosen field. A good strategy to make teachers ready for PD is for every school administrator and head to assume that every teacher wants to improve their teaching. To quote Tomsett (2015) 'It's this attitude that will gain cultural currency over a period of time.'

Where is the Time for PD?

If our survival or a school's survival depended on it, we would make time for professional development. Moreover, we have to move away from the notion that teachers need to work only the same number of hours or days as students. Nowhere is this written in stone—but teachers and school management and governments have become conditioned to this practice.

Besides, we don't need to set aside vast amounts of time for professional development, outside of school hours. With careful thought and planning, every minute that's spent by a teacher in class, engaging with students, throws up opportunities for reflection, feedback by a peer or a senior expert. Similarly, listening to a podcast by a specialist teacher, on the way to work, reading an article by an expert on early years education, sharing a teaching approach successfully implemented in one's class all offer ways to develop professionally. And apart from all the above, it is always useful to enroll for need-based formal professional workshops and courses on aspects of effective educational practice.

How Can we Measure the Impact of PD?

Like all good learning, professional development too needs to be evaluated based on what one wants to achieve in terms of learning for the teachers, and more importantly their learners, and then work backward from there. According to Thomas Guskey (2002a), there are five levels of evaluating professional development. The first level is that of gauging participants' immediate response and reaction to the learning experience. Here participants can share their opinion about the usefulness of the content, what they like and/or what they dislike. The second level measures participants' learning—did the participants achieve the intended learning outcomes from the professional development engagement. Level three to five are the evaluation levels—wherein at level three, the institution's support and change is assessed, participants' use of the new knowledge and skills in the classroom, is gauged in level four and finally how it gets reflected in students' learning outcomes in level five.

This informs us that when measuring impact of professional development, it is necessary to rigorously examine multiple methods and levels. Just getting feedback and testimonials doesn't accurately assess the real time benefit of PD. However, expecting marked improvement in student learning after a few days of PD is an unrealistic estimation.

How does PD Impact Teachers and Teaching?

Most academics in the past have attempted to design PD programmes that bring about a change in teacher beliefs, attitudes and perceptions, which they considered are vital precursors to bringing about change in classroom practices and behaviors. This to many practitioners seems a rather unachievable effort. However, Thomas Guskey (1986, 2002b) suggests an alternative and perhaps more practical model for explaining change after professional development. As explained by Guskey (2002b), this chain-like-sequential model suggests that the focus of PD should be to initially equip teachers with the competencies and confidence to change their classroom practices for the better. When these changes bring about an improvement in student learning outcomes, over an extended period of time, then and then only do teachers' beliefs and attitudes actually change.

So, how does all this add up for early childhood education practitioners?

These questions have for long been outside the purview of early years educators. It's important to place ECCE alongside the rest of school education, while recognising the special consideration of very young learners in a large and diverse population like

India's. The Government of India in its recently released National Education Policy (NEP 2020), has made decisive effort to put early childhood care and education as a fundamental part of its education policy for the country. It has proposed a 5+3+3+4 structure for schooling. The initial three years of ECCE have been integrated with the first two years of primary schooling. ECCE has been referred to by the Ministry of Human Resource Development (MHRD) as the 'Foundation of Learning'. ECCE has also been placed under the ambit of Right to Education (RTE) unlike in the first ten years after the law was enacted. However, it's still early days and there could be many gaps in how the national policy is finally implemented by every state. There are also many questions yet to be answered by the NEP 2020, such as, how will the first three years of ECCE (which, in a large, diverse and under-resourced nation like India occur in the informal anganwadis and balwadis), merge with the remaining two years of the Foundational Learning segment as stated in the NEP. The latter two years are currently part of formal primary schooling. How will the ECCE teachers be trained? What will be the ECCE curriculum? Will the ECCE teachers be paid as per government salary norms? The next 3–5 years will reveal what we have in store for India's very young and most vulnerable learners.

Notes

1. MHRD Data: 233 million students in Grades 1–10 and 255 million students enrolled in Grades 1–12; 8.3 million teachers (Grades 1–12). No data on Early Childhood Education in India from UNICEF.
2. Excerpts from the speech by Dylan at SSAT conference 2012 (https://www.youtube.com/watch?v=r1LL9NX1hUw).

References

A critical analysis of India's education policy: Determining objectives, outcomes and flaws. (2017, March 14). Accessed from https://nickledanddimed.com/2017/03/22/a-critical-analysis-of-indias-education-policy-determining-objectives-outcomes-and-flaws/.

Child Population (0–6 Age group). (n.d).Accessed from http://censusmp.nic.in/censusmp/All-PDF/4childpopulation0-6-21.12.pdf.

Dylan, W. (2012). How do we prepare our students for a world we cannot possibly imagine? Speech delivered at the SSAT National Conference, Liverpool.

Guskey, T. (2002a). *Does it make a difference? Evaluating professional development, educational leadership.* ASCD. Retrieved from http://www.ascd.org/publications/educational-leadership/mar02/vol59/num06/Does-It-Make-a-Difference%C2%A2-Evaluating-Professional-Development.aspx.

Guskey, T. (2002b). Professional development and teacher change. *Teachers and teaching: Theory and practice, 8* (3/4), 2002. DOI: 10.1080/135406002100000512.

Guskey, T. R. & Yoon, K. S. (2009). *What works in professional development?* Phi Delta Kappa, 90(7), 495–500. https://doi.org/10.1177/003172170909000709.

Ministry of Human Resource Development. 2020. *National Education Policy 2020.*

Ohara, Y. (2013, October 11). Early childhood care and education in India. Accessed from http://www.childresearch.net/projects/ecec/2013_13.html.

Tomsett, J. (2015). *This much I know about love over fear … Creating a culture of truly great teaching.* Crown House Publishing Ltd.

11

Implementing Inclusive Education in Early Childhood Settings
Preparing Teachers for the Role

Ankur Madan

The importance of providing a stimulating environment to children in the early years is well-established and founded on principles of long-term benefits to growth and development of young children. India's commitment to providing such an environment to *all* children in the age group of 0–6 years is reflected in its various policies and programmes. However, a large section of the population of children in this age group fails to find representation in such initiatives. These are children with disabilities.

According to a recent UNESCO report, there are an estimated 7.8 million children with disabilities aged 19 or younger in India. Of these, 1.3 million are in the 0–4 years age group and 1.9 million are in the age group of 5–9 years. Of these, three-fourths of the children under five years of age do not attend any educational institution (UNESCO, 2019). While this data is not quite representative of the actual number of children with disabilities in India, it is amply clear that a significant section of the population in the country faces marginalisation, which not only reflects the failure to achieve the objectives of creating an inclusive society based on principles of social justice and human rights, but also deprives very young children of the benefits of a stimulating environment in their formative years. In this paper I explore inclusive education in the context of early childhood education: the focus is on preparing teachers to work in inclusive settings with young children.

Inclusive Education

In India, from 1990 onwards, the concept of inclusive education made an entry into several important government policy and programme documents (such as the DPEP, PIED, PWD (1995), SSA, RTE, NECCE, the RPWD Act 2016, and most recently, the NEP 2020). While this has led to a fair amount of awareness and support for the 'idea' of inclusion, it has had very little impact on the ground. The fact that children with disabilities continue to remain outside the mainstream despite impetus from several robust policy measures is primarily due to insufficient engagement with the concept of inclusive education as it applies to the unique, diverse and complex situation of the Indian education system as well as the ambiguities that surround its implementation. In the Western world too where the concept of inclusive education originated much earlier than it did in India, inclusion is considered a complex matter with fissures appearing over time in practice because of the gap between conceptualisation and realisation. There is nevertheless a general consensus that inclusive education is concerned with *all* children and that it is a transformative process to increase access (or presence) of all children in school systems, enhance their acceptance and maximise participation and achievement levels of all children (and not just those from marginalised groups) (Artiles et al., 2006). According to Singal (2014), inclusion is achieved when every child's learning experience becomes equally meaningful, empowering, and provides them with resources, opportunities and capabilities to make the right choices for their own lives.

Despite the lack of a coherent understanding of the concept and the difficulties in its implementation, there is increasing consensus among academics and practitioners about the role that inclusive education can play in building an inclusive society and achieving the goal of 'education for all' for India. In the same context, the role of early childhood education is valued for its contribution towards ensuring retention and meaningful participation of all children in the education system.

Inclusion and Early Childhood Education

With impetus from initiatives at the international level, several policy measures in the recent years in India emphasise the importance of inclusion in the early years. For instance, the Salamanca Framework for Action, Article 53 (Chowdhury, 2011), to which India is a signatory, explicitly recommended setting up of early childhood programmes that recognised principles of inclusion. The National Early Childhood Care and Education Framework (2013) states: 'Inclusion in the early years implies that children with disabilities should have access to mainstream early learning environments which should accommodate them with a child-centred pedagogy, capable of meeting their individual needs' (Singh, 2005, p. 16). Likewise, inclusion finds a place in the vision statement of the National Early Childhood Care and Education Policy (2013). Support at the policy level comes with the wide recognition of the potential of early identification, intervention, and stimulation in improving impaired functions and disability during the early years.

However, even with such wide acceptance of the importance of inclusion, the reality is different. Children in the early years continue to remain out of the mainstream. For example, the Integrated Child Development Services (ICDS), the largest early childhood care and education programme in the country had until recently, actively excluded children with disabilities from all its services, including nutrition and monitoring of health (Alur, 2009). Preschool services, private or public rarely welcome children with disabilities in their settings, making inclusion a distant dream in India. It is beyond the scope of this paper to conduct a comprehensive analysis of the reasons for this failure at the systemic level. However, it may suffice to say that apart from the conceptual incongruities discussed earlier, one of the main reasons why children with disabilities in the early years remain out of the mainstream is the lack of preparedness and hence resistance from teachers to accommodate them in their preschool settings.

This includes Anganwadi Workers as well as trained preschool teachers working in private and public settings.

Preparing Teachers for Inclusive Classrooms

'The literature on inclusive education is unanimous about no matter how excellent the educational infrastructure might be, how well articulated educational policy might be, how well resourced a programme might be, effective inclusion does not take place until regular classroom teachers deliver relevant and meaningful instruction to students with disabilities' (Das, Sharma & Singh, 2012, p. 2).

This statement succinctly captures the importance of teacher preparedness for effective inclusion. Several research studies show that teachers have negative attitudes towards children with disabilities and show resistance towards including them in their classrooms due to the following reasons:

- lack of skills/knowledge of curriculum adaptation, instructional and evaluation methods, cooperative learning techniques
- poor sociological and psychological understanding of disability
- lack of availability of teaching and learning material and equipment
- poor classroom management skills and inability to cope with large class sizes
- extra demands on teachers' time (Das, Sharma & Singh, 2012)

Add to that the stigma and negative identity that is associated with disability due to the prevalent medical model of disability. These attributions lead to marginalisation and exclusion of children with disabilities from the mainstream at an early age, much of it because educational institutions resist including them in their classrooms.

At this point then, it might be pertinent to ask, what are some important capabilities that professionals working with children at the preschool stage must possess so that all children, irrespective of their learning needs, can be meaningfully included in preschool classrooms?

Competencies of Inclusive Teachers

Training of professionals working with children with diverse learning needs in preschool classrooms must aim to enhance teachers' knowledge about special needs, impart specialised skills to work with the children, and bring about an attitudinal shift in their thinking and beliefs about inclusion and disability in general. At the same time, it must be noted that while certain competencies are certainly essential for professionals working with children with special needs, an inclusive classroom caters to *all* children and hence, whatever capacities the teachers develop should be applied in working with all the children in an inclusive classroom and not just those with special needs.

Some of the competencies that early childhood education professionals must possess in this regard are:

- knowledge about theoretical and practical concepts and principles underpinning inclusive education within a local context
- knowledge about relevant policies that support inclusive education
- theoretical knowledge about different models of learning and teaching children in the early years
- capability to manage the physical and social environment of a classroom
- ways of identifying and then overcoming barriers to learning
- basics of differentiating curriculum and assessment for children based on their individual needs

In addition to this, inclusive preschool teachers must learn to appreciate that collaboration is the key to successful inclusion. For this, teachers need to develop effective communication skills, capability to recognise and utilise parents and community as an important resource for learning, and use peer support and cooperation to help children learn in the classroom. Collaboration also entails acquiring leadership skills and the capability to work as an effective team member who can lend support to colleagues in enhancing their capabilities and bringing about attitudinal change in them. A teacher of an inclusive classroom must also show lifelong commitment towards her own professional development. As a reflective practitioner, with belief in evidence-based practice, the teacher should be capable of applying action research methods to enhance her own teaching and learning as well as contribute to the learning of other stakeholders (EADSNE, 2012).

Given the ad hoc nature of professional development opportunities available to train preschool teachers in India, aspiring to develop these competencies in preschool teachers and Anganwadi Workers seems like a tall order. Valid questions can be raised about how such large-scale skill development can be undertaken when hardly any systematic means of providing professional development to preschool teachers at the pre-service or in-service level are in place. While such concerns are indeed legitimate, my submission in this regard would be that we need to understand at the outset that our resistance to the idea of preparing teachers for inclusion arises from our misconception about the concept of inclusion itself. We need to realise that any preparation that a teacher requires to work with special needs in her class prepares her to work better with all the children in her classroom. Hence, inclusion does not necessitate preparation that is over and above the skills that a teacher requires to be an effective preschool teacher. By acquiring these so-called specialised skills, she can become a more effective teacher who has the ability to recognise individual differences among her pupils and is prepared to take measures to address them. Besides, diversity of learning needs in any classroom is an inevitability that every good teacher must learn to appreciate and attend to.

Hence, all professional development programmes for preschool teachers, irrespective of the scale and context must incorporate within their curricula the above-mentioned competencies as integral to their preparation for the role of working with young children. In this regard, the following are a few recommendations that may help such training programmes at the micro level, that is, at the level of individual early childhood education programmes and at the macro level, that is, large-scale teacher programmes for Anganwadi Workers and preschool teachers:

1. Programmes that prepare pre-service and in-service early childhood professionals to work with children with special needs should adopt long-term, systematic staff development plans rather than one-time, short-term programmes in order to prove effective (David & Kuyini, 2012). A functionally sustainable train-the-trainer model should be adopted wherein supervisors and teacher educators are provided with skills to train workers in order to reach out to the largest number of functionaries in relatively short periods of time. Helping teachers overcome their negative attitudes and building in them a sense of confidence in their ability to work with children with special needs should be an important objective of the skill development. The curriculum, irrespective of the scale must incorporate competencies mentioned in the earlier section of the paper with opportunities for reinforcement of the learning on a regular basis.

2. At the individual preschool programme level, ongoing in-service learning opportunities should be created wherein peer learning and collaboration form the thrust of such initiatives. Colleagues could be led by more informed peers to engage in continuous dialogue and discussion to alleviate negative attitudes, share effective techniques for curriculum differentiation, classroom management

and assessment, learn systematic ways of parent and community involvement and create an atmosphere of tolerance and acceptance for differences and diversity. All of this can be accomplished at a scale and pace that the individual programme sees as suitable, based on the availability of resources at its disposal and access to expert knowledge. Needless to say, such initiatives work best only when the leadership is convinced about the ideology of inclusion and is willing to invest energy and time in making the institution inclusive. It is also worth mentioning here that efforts such as these when initiated from within the institution are likely to meet with greater success than when they are imposed from outside, as stringent diktats at the systemic level.

3. It is clear that efforts towards sensitisation and skill development of preschool professionals will require similar competencies to be developed in the teacher educators as well. Teacher educators' beliefs and notions about disability and commitment towards creating an inclusive society will impact the way in which they design their curriculum and the conviction with which they deliver the content. Hence, the training of teacher educators of Anganwadi Workers as well as preschool teachers must make inclusive education an important curriculum agenda. For this it is important that training institutions of teacher educators become centres for conducting research and generating scholarship in inclusive education. Exposure to evidence-based practices will enable them to make convincing arguments in favour of inclusion in their classrooms and help them generate realistic, contextually relevant, workable solutions to deal with complex situations of diverse classrooms. Teacher education institutions for training preschool teachers should be located in universities and affiliated with departments of higher education with proven record of sound academic scholarship and research.

Conclusion

Having remained at the fringes of the education discourse, inclusive education continues to be a vexed issue in India, in concept as well as in practice. On the other hand, considering that the potential of early childhood education in bringing about discernible differences to the physical and intellectual lives of young children has begun to be recognised, it is absolutely pertinent that a significant section of the population of children with special needs is not excluded from the potential benefits of an early childhood education. The role that the early childhood professional can play in this regard is crucial and must be duly recognised. The impetus provided to Early Childhood Education and inclusion in the National Education Policy (2020) is an encouraging beginning towards this end. Equipping the professional, especially Anganwadi Workers with basic skills to provide meaningful intervention to children with different learning needs in every early childhood setting, should be the goal of all professional development activities related to early childhood education in the future. A comprehensive and collaborative plan of action that involves all stakeholders must be formulated to implement the NEP 2020 vision in letter and spirit. A sustained dialogue to enable early childhood education functionaries understand the concept of inclusive education and helping them overcome the psychological and attitudinal barriers that come in their way of adopting inclusive practices, is the only way forward and must be followed if we wish to fulfil our commitment to creating an inclusive society.

REFERENCES

Alur, M. and Bach, M. (2010). *The journey for inclusive education in the Indian sub-continent*. Routledge.

Artiles, A, J., Kozleski, E. B., Dorn, S. and Christensen, C. (2006). Learning in inclusive education research: Re-mediating theory and methods with a transformative agenda. *Review of Research in Education*, Vol. 30, *Special Issue on Rethinking Learning: What Counts as Learning and What Learning Counts*, 65–108.

Chowdhury, P. R. (2011). The right to inclusive education of persons with disabilities: The policy and practice implications. *Asia Pacific Journal of Human Rights and the Law, 12*(2), 1–35.

Das, A. K., Sharma, S. and Singh, V. K. (2012). Inclusive education in India: A paradigm shift in roles, responsibilities and competencies of regular school teachers. *Journal of Indian Education,* XXXVII (4).

David, R. and Kuyini, A. B. (2012). Social inclusion: Teachers as facilitators in peer acceptance of students with disabilities in regular classrooms in Tamil Nadu, India. *International Journal of Special Education, 27*(2), 1–12.

European Agency for Development of Special Needs Education. (2012). www.european-agency.org.

Ministry of Human Resource Development. (2020). *National education policy 2020.*

Ministry of Women and Child Development (2014). National early childhood care and education curriculum framework, Government of India.

Odom, L. S. (2000). Preschool inclusion: What we know and where we go from here. *Topics in Early Childhood Special Education, 20*(1), 20–27.

Singal, N. (2014). Entry, engagement and empowerment: Dilemmas for inclusive education in an Indian context. In L. Florian (Ed.). *The Sage handbook of special education, Vol 1,* 203–216. Sage.

UNESCO (2019). *N for nose. State of the education report for India 2019 children with disabilities.* UNESCO.

12

Inclusive Classrooms

Challenges of Deaf Learners and Their Teachers

Kanika M. Agarwal

The paper aims to shed light on the necessary teacher attributes and dispositions that various educational policies for the d/Deaf school children in India propose and how these could benefit deaf children in inclusive educational setups.

Never having experienced deafness, teachers consider inclusion of a deaf child in regular classrooms as impossible. Though inclusive education is a difficult step ahead in Indian classrooms, persistent efforts, and insight into issues of d/Deaf learners by the teachers, families, and local bodies, such as state governments and non-governmental institutes, can bring a significant amount of change in the quality of education for the deaf children.

Of all the disabilities in India, deafness is the most prevalent form of disability. As per the Census data of 2011, India has a population of more than 50 lakh deaf people out of which more than 4 lakhs belong to age group of 0–6 years. It is known that 80% of persons with hearing loss live in rural areas, whereas 80% of the rehabilitation services are centred in the urban areas (Randhawa, 2006, p. 3). Furthermore, myths about deafness in India have prevailed for long and persist in many parts of the country. Deafness is looked down upon by many (though the extent has reduced considerably recently) in India. As such, it becomes difficult for the families to find an appropriate special school[1] for their deaf child, especially in remote areas. The paper will shed some light on the necessary attributes of a teacher of the deaf child in inclusive classrooms[2], as mentioned in various schemes and policies by the Government of India.

Concepts Related to Deafness

Deafness[3] is defined as a hearing loss above 40 decibels. Depending upon the degree of loss of hearing, deafness is categorised as mild, severe and profound.

Table 12.1 defines and explains the differences in views of medical and social models of deafness.

Table 12.1: *Medical and social models of deafness*

Detail	Medical Deficit Model	Social/Cultural Model
Focus	Focus on inability to hear	Focus on visual learning ability of the d/Deaf
View of the world	Child considered impaired and in need of correction (through hearing aids, cochlear implants, etc.)	Child considered as a part of a culturally diverse community— the deaf community
Solution for deafness	Treatment for hearing loss	Counselling family members to find effective ways of developing the child
Career and contribution to the society	Child is considered abnormal and dependent	Diversity is welcomed, child is included just like everyone else (with necessary modifications in accessibility)

Challenges of Deaf Learners

Table 12.2 explains the issues that a d/Deaf child and their parents face and the effects of these issues on development of the child.

Need for Inclusive Education

Throughout the document, the National Curriculum Framework (2005) has stressed upon the need for inclusive education. When considering deaf children, it can be taken that inclusive education

Table 12.2: *Causes and effects of challenges faced by deaf children*

Cause	Effect
Lack of early intervention programmes for deaf children in India	• No awareness among family members and general public • Confusion in families over choices for their child
Limited interaction with family	• Missing crucial years of language learning and cognitive development
Medical approach instead of cultural approach	• Exhaustive speech therapy sessions • No exposure to culturally deaf communities • Heterogeneity neglected. All children compelled to follow oral approach. It helps only some

will expose deaf children to hearing children and that is when development of both the children will take place. Daniel (2015) states that though special education was initially intended to be a part of special schools, with integration of more and more students in regular schools, special education in regular schools has become common now. She explains the importance of specially designed learning packages for optimal learning.

Deafness is not just one disability with certain benchmark levels of severity. It is an entire spectrum that impacts not just the ability to hear, but other areas of a deaf child such as communication, speech, cognition, instruction reception etc. The degree of deafness impacts these factors and hence, it is important to provide instructional input based on the children's individual needs. An array of research based multimodal teaching discourses are now available for the special educators to choose from. Ensuring use of appropriate discourse modality can help in better acquisition of first language, thereby leading to overall development of the deaf child.

Meeting the Instructional Needs of a d/Deaf Child

To ensure proper first language development, early intervention programmes are needed in schools. Based on the degree of deafness of the child, teachers can choose one of the following modes of communication to ensure that classroom instructions are fully accessible to the deaf child:

(a) ***Sign bilingualism:*** This method considers sign language as the first language of a deaf child and subjects are taught using sign language and another language.

(b) ***Total communication:*** This method uses a mix of various modes of communication: signs, written mode, gestures, or visual aids in spoken language syntax along with lip-movements/speech. A teacher can choose a combination of methods (one or more) depending on the individual needs of the child.

(c) ***Cued speech:*** This is a visual mode of communication that uses hand shapes and placements in combination with the mouth movements of speech to make the phonemes of a spoken language look different from each other. The hand-shapes help a deaf child to understand the lip-movements.

(d) ***Oralism:*** Education is imparted through spoken dialect only. The child has to lip-read the teacher to understand her instructions. Child can be given speech therapy sessions to help him improve his lip-reading ability.

Inclusion Outside Classrooms

A teacher of the deaf child should ensure active socialisation, at par with non-deaf children (Shirin, 1999), for example, by making sure the child is involved with peers and is an active participant in all sports or activities that interest him/her. Such inclusion will need modification in instructional design. Consider a deaf child who is enthusiastic about football. If he is involved in a team with hearing peers, some of the visual modifications that will need to be brought in are providing written (visual) boards and signs (for sign language user) for spoken content, use of flash-lights along with a whistle, etc.

Ensuring that the child has direct and fully accessible communication established between his peers and other teachers will help the child's self-confidence. Just like trips or camps held for regular school children, deaf children should be provided with accessible academic outings (with interpreters) and/or guided to camps held exclusively for the deaf.

Providing Aid to Families

Most parents who have never interacted with a deaf child/adult before, have no idea how to deal with their child. As a result, the onus of having the child bond with the parents, falls on the teacher of the deaf child. Thus, it is important for the teacher to keep knowledge of both medical and cultural models of deafness and give open and broad options to parents to choose from. Further, the teachers should also assess the level of deafness of the child, the precise communication needs, psycho-emotional and cognitive needs of the deaf child and then counsel the parents on the possible course of action to enable them to mould their child into a responsible, self-sufficient adult.

Training Module on Hearing Impairment, developed by SSA (Sarva Shiksha Abhiyan), defines various concepts surrounding deafness and a chart of developmental milestones for a deaf child as per his age. The latest National Education Policy (NEP 2020) also emphasises the importance of multifaceted (flexible, multi-level) education that is safe and accessible to every child. Both of these documents focus on providing high-quality education to every child, that would help provide sustainable development of the child, thereby making him a global citizen.

Being in touch with NGOs, deaf right activists and other organisations that work for the deaf children can enhance the knowledge base of the teachers.

Procuring Aid from Third-party Agencies

The Rights for Persons with Disabilities Act (2016) (hereafter referred to as RPWD 2016) has mandated accessible material to all children studying in schools. In the case of children using sign language, accessibility may be provided by creating digital resources where written curriculum is translated in Indian Sign Language or a more visual format. Calling in third party agencies to provide signed interpretations of the textbooks for signing d/Deaf children could help the teachers make the curriculum accessible to signing children. The most recent development in this direction has been an exchange of MoUs between Indian Sign Language Research and Training Centre (ISLRTC) and NCERT to translate English- and Hindi-medium textbooks into Indian Sign Language.

Social organisations and associations such as National Convention of Educators of the Deaf (NCED), ISLRTC, etc. organise educational conferences exclusively for teachers of d/Deaf children. Attending workshops for special educators with focus on deafness can help the teachers express their concerns to other teachers and also receive suggestions/solutions for the issues they face.

Some organisations like Deeds, Deaf Enabled Foundation, v-shesh, undertake literacy programmes for d/Deaf schoolchildren. These organisations hire d/Deaf trainers and train them to cater to the needs of d/Deaf children. Though there has been no research on the effectiveness of d/Deaf trainers, it is seen that these d/Deaf trainers, having experienced similar and myriad challenges, understand the needs of the d/Deaf learners better and are thus able to establish better rapport with them. The institutes also arrange meetings with prominent deaf role models. Meeting such role models can enhance confidence of the child, the family, and teachers. Names of some of the organisations are listed below.

Huge student-teacher ratio in Indian classrooms is another hindrance for the teachers in providing special attention to the d/Deaf child. Assistance from volunteers through NGOs and individualised education plans (IEPs), based on the learning needs of the children, can help the teacher plan and execute her lessons better.

Some organisations that hire deaf trainers are:

1. Deaf Enabled Foundation—A d/Deaf-led NGO working with d/Deaf youth in the fields of skill development and promotion of higher education. Additionally, DEF is rolling out the DEF e-academy providing online courses for the deaf. In order to promote the use of Indian Sign Language DEF has developed an App called DEF-ISL
2. Indian Sign Language Research and Training Centre (ISLRTC)—The first government body in India working towards research and development of Indian Sign Language and developing digital resources like signed dictionary
3. v-shesh—A for-profit impact enterprise that works in bridging the opportunity divide for persons with disabilities in accessing employment and education. As a part of its d/Deaf education operations, v-shesh has created English learning resources in digital/other formats customised for d/Deaf school children
4. Speech and Hearing Action Society (SAHAS)—An organisation working with parents of deaf children, guiding them on appropriate methods for early detection of deafness and intervention for appropriate language and cognitive development
5. Haryana Welfare Society for Persons with Speech and Hearing Impairment—A society with eight centres in Haryana working with special schools to provide early intervention, creation of digital content in sign language and teacher training courses like D.Ed. in special education and Diploma in Teaching Indian Sign Language (DTISL)
6. National Institute of Speech and Hearing—A government based institute in Kerala, that provides an array of teacher

training programmes, academic courses for d/Deaf adults, early intervention programmes for d/Deaf children between the ages of 0 and 6 years, among other resources
7. ISL Connect—An online platform for d/Deaf individuals that offers live classes from d/Deaf teachers on a variety of subjects, using Indian Sign language
8. Deaf Child Worldwide—An international arm of the National Deaf Children's Society in the UK provides training to support partners with technical knowledge and expertise that can be utilised by teams within communities including schools
9. Yunikee—A platform that creates learning, skill building and lifestyle content that is accessible by the deaf community in sign language

Adaptation

While the Training Module on Hearing Impairment developed by SSA (pp. 59–60) mentions the need for adaptation of appropriate curriculum, NCERT (2006) and NEP 2020 papers emphasise this throughout the document. The onus is on trying various teaching strategies and ensuring effective usage of these strategies in inclusive classrooms to ensure internalisation of knowledge rather than rote learning. The documents also emphasise the need for Individualised Education Plans (IEPs) for d/Deaf children (and other children with disabilities). This is because the child may be unable to follow the instructions in classroom due to one of the many reasons such as, inability to follow speech and lip movements, presence of multiple disabilities, limited cognitive understanding, etc. It is thus the responsibility of the teacher to assess the exact level of the child and approach school authorities for appropriate modifications in curriculum and assessment, instead of lowering expectations from the child.

The curriculum should be such that it matches the cognitive needs of a child along with the language level. The topics should resonate with the child's prior knowledge-base to make the learning experience meaningful. As an example, consider a d/Deaf child studying in class V. The textbook curriculum for environmental science involves concepts like water management systems, food chains and food webs. If the child has never had exposure to these concepts earlier, it might become difficult for the child to make sense of the topics now. Further, if the language (reading) level of the child is not upto the grade level, the situation may get further complicated for the teacher, since the child may not be able to read and learn. A special educator may then need to make the following adaptations to the curriculum:

1. Add background information on the topics in her lessons
2. Add real-life experiences for the child to make concepts clearer
3. Add labelled pictures of the topic for easier retention
4. Simplify vocabulary and sentence structure of the text to match the current reading level of the d/Deaf child, or convert the text into sign language if the child is an extensive signer
5. Provide glossary for difficult/new vocabulary in written/visuals/signs

Assessment can be adapted in a similar manner. The language of the assessment should be accessible to the d/Deaf child, that is, the questions should be in simpler language or in sign language. For subjects like EVS, Moral education etc., students using sign language should be provided scribes.

Conclusion

With the growth of number of d/Deaf school children in India, inclusive education has become a need of the hour. Huge student-teacher ratio in schools, does not allow teachers much time for attending to the needs of a d/Deaf child. However, a teacher of a d/Deaf child can provide a child with sustainable development through simple steps:

1. Stay up-to-date with understanding of medical aspects and social models of deafness
2. Stay up-to-date with various communication modes with d/Deaf children
3. Counsel parents on making informed choices regarding the preferred mode of communication with their child
4. Create IEPs specific to needs of the d/Deaf child
5. Act as a bridge between the d/Deaf child and his/her hearing family
6. Adapt curriculum and assessments to suit the needs of the child
7. Provide complete access to the child both inside and outside the classroom so as to make the child feel included
8. Take help from third-party agencies to develop accessible content resources
9. Talk to d/Deaf role models and d/Deaf teachers, and introduce the child to them

Notes

1. Special schools are the segregated schools where only children with a specific disability are taught.
2. An educational setup that includes regular children as well as children with deafness and/or other disabilities.
3. Based on the degree of hearing loss, the Government of India in SSA module for hearing impaired explains *deafness* as profound hearing loss, and *hearing impairment* as a spectrum of various degrees of losses. Despite the norms given by the government, Deaf people in various part of India prefer various terms. While some prefer being called Deaf others prefer Hearing Impaired, irrespective of the degree of hearing loss. Deaf Studies define 'Deaf' (with a capital 'd') as a person who considers himself a cultural minority and others are notified as 'deaf'. This paper uses only one term 'd/Deaf' to signify children with various degrees of hearing losses, for ease of reference.

References

Ministry of Home Affairs. (2011). *Distribution of disabled in the age-group 0–6 by type of disability, sex and residence – 2011.* Retrieved from https://censusindia.gov.in/nada/index.php/catalog/2140.

Albertech, G. (2006). *Encyclopedia of disability.* Sage.

Brueggemann, B., & Burch, S. (Eds.). (2006). *Women and deafness: Double visions.* Gallaudet University Press.

Daniel, V. (2015). *Effectiveness of learning package in learning environmental science with reference to academic achievement, communication and visual performance of hearing impaired students at primary education level.* http://hdl.handle.net/123456789/16181.

Ministry of Human Resource Development. (n.d.). *National education policy (2020).* Retrieved from https://www.mhrd.gov.in/sites/upload_files/mhrd/files/NEP_Final_English_0.pdf.

Ministry of Law and Justice. (2016, December 28). *Rights for persons with disabilities.* Retrieved from https://www.tezu.ernet.in/PwD/RPWD-ACT-2016.pdf.

National Council of Educational Research and Training. (2006). *Education of children with special needs.* Publication Department, National Council of Educational Research and Training.

National Council of Educational Research and Training. (2005). *National curriculum framework.* Retrieved from https://ncert.nic.in/pdf/nc-framework/nf2005-english.pdf.

Randhawa, S. (2006). *A status study of special schools for the deaf and identification of intervention areas* (Unpublished doctoral thesis). Indian Institute of Technology (IIT), Roorkee, India.

Sarva Shiksha Abhiyan. (2001). *Training module on hearing impairment.* Retrieved from https://dsel.education.gov.in/sites/default/files/publication/modulea6.pdf.

Section 3
In-service Professional Development of Early Childhood Teachers

13
Role of DIETs in Training Preschool Teachers

Padma Yadav

For successful implementation of Sarva Shiksha Abhiyaan (SSA), now known as Samagra Shiksha (an overarching programme for the school education sector extending from preschool to class 12), Right to Education Act 2009 (RTE) and the National Education Policy (NEP 2020), there is need to have better coverage of children in ECCE and enhancing children's readiness for school. The National Curriculum Framework (NCF) 2005 envisages ECCE for all children before they enter primary school. The Right to Education Act, 2009 confines the right to education to the age group 6–14 years. NEP 2020 recognises the importance of ECCE in all-round development of children, its role in developing foundational literacy and numeracy and its impact on later year life outcomes. It also aspires to universalise preschool education and lays special emphasis on the attainment of foundational literacy/numeracy in primary school by 2025. Research supports the need for a sound preschool education programme for all children. But due to lack of facilities of training in the states and lack of resource persons in this area, the quality of ECCE has remained a big concern. SCERTs and DIETs are also inadequately equipped to conduct training programmes in ECCE effectively.

In the wake of new demands for ECCE from time to time, teacher educators either qualified for higher level or under qualified for ECCE take on the task of training in ECCE. The mushrooming of private Nursery Teacher Training Institutions (NTTI) is the result of great demand for ECCE. The demand for teachers in the private sector is being filled through a network of unrecognised and unregulated private NTTIs. These training institutions run, in a majority of cases, without qualified and trained staff. It has been difficult to regulate these institutions so far.

District Institutes of Education and Training (DIET)

The District Institute of Education and Training (DIET) is a nodal agency for providing academic and resource support at the district and grassroots levels for the success of various strategies and programmes undertaken in the areas of elementary education. Until the adoption of NPE 1986, academic and resource support in the area of elementary education was being provided largely at national and state levels only by institutions like the NCERT, National Institute of Educational Planning and Administration (NIEPA) and SCERTs. Below the state level, there were elementary teacher education institutions. The National Policy on Education (NPE) 1986, and Programme of Action (PoA) 1992, envisaged the addition of a third, district-level tier to the support system in the shape of DIETs. These were established with financial support from the Central Government in pursuance of the NPE 1986. The New Education Policy 2020 recommends strengthening of DIETs and emphasises that capacity building of personnel will be strengthened to support the implementation of ECCE.

Functions of DIETs

The major functions of DIETs are:
- pre-service education at primary level
- in-service education to primary teachers and to non-formal and adult education functionaries
- resource support to primary schools and adult education centres
- conducting action research in the area of Primary Education and Adult Education

The NCTE offers a diploma in early childhood education programme leading to Diploma in Preschool Education (DPSE), through the DIETs. There are approximately 600 DIETs in India not all of which offer a DPSE. Recently a unit on ECCE has been added to the revised Diploma in Elementary Education (D. El. Ed) course.

Role of DIETs in Professional Development of Preschool Teachers

The DIETs play a role in teacher development in the following areas:

- Provide leadership in innovating pre-service preschool teacher training
- Contribute to development of quality learning materials for preschool education
- Carry out innovations for improving the functioning of preschools
- Conduct in-service training programmes for preschool school teachers
- Carry out field-based empirical studies to improve preschools
- Train functionaries of NGOs and volunteers
- Provide support to district authorities in implementing quality preschool education

NCERT organises teacher training programmes in the field of School Education for teacher educators working in SCERTs and DIETs. Preschool is one of the focus areas of the NCERT as it is the foundational stage of school education.

For professional development of teachers and teacher educators, a diploma course in ECCE was initiated by the NCERT in 2006 and was found beneficial for state level training institutions and private and voluntary agencies running nursery teachers' training.

The objectives of the diploma course in ECCE were:

- To increase the knowledge-base of teacher educator (trainees) in the area of ECCE

- To develop competence in conduct of quality ECCE programmes in different settings
- To orient participants on various teaching-learning strategies to be used in training of teachers
- To provide hands-on experience to participants for conducting research studies

The duration of the course was 25 weeks (six months) broken up as follows:
  (a) 13 weeks (three months) face-to-face training at NCERT
  (b) 10 weeks (two and a half months) on-the-job exercise in own place of work
  (c) Two weeks contact programme at NCERT after on-the-job exercise

The Course and its Transaction

The course was targeted at teacher educators working in DIETs, SCERTs, ICDS and private nursery teacher training institutions including NGOs catering to disadvantaged population of society. It aimed at developing a cadre of resource persons who would be equipped with skills and knowledge for organising state level ECCE training programmes and extension activities for generating awareness among communities about the need, significance and good quality ECCE programmes, conduct training programmes for ECCE functionaries, develop resource material for different levels of functionaries, prepare learning material for children and conduct research studies in the area of ECCE.

The course was visualised as an innovative, interactive, participatory and learner-centred programme with minimum lectures. It was divided into 10 units inclusive of 12 days of internship. The course was conducted through practical workshops, case studies, role-play, simulation exercises, hands-on experiences, observations, field visits, utilisation of various resource materials, and audio-visual aids, such as films on early childhood education, extracts from books, articles, pamphlets.

Group discussions, panel discussions, assignments and library work were the core of the transactional strategy. Internship and practical activities were given emphasis. The internship was of two weeks in the Anganwadi Centres, nursery schools or government schools. During the period of internship, the trainees were expected to plan ECCE activities and carry out child development activities in specific ECCE centres. They would develop teaching-learning material to impart developmental activities, along with children. They would thus get the chance to work with the community, organise parent-teacher meetings or advocacy programmes to seek support from parents in strengthening ECCE centres. Evaluation strategies included assessment through observations, assignments, and peer evaluation. Such a process enabled the teacher educators to transmit the message of innovative teaching learning methods to teachers. Follow-up of all the batches was done and the results were positive. States like Nagaland, Sikkim, Assam, Karnataka, Tamil Nadu, and others made efforts for quality improvement. A total of 168 teacher educators/teachers were trained through seven batches from 2006 to 2012.

Feedback was collected from the trainees. Trainees felt enriched after participating in the course. They developed the competence in planning and implementation of ECCE activities. They learnt to develop low-cost/no-cost, age appropriate, teaching-learning material. A follow-up study was conducted to assess the post-training involvement of ECCE diploma holders. Findings of the study revealed that states had started taking initiatives in ECCE programmes under SSA. They began providing support to anganwadis (SCERT, Haryana), offering certificate/diploma courses in ECCE (Regional Institute of Education Shillong, SCERT Nagaland), and establishing linkages between ICDS and Education department (Rajasthan, Uttarakhand, West Bengal).

Some learnings related to teacher and teacher education programmes in ECCE organised in DIETs are as follows:
- There should be uniformity to some extent in the structure of teacher education programmes in DIETs of all the states

and union territories with respect to duration, nomenclature, content, pedagogy, assessment, etc.
- The access and coverage of nursery teacher training institutes needs to be enhanced (in DIETs or otherwise). There is inequitable distribution of ECCE teacher education institutions across states at present (both in-service and pre-service). Infrastructure and facilities are also poor.
- Teaching methodology should be interactive and not limited to copying of notes or lectures or rote learning.
- There is no lab facility available for internship in majority of the DIETs. So, ECCE centres attached to primary schools should be made available for internship; alternatively, neighbourhood schools should be adopted by SCERTs or DIETs.
- It is observed that admissions to the teacher training courses is delayed in DIETs. Also, after enrolment trainees are attached to schools for internship but have not been adequately briefed about what to do in the field and how to go about it. As a result, they lack understanding of programme planning, development of teaching-learning materials, teaching methods, assessment procedures, etc.
- Capacity of ECCE teacher educators and teachers is to be strengthened to handle multi-age and multilingual contexts (National ECCE Policy, 2013).
- The role of open and distance education in teacher preparation needs to be clearly conceptualised and regulatory norms and standards need to be developed for offering courses through the distance mode for pre-primary and grade 1 and 2 teachers, which are at present lacking in the NCTE regulations. For example, the Nagaland SCERT offers a diploma course in ECCE to all primary teachers in blended mode to cater to the needs of pre-primary children. The Directorate of School Education deputes 35 teachers from the government schools for the course. Teachers who

are not D.El.Ed. have three-years' time to complete D.El. Ed. from IGNOU.
- Creating a single cadre of teachers for the pre-primary and primary levels of education, which together form the foundation of all school education, would go a long way in giving this stage its due importance. An integrated approach will also allow the preschool teacher to move with a group of children through grades 1 and 2, thus providing the much-needed continuity and emotional stability to children during this tender age. A common cadre of teachers for ECCE and primary stage with similar nomenclature and pay scales and terms of employment is required to be formed.
- Training of functionaries (both pre-service and in-service) is very essential particularly because of the specialised nature of early childhood care and education. Organisations offering ECCE programmes should ensure that there are regular refresher courses, workshops, visits to other schools and self-evaluation techniques for teachers and assistant teachers so that they can update their knowledge and enhance their efficiency. Given these concerns, the training of professionals in the field of early childhood requires new thinking and careful consideration.

With NEP 2020 and its recommendations, the NCERT has a critical role to play in realising the vision of NEP 2020, which proposes a new school education structure with a strong base of ECCE and extending it up to class 2, covering ages 3–8 in continuum. The new National Curricular and Pedagogical Framework for Early Childhood Care and Education will be in two parts: a sub-framework for 0–3-year-olds, and a sub-framework for 3–8-year-olds, aligned with the above guidelines, the latest research on ECCE, and national and international best practices from NCERT.

According to NEP 2020, teachers will be trained through a systematic effort in accordance with the curricular/pedagogical framework. Teachers with qualifications of 10+2 and above shall be given a 6-month certificate programme in ECCE; those with lower educational qualifications shall be given a one-year diploma programme covering early literacy, numeracy and other relevant aspects of ECCE. These programmes may run through digital/distance mode using DTH channels as well as smart phones, allowing teachers to acquire ECCE qualifications with minimal disruption to their current work. The ECCE training will be monitored by cluster resource centres of school education departments and in the longer term, state governments shall prepare cadres of professionally qualified educators for early childhood care and education through stage-specific professional training, mentoring mechanisms and career mapping. Necessary facilities will also be created for the initial professional preparation of these educators and their Continuous Professional Development (CPD). The responsibility for ECCE curriculum and pedagogy will lie with the MHRD to ensure its continuity from pre-primary school through primary school, and to ensure due attention to the foundational aspects of education. The planning and implementation of early childhood care and education curriculum will be carried out jointly by the Ministries of HRD, Women and Child Development (WCD), Health and Family Welfare (HFW), and Tribal Affairs. A special joint task force will be constituted for continuous guidance of the smooth integration of early childhood care and education into school education.

Initiatives of NCERT to Realise the Vision of NEP 2020

- NEP 2020 expects the development of a National Curricular and Pedagogical Framework for ECCE for children up to the age of 8. A developmentally appropriate curriculum for 3 years of preschool education has already been developed by NCERT, which aims at holistic development of the child through play, activity and enquiry-based learning. There is a need to provide an upward linkage of this curriculum to classes 1 and 2 to strengthen foundational literacy and numeracy and lifelong learning. NCERT has also developed the guidelines on preschool education which provide the details of infrastructure, play material, indoor and outdoor play spaces, classroom organisation, manpower requirements, duties and responsibilities of preschool staff, records and registers to be maintained, parent and community participation as well as on developing strong linkages for smooth transition to primary grades and can be used by teachers, teacher educators, administrators and researchers.

- NEP 2020 recommends flexible, play- and activity-based pedagogy for both ECCE and up to class 2 in continuum for which trained teachers will be required. NCERT plans to develop training programmes that will provide opportunities for teachers to teach in any programme that caters to children up to eight years, introducing flexibility in training by creating modular programmes, which help teachers to move from a certificate to a diploma to a degree; each of these achievements will make them eligible for specific programmes, like being a crèche worker, day-care workers or anganwadi/balwadi teachers or school teachers. Emphasis will be on practical hands-on training rather than resorting to outdated, formal, and heavily theoretical approaches, particularly in those aimed at grassroots-level workers. Emphasis will be on short- and medium-term in-service training programmes (face-to-face or online) rather than pre-service training.
- Innovative and practical in-service courses, distance education models, etc. may be spread over a period of time, to meet the needs of vast numbers of so-called untrained personnel, especially in the private sector.
- Training approaches and courses employing participatory methods may be developed to involve the various stakeholders, especially teachers.

- ECCE training may be certified and recognised to promote both self-employment and employment that can deliver quality services.
- Inter-sectoral development, sharing, and networking of resources, expertise, and resource materials etc. in ECCE may be strengthened.
- There is a need for developing a readiness package for children before class 1, which will focus on play-based learning with a focus on developing cognitive, affective and psychomotor abilities and early literacy and numeracy.
- Longitudinal and cross-sectional research studies in different dimensions of ECCE as per need should be conducted to find out the implications for the policy as well as the field. Seminars, conferences, and workshops need to be organised to know about the new initiatives, innovations in the field.
- Teachers should be given continuous opportunities for self-improvement and to learn the latest innovations and advances in their profession.

Conclusion

Teacher education is vital in creating a pool of schoolteachers that will shape the next generation. The role of DIETs in training teachers cannot be overlooked. DIETs need to be strengthened with modern infrastructure and teacher training facilities because teachers will require training in high-quality content as well as pedagogy to achieve the vision of NEP 2020. Teacher educators working in DIETs need to be professionally empowered in multidisciplinary perspectives and knowledge, formation of disposition and values, and development of best practices under mentors to implement the recommendations of NEP 2020 and contribute to the development of professionally trained teachers.

REFERENCES

CECED, AUD. (2012). *Preparing teachers for early childhood care and education.* Ambedkar University.

Ministry of Women and Child Development. (2013). *National early childhood care and education (ECCE) policy.*

Kaul, V, Ramachandran C. & Upadhyay, G. C. (1994). Impact of ECE on retention in primary grades: A longitudinal study. NCERT.

Ministry of Human Resource Development. (2020). *National education policy 2020.*

National Council of Educational Research and Training. (2005). *National curriculum framework.*

National Council of Educational Research and Training. (2006). *National focus group report position paper on ECE (3.6).*

National Council of Educational Research and Training. (2012). *Course outline diploma course in ECCE.*

National Council of Teacher Education. (2005). *Report on ECCE teacher education curriculum and framework and syllabus outline.*

National Council of Educational Research and Training. (2015). *Exemplar guidelines for implementation of national ECCE curriculum.*

14

Strengthening ECE in Anganwadis Through Ankur

Nilesh Nimkar

Sulabha Kakade (name changed), a primary school teacher in Wada block of Palghar district of Maharashtra decides to admit her daughter in the Anganwadi Centre close to her school. She and her husband, Sudheer, who too is a primary school teacher, are convinced that an Anganwadi Centre, with a developmentally appropriate Early Childhood Education (ECE) programme, is the best place for the holistic development of their daughter. This decision is unusual and their relatives and well-wishers are surprised when both of them, with no issue of affordability, chose an anganwadi over a private preschool. Sulabha has been teaching the first grade for the past few years. She has realised that a sound Early Childhood Education (ECE) programme in the preschools, which the anganwadi in her village offers, is extremely critical for better performance in the primary school. She herself has noticed a stark difference between the children who entered grade 1 after undergoing a good ECE programme. 'I have been teaching grade 1 for quite some time. The children (coming from Palavee intervention) are ready for the school. Their pace is astonishing. Almost everyone is on the way to becoming an independent reader by the end of grade 1,' she explains.

This is one of the many anecdotes we have collected through interviews of stakeholders in the Palavee programme. The programme focuses on strengthening of ECE in anganwadis through systematic input to Anganwadi Supervisors and Workers over a period of three years. It transforms anganwadis into vibrant ECE centres step by step. In this paper I present the genesis of the

Palavee programme in brief, discuss the results obtained from the pilot programme, describe the Palavee model of capacity-building and towards the end, share some challenges and future direction of the work.

Genesis of Palavee Programme

India's Integrated Child Development Services (ICDS) scheme is one of the world's largest outreach programmes that provides Early Childhood Care and Education service to children in the age group of zero to six years. The scheme reaches out to children in urban, rural and tribal areas through a large network of Anganwadi Centres (AWC). In Maharashtra this network consists of 88,272 AWCs spread across the 553 projects. Out of these 364 projects are in rural areas while 85 and 104 projects cater to the tribal and urban slums, respectively (ICDS). Typically, a child development project officer (CDPO) is in charge of the project. Around eight to ten supervisors, who are in charge of a beat, report to the CDPO. Usually, the beat comprises 20–25 anganwadis with one worker and a helper in each anganwadi. The size of an ICDS project varies from 100 to 250 anganwadis depending on the area. The tribal projects have fewer anganwadis due to scattered habitation, resulting in large geographic jurisdictions.

The Anganwadi Worker (AW) is the field level functionary of the ICDS. Her role is extremely critical and complex, as she has to deliver all the six child development services offered under the ICDS scheme, namely, Health Check-up, Immunisation, Health and Nutrition Education, Referral service, Supplementary Nutrition and Early Childhood Education (ECE). Each service requires a different knowledge base and skill set. Any woman with qualification ranging from high-school to postgraduation can work as an Anganwadi Worker (AWW). There is no pre-service training required to work as an AWW. The in-service training imparted doesn't place adequate emphasis on the ECE component. As a result, ECE remains the weakest service of ICDS

(Kaul et al., 2017; Kaul & Bhattacharjea, 2019). AWs being the everyday work-force for the implementation of the ICDS scheme, there is a great limitation for taking them out of their work for imparting professional development (NIPCCD, 2009). Hence it was necessary to evolve a model of in-service professional development that could offer quality inputs on ECE at the local level and help AWs to strengthen the ECE service in anganwadis. This also runs parallel to the point 1.7 made by the new National Education Policy (MHRD, 2020, p. 8).

Quality Education Support Trust (QUEST), an organisation working in the field of ECE for the past decade, developed a step-by-step approach to strengthen the ECE service in the anganwadis through its pilot programme named Ankur, supported by Tata Trusts. The insights generated from the implementation of Ankur formed the backbone for the Palavee intervention. Under Ankur, 112 AWs were given inputs through short workshops over two years. Between the two workshops, experienced ECE educators from QUEST provided onsite support to the AWs. During the implementation of Ankur, the need for involving the entire machinery (CDPO, supervisors and the helpers) into the process right from the start of the intervention was felt. The Palavee model was developed based on these insights.

The Palavee Model

The CECED report on impact of ECE states that the key challenge in the field is to create an intervention that can provide a quality preschool programme at scale which can make children in pre-school 'school ready'. The challenge is particularly acute for first-generation learners (Kaul et al., 2017). The Palavee intervention is QUEST's attempt at tackling this challenge. This also echoes the goals set out by National Education Policy 2020 in the Foundational Learning section (MHRD, 2020, pp. 8–9)

The three-year Palavee intervention begins with signing of an MoU with the district administration, one of the key stakeholders in the ICDS scheme. The unit of intervention is minimum; one ICDS project in the jurisdiction of the district. The financial support for the intervention is normally provided by the external funding partner, the administration takes the responsibility of implementation and QUEST provides technical expertise. One of the key insights from Palavee intervention is that it requires a fair amount of time and effort to bring all the three stakeholders on one page. It seems that the importance of ECE service in the anganwadis is often not recognised by the administration and the funding partners. It takes several rounds of meetings with the administration and funding partners before the actual implementation starts. This process may take 10–13 months.

Palavee intervention has two phases. The first phase lasts a year while the second phase lasts two years. In the first year of the implementation, Palavee intervention focuses on building a resource team in every beat. The beat level resource team consists of the respective supervisor of the beat, two or three Anganwadi Workers selected by the supervisors and the helpers from these selected two anganwadis. This resource team receives direct inputs from the ECE experts from QUEST for two consecutive years. In year one, they complete three out of six stages of input. The objective of the first year is to set up 2–3 model anganwadis in each beat, which would serve as training and demonstration sites for the next phase of universalisation. The supervisors too conduct activities in the model anganwadis in these two years at regular intervals. In the second year of the implementation, the resource team conducts beat level training workshops, which is the first step towards universalisation of the programme within their beats. In the third year the programme stabilises to a great extent and the external agency can start the gradual withdrawal of the resource support. The inputs under Palavee are provided mainly through workshops and continuous onsite support. Table 14.1 gives the details of the inputs.

One of the important steps towards the implementation of the programme is a joint field visit at the beginning, by the

Table 14.1: *Input provided through Palavee*

Stakeholder	Days	Description
District and Block Administration	4 days	2 days: exposure visit in every year of the intervention
		2 days: planning meeting in every year of the intervention
Resource team (Supervisors + Workers and helpers from the model anganwadis)	12 days	6 residential workshops of 2 days each over two years
		Regular onsite support by QUEST team
Anganwadi workers	18 days	18 one-day workshops at beat over two years
		Onsite support mainly by Resource team
		Troubleshooting support by QUEST team
Helpers	8 days	4 workshops of 2 days each over two years at beat level

representatives of district administration, CDPO and supervisors to the anganwadis where the Palavee intervention is being effectively implemented. This exposure visit builds considerable confidence about the workability of the proposed intervention. Such visitors often pose questions to the supervisors and workers undergoing the intervention. The questions are usually about their motivation to participate in the intervention, the time management challenges one may face, the relations with the external agency (QUEST in this case) and resource mobilisation. It is obvious that not all the questions have definite answers, but the exposure visit strengthens the belief that a lot could be done even within the given constraints, if there is a good plan.

The Palavee model has some clear strengths and inherent limitations. It creates a resource team within the system, by building capacities of functionaries that ensures the sustainability of the programme. The training for the Anganwadi Workers is made available in a highly decentralised model (at the beat level) which reduces the costs drastically. It achieves universalisation of ECE on a small geography at fairly reasonable cost and thus becomes a replicable model. One of the limitations from the perspective of the funders is its long-term nature. The model requires sustained efforts at one place for a minimum of three years to yield results. Another limitation of the model is that the administration feels it needs to be implemented with external support of funders and competent technical partners, which are difficult to find. Having said that, the model looks like a pragmatic solution to achieve strengthening of ECE service under ICDS.

The Pilot

The pilot for Palavee programme, named Ankur, was conducted in Wada block of Palghar district. All the children between the age of 46 to 50 months were selected for testing because these children were going to recieve a complete intervention cycle of the pilot programme. Another cohort was selected from an adjacent project as a control group. Both the projects are tribal projects and have similar scocioeconomic background.

The selected children from both the groups were tracked during the intervention cycle and also for three years following the intervention. During the intervention the children were administered a school readiness test focusing on language and cognitive development tasks. For baseline, midline and endline the same school readiness test was used and after that grade-appropriate tests in literacy were administered to both the groups.

After three years of intervention a significant difference of about 19 percentage points on school-readiness test can be seen between the control and intervention groups. This gap fluctuates but persists after the intervention has stopped which shows that early intervention has long-term impact on children's learning. The CECED report had concluded that participation in preschool improved retention in primary grades (Kaul et al., 2017). This

Table 14.2: *Results of pilot study*

DATE	Test	CONTROL			EXPTAL			Mean Difference	
		N	Mean %	SD	N	Mean %	SD	In %	p*
Mar-14	BASELINE	43	6.943	6.960	37	8.99	10.17	2.05	0.29
Feb-15	MIDTEST	40	15.46	8.853	32	24.37	10.92	8.91	0
Jan-16	ENDTEST	40	24.25	11.48	31	43.31	18.66	19.07	0
Mar-17	Grade 1	38	31.01	23.50	31	52.26	26.45	21.25	0
Mar-18	Grade 2	38	28.43	20.35	30	53.37	22.46	24.94	0
Mar-19	Grade 3	38	23.49	15.19	30	42.42	23.08	18.93	0

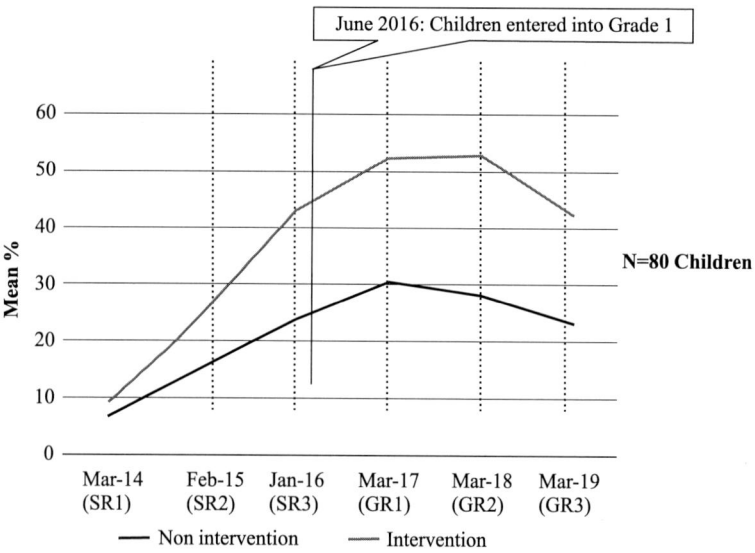

Figure 14.1: *Palavee intervention longitudinal data (graph)*

sustained impact of preschool intervention on scores in primary grades, as observed in this study, may perhaps be the reason for that.

Two important conclusions can be drawn from this study. First, effective instruction of ECE shows significant impact on children and that this impact persists even after the input is completed. This is evidence for the argument which posits that investment in early years can lead to sustained effect in later years.

For example, Kaul reports in her chapter that there was evidence of 'linear association' with school readiness, particularly in literacy and numeracy domains, with children's scores in same domains in primary grades (Kaul & Bhattacharjea, 2019).

The Ankur project continued testing children after they entered first grade to understand how the impact of school readiness sustained in primary grades. The results of this extension of assessment lead to the second important conclusion, which is, while this impact is significant and persistent, it also seems to reduce in intensity as both the groups show lower scores in grade 3. The third year also shows a significant gap between the groups though both the groups' scores have dropped on grade-appropriate tests. It is clear that the gap created at the beginning of the schools persists till the grade 3 at least. The drop seen in the performance in both the groups could possibly be attributed to the input received in the primary schools on grade-appropriate competencies. This finding perhaps calls for an ECE curriculum that includes grades 1 and 2, which the NEP 2020 accepts by restructuring the curriculum to include the 'Foundational Stage' (MHRD, 2020, pp. 8–9). However, it is necessary to undertake a longer intervention along with a longitudinal study to confirm this. Palavee is planning an upward extension programme to study this claim more robustly in one of its intervention areas.

Stages of the Palavee Programme

The total input to be provided under the Palavee intervention has been divided into six stages. Each stage has well-defined objectives. The Anganwadi Workers are informed about what they are supposed to achieve at the end of a particular stage. The progress of the Anganwadi Worker is observed using specially designed observation tools and corrective feedback is given immediately during onsite support. This handholding is critical for the progress of the Anganwadi Workers and it has been observed that several gaps in what the worker has learnt in the workshops could be bridged through this process. This support is provided to the resource team from QUEST while the resource team members are expected to extend this type of support to the AWs during the universalisation phase. The objectives of the six-stage training programme are given in Table 14.3.

Table 14.3: *The six stages of the Palavee programme*

Stage	Objectives (incremental)
One (1 to 4 months)	– To set up physical facilities and environment in the anganwadis – To set up routine of ECE activities (which would last for about 20 minutes) – Introduce one or two activities such as shared reading which are instructionally demanding for Anganwadi Workers – To understand the basics of child development
Two (5 to 8 months)	– To create print-rich environment in anganwadis – To focus on oral language development – To introduce art experience activities – To introduce activities aimed at manipulating sounds in the language (phonological awareness)
Three (9 to 12 months)	– To introduce emergent literacy ideas – To increase the proportion of instructionally demanding activities for cognitive development and math – To introduce some EVS activities
Four (13 to 16 months)	– To introduce some more emergent literacy ideas such as LEA (the language experience approach) – To introduce differentiated planning for different age groups – To introduce theme-based learning
Five (17 to 20 months)	– To introduce the idea of sound-letter correspondence – To introduce activities related to use of number knowledge acquired by children so far – To introduce conventional script and decoding – To set 2.5 hours routine of ECE activities in the anganwadi

(Contd.)

Table 14.3: (*Contd.*)

Stage	Objectives (incremental)
Six (21 to 24 months)	– To consolidate what the worker has learnt over two years – To introduce the idea of observation-based assessment – To refine planning skills

The stages are designed keeping in mind that the Anganwadi Workers are on a learning curve and require sufficient time to acquire the complex skills. Activities like free play, activities for gross and fine motor development are introduced in earlier stages while activities for cognitive and literacy development, that are instructionally demanding, appear later. The duration of the ECE activities in the anganwadi increases gradually from 20 minutes to 2.5 hours across the stages. This type of design helps the Anganwadi Workers to cope better with the changes that the anganwadi undergoes because of the intervention. The success and response in the earlier activities increases the motivation to take up higher challenges. The process of going through these stages appears to be lengthy but our experience shows that considering the workload, educational backgrounds, and exposure of the Anganwadi Workers, smaller chunks of inputs over a longer period of time yield more sustained results.

Material Resources

During the intervention period high quality, low-cost resource material is supplied to the anganwadis along with the training input. The material includes manipulative toys such as blocks and puzzles, printable material such as interactive charts and cards, storage facilities such as pocket boards and transparent containers, and children's books. Most of the printable material is designed internally by the QUEST team and has been kept in the public domain so that after the intervention it could be made available to anganwadis at printing cost by the department. The imagery used in this material is culturally and contextually appropriate. The material is supplied stagewise during or immediately after the workshops. Along with the materials supplied in the anganwadis, the workers are expected to collect indigenous material such as seeds, clay, bottle tops, cloth pieces, etc. The timely supply of the material helps the Anganwadi Workers to conduct the ECE activities smoothly.

The ECE curriculum, adopted in Maharashtra named Akar, recommends practising the emergent literacy approach. In order to make this a reality it is absolutely necessary to have good quality children's books in the anganwadis. The Palavee programme not only ensures the availability of the books in the anganwadis but also imparts the necessary knowledge skills to the workers to use these books effectively. The set of books provided under the Palavee intervention is carefully chosen keeping in mind the sociocultural context of the children.

The insights from the field implementation of Palavee have been coded systematically into manuals for Anganwadi Workers and Supervisors. It's a series of six well-illustrated manuals written in a narrative form. Each manual roughly corresponds to the objective expected to be achieved at the end of a given stage. The content actually appears through the story of an Anganwadi Worker Bhavanatai and a helper who want to convert their anganwadi into a vibrant ECE centre. Their journey provides the reader in-depth understanding of the process to be followed under the Palavee intervention. More than 250 photographs from the field have been used for the purpose of illustration across six manuals. The manual uses data collected from the field to exemplify the points. For example, to emphasise that the Anganwadi Worker should accept, respect and use the child's home language in the anganwadi, actual conversations between the Anganwadi Worker and a child captured from the field have been used. The manuals show icons representing various developmental areas such as cognitive development, motor development etc. near the relevant activity.

These manuals serve as a strong pillar of the programme. It would have been difficult to conduct decentralised training programmes in every beat in the absence of these manuals. The narrative form makes it easy for the workers to comprehend; the resource team members often read out portions of the manual during the training. The constant linkage of the activity with the developmental areas through the icons makes it easy for the Anganwadi Workers to link the theory with practice.

Some Challenges

The challenges faced by the Palavee programme are wide-ranging and differ from area to area; a local approach is needed to overcome them.

One of the most common challenges faced by the programme, especially in the non-tribal areas, is different conception of ECE among parents and functionaries of ICDS. On the demands from parents, the department has started interventions like digital-anganwadi or semi-English anganwadis. These interventions are largely an attempt to attract parents who prefer a private English-medium school over the anganwadis. There is fear that children may drop out of the anganwadis in the absence of such intervention. As a result, unless some profound change is seen in the functioning of the anganwadis, ICDS functionaries do not feel confident about Palavee. Hence ongoing discussion, support and handholding during the first year of the programme is critical.

The infrastructure of anganwadis, especially in the tribal and high rainfall area poses an altogether different challenge. Sometimes the leaks in buildings are so serious that it becomes difficult to use the buildings; often the resource material is damaged because of damp walls.

Anganwadi Workers are probably at the bottom of the pyramid and one of the lowest paid functionaries associated with the government schemes. They often do not receive the (meagre) compensation on time. As a result, the protests organised by the

AWs unions interrupt the programmes. Strikes may sometimes cause delays. However, the general acceptance of the programme has been found to be quite high and some of the workers have gone out of their way to support critical activities like testing or data collection planned on the day of a protest.

Future Plans

As of November 2022, the Palavee programme has impacted the ICDS system in following manner.

Table 14.4: *Palavee outreach*

Unit	Number (covered under the programme)	Details
Districts	8	Palghar, Pune, Parbhani, Amaravati, Yavatmal, Gadchiroli, Hingoli, Raigad
Projects	13	Wada, Vikramgad and Jawhar in Palghar district, Baramati in Pune district, Pathari and Manwat in Parbhani district, Dharni and Teosa in Amaravati district, Ner in Yavatmal district, Dhanora in Gadchiroli district, Khalapur and Mangaon in Raigad district and Basmat in Hingoli district
Anganwadis	2319	
AW supervisors	84	
AW workers	2319	
AW helpers	2319	
Children	48000	Age group of 3 to 6 years

The Palavee programme, by 2025, aims to reach out to around 5000 anganwadis impacting 75,000 students. The Palavee programme has also constructed an upward extension for grades 1 and 2 in accordance with FLN (Department of School Education and

Literacy 2022) and its implementation will have to be studied robustly to understand its impact on children's learning outcomes in further schooling. QUEST aims to create a robust model to make foundational stage a reality by strengthening the anganwadis along with the first two grades of primary schools.

Many questions have also risen during the implementation of the programme and finding answers to these questions needs further research. The basic question of reliable school readiness scores of children in different areas in Maharashtra needs to be investigated and reported; as the Palavee programme is set to grow, this question can be tackled. There is also the question whether the impact of intervention on the children's school readiness scores remains constant or changes in rural or urban areas. There are other questions regarding the nature of the intervention, or the tools used or the nature of children's growth as reflected in the scores that need to be investigated. The Palavee programme offers many opportunities for data collection and analysis along with experimentation to further our understanding in ECE.

References

ASER. (2019). *Annual status of education report 'Early Years'*. Retrieved from http://www.asercentre.org/p/359.html on February 2020.

ICDS: http://www.icds.gov.in. (n.d.).

Kaul, V., & Bhattacharjea, S. (2019). *Early childhood education and school readiness in India*. Springer.

Kaul, V., Bhattacharjea, S., Chaudhary, A. B., Ramanujan, P., Banerji, M., & Nanda, M. (2017). *The India early childhood education impact study*. New Delhi: UNICEF.

Ministry of Human Resource Development. (2020). *National Education Policy, 2020*.

NIPCCD. (2009). *Research on ICDS: An overview (1996–2008)*.

UNESCO. (2019). *Early childhood care and education*. Retrieved March 3, 2020, from UNESCO: https://en.unesco.org/themes/early-childhood-care-and-education.

UNICEF. (2012). *School readiness: A conceptual framework*. New York: United Nations Children's Fund.

15

Professional Development Strategies
Akshara Foundation's Experience

VAIJAYANTI K. and GAYATRI KIRAN

It is an undeniable fact that the first six to eight years have a direct, decisive bearing on children's lives. These early years are crucial to the later development of an individual. That is when minds develop and skills are acquired. The importance of early stimulation cannot be underestimated. Good quality early childhood care and education (ECCE) becomes an indispensable intervention, particularly for children from disadvantaged families.

The National Early Childhood Care and Education (NECCE) Policy and Curriculum Framework (2013, 2014) expects early childhood educators, or Anganwadi Workers, to have a high degree of understanding of child development, pedagogy and curriculum content, as well as the skill sets to manage a preschool within the restricted facilities of an Anganwadi Centre.

ECCE programmes can contribute to better nutrition and health, and better rates of school enrolment (Myers, 1995). A study of about 33,000 children across eight Indian states shows a significant impact on retention (estimated to increase by 15–20 percent) in primary grades (Kaul et al., 1994). The India Early Childhood Education Impact Study (IECEI, 2017) recommends the need to acknowledge and address the professional needs of preschool educators through professional training. Further, it also stresses institutional mechanisms for training. Most accepted practices in the professional development of early childhood educators converge on the need to look at the method and content of their skill-building, rather than at the routine processes of capacity building (Sheridan et al., 2009). It becomes essential to look at other methods rather than just the transfer of knowledge common to most training models. The inclusion of mentoring, coaching and on-the-ground support is essential to build the capacity, motivation, and skills of the early childhood educator in any setting.

Research is clear that teachers with more experience and training are more likely to practice a child-centered pedagogy and deliver better learning outcomes for children (Raikes, 2015; Banu, 2014; Thao & Boyd, 2014).

A review of the professional development of early childhood educators in low- and middle-income countries presents a common profile which our experience also reiterates (UNESCO, 2015). It notes that most Early Childhood Education (ECE) educators are younger as compared to other educators, and are predominantly female. They are less educated and receive less rigorous training at the time of appointment, which is of lesser duration than for any other section of educators. The review also observes that most countries are not strict about adhering to basic minimum qualifications for early childhood educators.

In addition to this, the quality of supervision and support to the ECE educator, especially in rural and remote areas where they are most required, is also poor (Sun et al., 2015). The sheer diversity of backgrounds and the services to be delivered, coupled with the volume of reach, make it difficult to monitor, given the minimum skill sets, monitoring tools, and qualifications of the supervisory and monitoring staff.

The IECEI (2017) study reports that the duration of training for Anganwadi Workers (AWWs) is highly inadequate to enable them to transact a good quality preschool programme.

All the literature reiterates that at the core of all successful ECCE programmes are well-trained, well-equipped and well-supported personnel.

Early Childhood Education and the ICDS

Launched on 2 October 1975, the ICDS is a flagship programme of the Government of India and represents one of the world's largest and unique programmes for early childhood care and development. Among the several functions of the ICDS is the delivery of early childhood education to children aged 3–6 years. This is in addition to other duties entrusted by the state government and local panchayats from time to time (Sandhyarani, 2013). The tasks of the anganwadi helper include cooking and all the secondary support functions that keep an anganwadi running.

The real challenge for the ICDS is to improve its services and offer universalisation with quality. This is where Anganwadi Workers have a crucial role to play. Indeed, the success of an anganwadi depends first on the skill and motivation of its workers and the support they get from the administration and the community. Realising that the successful implementation of the ICDS depends on the capacity of the functionaries involved, the government launched a countrywide training programme called Project Udisha with financial assistance from the World Bank. It stated that improved worker training was crucial to the success of the ICDS programme and designed a progressive training model to be the centrepiece of the project. ICDS implemented Project Udisha in mission mode in 1999–2000.

The Position Paper on ECCE of the National Curriculum Framework (2005), says that while the staff implementing ECCE is the most important factor in determining the quality of the programme, it is also the most neglected aspect of the educational system, and further questions the prevailing perception of 'any person who likes children, or who is herself a mother, will be a good staff member in early childhood programmes (p. 28).'

Akshara Foundation's internal study in Karnataka revealed that an Anganwadi Worker has as many as 21 tasks to perform. From community surveys to maintaining records of births and deaths, assisting the health staff, and interacting with pregnant and nursing mothers, to distributing food. It was found that ICDS functionaries/staff[1] are good at target-oriented, record-keeping tasks and preschool education is only one of the six services the anganwadi caters to. They are not expected to achieve any targets or maintain any records on preschool education.

The National Institute of Public Cooperation and Child Development (NIPCCD) is a premier institution in India for training functionaries of the ICDS programme at the regional and national levels. The NIPCCD facilitates a three-month induction training to Anganwadi Workers at the time of their appointment and occasional refresher training delivered by the Mid-Level Training Centres. Many documents including the World Bank report[2] inform that these training curriculums have limited ECCE component, indicating insufficient focus on capacity building around ECCE.

The IECEI 2017 study recommends that the professional needs of preschool educators should be acknowledged and addressed through expert training. Further, the study stresses upon the need for strengthening the institutional mechanisms for training.

The National Policy on ECCE 2013 also recognises the need for trained manpower and stresses the professionalisation of ECCE at all levels and the capacity building of ECCE personnel with comprehensive training and skill development strategies.

The National Education Policy 2020 recognises the need for universalising quality ECCE. The policy talks about the professionalisation of teachers for ECCE/Foundational Stage as a core element and recommends to State Governments to develop cadres of professionally qualified teachers for ECCE through stage-specific professional training and provides for their Continuous Professional Development. However, it is not clear whether there will be an additional trained Anganwadi Worker who will cater to the 3–6 year age group or if the existing Anganwadi Worker is expected to execute the curriculum for 3–6 years, in addition to her existing responsibilities.

For the Anganwadi Worker, preschool education will continue to be one of the six services that she is mandated to deliver; with shifting priorities within the ICDS, this may affect the regularity and quality of the preschool education available to children. The proposed system of early childhood education is likely to continue with the current quality of education in ICDS anganwadis if these challenges are not addressed, especially within the system.

The gaps in the capacity building of ICDS functionaries, more so the Anganwadi Workers, have been recognised, and rightfully so, as elaborated in the above literature. Against this backdrop, this paper presents Akshara Foundation's experience in capacity building strategies designed to professionalise the ICDS workforce. It followed as a natural corollary of its preschool programme in Karnataka and became embedded in implementation.

Akshara Foundation's Preschool Model

Akshara began its School Preparedness Programme across 200 ICDS anganwadis in Bengaluru in 2006–07 with the help of paid instructors who delivered a preschool component for two hours a day. In 2009, this programme was redesigned as the Preschool Education (PSE) programme by providing teaching-learning materials (TLMs) to support a developmentally appropriate, play-based curriculum aligned to the curriculum implemented by the Department of Women and Child Development (WCD), the flagship of the Integrated Child Development Services (ICDS), which runs anganwadis. Akshara has implemented its preschool programme in an action-research mode in other pilots like preschool centres in non-notified slums in Bengaluru; independent balwadis being run by women entrepreneurs; and preschool modules delivered through a third worker in selected anganwadis of Karnataka (Vaijayanti. K, 2014, pp. 85–87).

However, the largest reach has been in Anganwadi Centres in collaboration with the WCD. The main objective of Akshara's preschool education programme is to put a *structured* preschool programme in place with key inputs of high quality TLMs and capacity building of teachers. To this end, the programme trained instructors to deliver 90 minutes of daily preschool education. This was supported with a well-designed, research-based preschool kit for supporting development across multiple domains. The programme had a robust training curriculum and assessment framework and indicators for measuring learning outcomes, guidelines for tracking children's progress, capacity building, and monitoring tools. The programme put into effect a rejuvenation plan for Bal Vikas Samiti (BVS) that the government envisaged as a community outreach and support mechanism for anganwadis. Akshara implemented the preschool programme in all 1776 anganwadis in Bangalore Urban District from 2009 to 2012. During this period the learning outcomes of children were measured and tracked. All 1776 anganwadi workers were trained and around 18,000 BVS members were also trained. The following sections focus on the capacity building component of the preschool programme implemented by Akshara Foundation in ICDS centres.

Capacity Building Strategy

Akshara's preschool education programme developed a training model to establish a sustainable capacity building strategy for preschool delivery in Anganwadi Centres. The strategies evolved over some time with learnings from field experience. They followed three stages of training, covering different levels of the ICDS vertical in a cascade model.

The key strategies involved in capacity building included buttressing the skills of functionaries working at different levels, layered stages of training, a training curriculum, and training delivery modules.

Stage 1. Akshara selected Field Coordinators to work alongside ICDS Supervisors and provide on-site mentoring, demonstrations, handholding, and guidance to several Anganwadi Workers. Each Field Coordinator supported 25–28 AWWs. Akshara's training team provided the field staff with an intensive 10-day induction and orientation. The shelf life of a typical on-site mentoring module was three years.

Stage 2. A 3–5-day training was conducted for Child Development Project Officers (CDPOs), Assistant Child

Development Project Officers (ACDPOs) and Supervisors of the ICDS Circles. The training content was the same as for Stage 1. However, additional inputs on monitoring mechanisms were provided to trainees. They were trained to take over as Master Trainers.

Stage 3. In this stage, the trained CDPOs, ACDPOs and Supervisors trained AWWs at ICDS Circle level. ICDS conducted this training, with Akshara's Field Coordinators acting as co-trainers. The Supervisors needed to plan and implement the training utilising the contents and strategies Akshara Foundation provided. The Foundation played a supportive and facilitative role during the training of the AWWs. A strong component of on-field support and mentoring was included.

Stage 3(a). Over time Akshara Foundation understood and appreciated the role that helpers played in the centre. The strategy was modified and the training was extended to anganwadi helpers in some aspects of PSE and keeping children engaged.

Curriculum for Capacity Building

The core objective of the curriculum was to build the capacity of ICDS staff and enable them to deliver ECCE effectively. The curriculum of the training underwent several iterations. Initially, the training of ICDS staff (Vaijayanti, 2014) focused on the usage of the TLMs that Akshara Foundation provided. Gradually, as gaps became evident, the training modules were revamped and modules on classroom transactions and management were added. An external evaluation conducted by a renowned ECCE assessor influenced the inclusion of strategies for child development and the principles of preschool education and developmentally appropriate practices.

Training Delivery Strategies

One of the key strategies of the training was a design of interactive sessions. All trainees were made to work in groups and make presentations on how to use the TLMs, create activities around

Table 15.1: *Contents for capacity building*

	Content for Stage I and II Training. Purpose was to build capacity as trainers and support preschool education at the field level	Content for Stage III Training. Purpose was to build capacity to deliver effective preschool education
Target group	• ICDS supervisory staff	Anganwadi Workers
Methods for effective training	• Effective communication skills • Techniques used in training	Not Applicable
Monitoring skills	• Classroom observation skills • Random assessment skills	Not Applicable
Child Development	• Principles, domains and milestones of development • Developmental delays and special needs in the early years	• Principles, domains and milestones of development • Developmental delays and special needs in the early years
Preschool education	• Principles of preschool education • National policies (ECCE policy 2013) • Preschool curriculum • Methods of preschool education	• Principles of preschool education • National policies (ECCE policy 2013) • Theme-based approach and how to navigate • Preschool curriculum linking with Chili-Pili • Methods of preschool education
Classroom management	• Centre set-up • Behaviour management	• Centre set-up • Segregation of children by age

(Contd.)

Table 15.1: (*Contd.*)

Content for Stage I and II Training. Purpose was to build capacity as trainers and support preschool education at the field level		Content for Stage III Training. Purpose was to build capacity to deliver effective preschool education
	• Instruction strategies for young children • Use of teaching aids • Making low-cost teaching aids	• Strategies for meaningful engagement of children • Behaviour management • Instruction strategies for young children • Use of teaching aids • Making low-cost teaching aids
Techniques used for teaching children	• Techniques suggested by ECCE policy • Framework on techniques used in teaching like play, storytelling • Activity-based learning	• Strategies on group activities, personalised teaching • Activity based learning • Play, indoor and outdoor • Storytelling • Dance, drama, music • Art, craft and creativity • Use of TLM as teaching tools • Directed free play • Use of teacher handbook and calendar
Assessment Techniques	• Assessment framework • Use of assessment for improvements in classroom transactions	• Assessment methods, facilitation • Use of assessment manual • Baseline and endline assessments • Assessment reporting • Connecting with community

(*Contd.*)

Table 15.1: (Contd.)

Content for Stage I and II Training. Purpose was to build capacity as trainers and support preschool education at the field level		Content for Stage III Training. Purpose was to build capacity to deliver effective preschool education
Community Engagement	<ul><li>Community engagement strategies</li><li>Centre Indicators and planning</li><li>Role of Bal Vikas Samiti</li></ul>	<ul><li>Community engagement strategies</li><li>Bal Vikas Samithi</li><li>ECCE day</li><li>Involvement of parents and creation of Friends of Anganwadi</li></ul>

Source: Akshara Foundation

them, and practise pedagogic strategy. Demonstrations, field visits to Anganwadi Centres functioning more efficiently, and simulation of classroom arrangements and organisation during the training were reported to be more effective. The training covered several skills for holistic development and introduced AWWs to the methodology and use of the TLMs aligned to the curriculum. In the first year of implementation, the trainees were exposed to a preschool as a real-time experience. It was an activity that brought all the trainees together as a team to set up a model preschool centre, following which they discussed the challenges of doing so and gave suggestions about how to start one and how it should develop and flourish.

Between 2006 and 2014 Akshara trained more than 3000 AWWs and helpers and around 200 supervisory staff from different parts of Karnataka on the modules explained above.

The section below captures anecdotal evidence on the impact of capacity building as perceived by the supervisory functionaries and Anganwadi Workers.

Narratives from the Field

Given below are some narratives of people involved with PSE programmes:

- A Supervisor, ICDS Bangalore South Project, (2014), said that, 'Akshara Foundation's ECCE curriculum framework is excellent. In my Circle, only eight anganwadis were included in the programme and they are conducting it according to the training given to them by Akshara Foundation. However, I have 28 anganwadis in my Circle. I wish to run all the centres in my Circle along similar lines. Therefore, I have started the same training for the other Anganwadi Workers during the monthly meetings with them. They too are following the same guidelines and models for early childhood education in their centres. I hope to follow all the ECCE guidelines whenever a new anganwadi is sanctioned and constructed in my Circle.'
- An Anganwadi Worker, Bangalore South Project (2015), reflects, 'There are many changes in my anganwadi since the training. The way we talk to the children and interact with them, the best use of teaching-learning materials in the classroom, the age-appropriate development of the children, and classroom management are some things I have learned since then. This change in me is due to the training Akshara Foundation provided. I feel it is because of the training that I was awarded the Best Worker of the District for Bangalore Urban district. My anganwadi is as good as any English-medium play home. The community has started appreciating and supporting me and my work with the children. Enrolment has also increased in my centre.'
- A Project Coordinator, Akshara Foundation, says, 'I have seen many changes in the centres where the Anganwadi Workers were trained by us. There are significant changes in the ECCE component of the anganwadis from the time we started up till now. I have seen changes in Anganwadi Workers' awareness of their roles and responsibilities regarding ECCE, the maintenance and arrangement of

teaching aids, usage of teaching-learning materials, teaching according to developmental norms, and techniques for teaching larger numbers of children.'

Concluding Remarks

Akshara Foundation's capacity building strategies evolved progressively over the years to address field realities. In summary, the main components that showed a positive impact on the professional development of the ICDS functionaries were the design of the training modules that helped build perspectives around the principles of child development and the milestones of foundational learning. The facilitation strategies of training, that is, interactive, hands-on experience, debate, and openness as well as the scaffolding through on-site support contributed to the success of the programme.

The external evaluation by the Centre for Early Childhood Education and Development (CECED) in 2013 observed that Akshara's capacity building modules on classroom arrangement and management, the strategies of mentoring, handholding and demonstration in the field as part of training and empowering the supervisory level of the system to deliver training using the cascade model were effective.

Some of the learnings from this extensive exercise include: sustained and structured systemic efforts would need to be made to see any impact of the programme in quantifiable terms; longer durations and frequency of interactions with the Anganwadi Workers would yield better results; and inclusion of parents and other community stakeholders in planned capacity building exercises would yield optimal benefits to early childhood education.

The new National Education Policy 2020 includes some path-breaking strategies that may align with a promising vision for the future of ECCE in the country. As pointed out earlier, NEP should guide the state governments to address the concerns about the capacity building of ICDS functionaries along the lines of strategies followed in school education aligned with local contexts.

Looking ahead, Akshara believes that there is an urgency to bring about a paradigm shift in the strategies of capacity building of ICDS functionaries in the country to ensure that children get appropriate preschool education. The National Education Policy 2020 has created an opportunity to work towards the institutionalisation of capacity building in the years to come for ICDS functionaries along the lines of school education.

Notes

1. ICDS staff include the Anganwadi Worker, helper and the supervisory staff of Assistant Development Programme Officer, Child Development Programme Officer and the Supervisor.
2. 'Reaching Out to the Child': An Integrated Approach to Child Development, Human Development Sector, South Asia Region, World Bank, September 2004.

References

Banu, M. S. (2014). Teachers' beliefs and perceptions of quality preschool education in Bangladesh: A postcolonial analysis. *Australasian Journal of Early Childhood, 39*(4), 3744.

Barnett, W. S. (2008). Why governments should invest in early education. CESifo-DICE report, Journal for Institutional Comparisons, *Early Childhood Education and Care, 6*(2), 9–14.

Bartlett, S. (2013). *Learning about learning: Reflections on studies from 10 countries.* Aga Khan Foundation.

Behrman, J. R., Engle, P., & Fernald, L. C. (2013). Preschool programmes in developing countries. In P. Glewwe (Ed.). *Education policy in developing countries: What do we know, and what should we do to understand what we don't know?* (pp. 65–105). University of Chicago Press.

Das, Deepa. (2003). *Case study of the status of India's early childhood care and education services.* UNESCO.

Das, Subrat, & Kundu, Protiva. (2014). *Public investment in young children in India.* Centre for Budget and Governance Accountability (CBGA). Public-Investment-in-Young-Children-in-India-final-paper-red.pdf.

Devarakonda, Chandrika. (2013). India: Early childhood educators: In changing patterns of early childhood education and care. *International Perspectives on Early Childhood Education and Care, 114.*

CECED. (2013). *Evaluation of Akshara Foundation's engagement with the ICDS system in Karnataka*, CECED, Ambedkar University. https://akshara.org.in/wp-content/uploads/2014/12/Impact-Assessment-of-Akshara-Foundations-Engagement-with-the-ICDS-system-in-Karnataka.pdf.

Gupta, S. S. (2013). *Restructuring of ICDS: An opportunity to focus on under-three children.*

Kaul, V., Chaudhary A. B., Bhattacharjea, S., Ramanujan, P., Banerji, M., & Nanda, M. (2017). *The India early childhood education impact study.* UNICEF. http://img.asercentre.org/docs/Research%20and%20Assessments/Current/Education/Research%20Projects/IECEIStudyReport2017.pdf.

Ministry of Women and Child Development. (2013). *The National early childhood care and education (ECCE) policy.*

Ministry of Women and Child Development. (2006–2012). *Integrated Child Development Services (ICDS), Annual Report.* Retrieved from http://goo.gl/8aLrC.

Marope, M. & Kaga, Y. (Eds.). (2015). *Investing against evidence: The global state of early childhood care and education.*

Ministry of Human Resource Development. (2020). *National education policy 2020.*

Neuman, J. M., Josephson, K. & Gee, P. (2015). *A review of the literature—ECCE personnel in low- and middle-income countries.* UNESCO.

Raikes, A. (2015). Early childhood care and education: Addressing quality in formal preprimary learning environments. (Unpublished). UNESCO.

Sheridan, S. M., Edwards, C. P., Marvin, C. A., & Knoche, L. L. (2009). Professional development in early childhood programmes: Process issues and research needs. *Early Education and Development, 20*(3), 377–401. DOI: 10.1080/10409280802582795.

Sandhyarani, M. C., & Rao, U. C. (2013). Roles and responsibilities of anganwadi workers, with special reference to Mysore District. *International Journal of Science, Environment ISSN 2278-3687 (O) and Technology, 2 (6).* (1277–1296).

Thao, D. P. & Boyd, W. A. (2014). Renovating early childhood education pedagogy: A case study in Vietnam. *International Journal of Early Years Education, 22*(2), 194–96.

UNICEF. (2011). *Early childhood education—Building on Integrated Child Development Services.*

Vaijayanti, K. (2014). Creating an ecosystem for effective engagement with the ICDS system—Akshara Foundation's pre-school education programme. *Learning Curve (22),* 85–87.

16

A Multimodal Approach to In-Service Capacity Development of Anganwadi Teachers

Yogesh G. R., Kinnari Pandya and
M. Sreenivasa Rao

The Azim Premji Foundation recognises that quality Early Childhood Care and Education (ECCE) makes a positive contribution to children's long-term development and learning. Further, it recognises the relevance of ECCE for a smooth transition from home to preschool, and preschool to primary education.

The Sangareddy Early Childhood Education (ECE) Initiative focuses on capacity development of Anganwadi Teachers to become reflective practitioners with the aim to transform anganwadis into vibrant learning centres for the holistic development of 3 to 6-year-old children. The intervention is within the existing systemic resources of the ICDS scheme. Teacher capacity development is at the heart of a quality early childhood programme and early learning opportunities available to children. Our experience suggests that such a 'holistic in-service capacity development model' can effectively develop teachers' competence to transact developmentally appropriate curriculum for children.

The intervention aims to understand processes and procedures involved in implementing a quality ECE programme for public preschool setting, that is, the Anganwadi Centre. Like all other efforts of the Foundation, this initiative also engages with the public preschool system that is in the form of a large-scale programme—the Integrated Child Development Services (ICDS) scheme. The efforts of the initiative are across all levels of ICDS functionaries, and especially the Anganwadi Teachers (AWTs) who are at the heart of the effective delivery of the ECE programme. Our approach has been to develop professional capabilities of Anganwadi Teachers and functionaries (supervisory staff) in-service to enable them to implement the quality ECE programme with existing resources. It has proved to be an effective model given the tangible changes.

This paper first presents the various challenges in implementing quality preschool education programme by Anganwadi Teachers. Second, we discuss the various efforts made by the Foundation for continuous support and capacity building of Anganwadi Teachers in-service. We thereby outline the multi-modal approach that is critical to strengthening the existing ICDS structure. Finally, we present the effects the intervention has had on the Anganwadi Centres to offer quality early years environment and learning opportunities to young children.

Challenges in Offering Quality ECE Programme to Anganwadi Children and Possible Solutions

Our decade-long observation and intervention in Anganwadi Centres and work with Anganwadi Teachers of Sangareddy indicate a range of challenges that Anganwadi Teachers encounter while performing their role as teachers and providing ECE inputs to children. We suggest below some possible solutions to overcome these challenges that may enable effective implementation of a quality Early Childhood Education programme.

Challenge 1: A large part of the duration of Project meetings and Sector meetings go in completing administrative activities, leaving little time for Anganwadi Teachers and Supervisors and Child Development Project Officers (CDPOs) to discuss and plan for pre-school education related activities.

Possible Solution: Supervisors and CDPO's to be enabled and trained as Master Trainers of ECCE. Mandatory allocation of fifty percentage of time during Project meeting and Sector meeting for mentoring Anganwadi Teachers in planning ECE activities, rehearsing and clarifying concepts, sharing their plans; TLMs for implementing developmentally appropriate practices at Anganwadi Centres.

Challenge 2: Anganwadi Teachers have limited ECCE preparation despite being in service for many years. They need continuous mentoring and professional support in implementing curriculum.

Possible Solution: Our experience shows that the duration of preschool activities in the centres has gone up by 38% and usage of running blackboard by children has increased by 40% in the centres of teachers who received continuous support through weekly mentoring at the centre level. It is imperative therefore for Supervisors and CDPOs to spend quality time in Anganwadi Centres observing and mentoring Anganwadi Teachers on actual implementation of learning activities.

Challenge 3: Several responsibilities are thrust on Anganwadi Teachers resulting in their inconsistent presence and lack of focus on implementing the preschool curriculum. Their absence from the centre for other work further results in lower attendance among children.

Possible Solution: Regularity in implementing ECE curriculum at the Anganwadi Centre is most critical. We have observed that regularity in conducting preschool activities at the centre has resulted in increase in working hours of the Anganwadi Centre by 50% and attendance of children increasing by 17%. Anganwadi Teachers' presence at the centre, in planning and conducting activities with children is critical. If Supervisors and CDPOs regularly spent 50% of their time in visiting the Anganwadi Centres for guidance and recognising the Anganwadi Teachers' role, it would significantly aid the delivery of quality preschool education.

Challenge 4: It is not easy for the Anganwadi Worker to prioritise the various responsibilities they need to perform as a part of their routine work. Juggling various responsibilities such as immunisation, record maintenance, growth-monitoring registers, nutrition supplement distribution, counselling and referrals is a trying task. Preschool education, given its nature of continuous engagement on the part of the teacher, is as a result severely compromised.

Possible Solution: Professional effectiveness programmes conducted indicate that time-management, multi-tasking, prioritising work, self-care require explicit inputs. These inputs assist Anganwadi Workers to perform their roles effectively. Periodic professional development programmes should become a part of in-service capacity development programmes for Anganwadi Teachers and functionaries.

Substantial amount of time and effort of Anganwadi Teachers can be saved and used in centre level activities if the data collection processes through various departments (Health and Women and Child Development) is streamlined.

Challenge 5: Lack of basic facilities at workspace, such as hygiene facilities at the Anganwadi Centres, toilets and water supply at the centres, etc. These signal the overall status and respect she garners as a frontline worker.

Possible Solution: A collective response from the ICDS scheme, Women and Child Development department, elected representatives, parents and community at the village level to improve physical environment and conditions in Anganwadi Centres. This is critical for Anganwadi Teachers and as well as children's health and hygiene provisions at the centre.

Challenge 6: Limitations in undertaking extensive enhancement of physical environment with child-friendly material in rented Anganwadi Centre premises.

Possible Solution: Empowering Anganwadi Teachers to talk to village heads and look for a conducive place for running a preschool centre. It is critical that the Anganwadi Centre has essential physical infrastructure with outdoor play equipment and indoor spaces that are safe and child-friendly to run a quality early years programme.

Key Factors Enabling Children's Learning Within Teacher's Circle of Influence

Based on the assumptions about the teacher's role and early learning, we have identified the key elements of a good ECE programme that enable learning and development in the children attending the centre regularly. The key factors in the Anganwadi Teacher's control that we enable teachers within our intervention areas to achieve are listed below.

1. Every day, the teacher provides hygienic and nutritious food and ensures that the children wash their hands before and after food and a minimum of one hour of naptime after lunch.
2. Every month, the teacher measures children's growth (height and weight).
3. The teacher maintains a first aid kit in the centre and ensures a clean and safe environment in and around the centre.
4. The teacher organises a stimulating learning environment as per a thematic timetable and makes play material accessible to children.
5. The teacher records and displays the children's work.
6. The teacher treats children with care, respect and uses positive methods of disciplining.
7. The teacher engages in conversations, and encourages social interaction among children during play and mealtime.
8. The teacher executes a minimum of three to four hours of ECE programme daily.

ECE curricular components enhanced by the Anganwadi Teacher are presented in the Figure 16.2.

Overall Model of Intervention—In-service Teacher Capacity Building of Anganwadi Teachers

Our Journey

Based on an exploratory study conducted to understand the ICDS system and working of Anganwadi Centres in 2012, in

Figure 16.1: *Anganwadi teacher facilitates concept development activities for children*

Source: Azim Premji Foundation photo repository

Figure 16.2: *Components of ECE programme regularly followed by Anganwadi teachers*

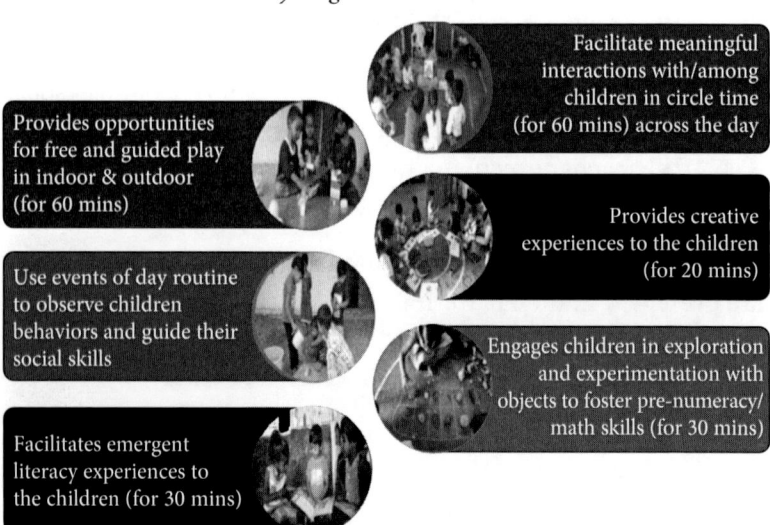

- Provides opportunities for free and guided play in indoor & outdoor (for 60 mins)
- Use events of day routine to observe children behaviors and guide their social skills
- Facilitates emergent literacy experiences to the children (for 30 mins)
- Facilitate meaningful interactions with/among children in circle time (for 60 mins) across the day
- Provides creative experiences to the children (for 20 mins)
- Engages children in exploration and experimentation with objects to foster pre-numeracy/math skills (for 30 mins)

Source: Sangareddy District Institute, Azim Premji Foundation. Used with permission

2014 we conducted a baseline study of a sample of Anganwadi Centres of Sangareddy (erstwhile Medak district). Following the baseline study, 40 Anganwadi Centres across four sectors in Sangareddy were identified for intensive engagement and gauging improvement in the preschool programme. We worked intensively with these 40 centres for a period of five years to understand what it takes to build their in-service capabilities. In parallel, several other modes of engagement were initiated to work with other Anganwadi Teachers (AWT) in the district, and we now reach out to AWTs across the whole district with intensive engagement with 200 teachers. A team of 30 members facilitate this work on the ground. Figure 16.3 below presents the overall timeline of work in Sangareddy since 2012.

Strengthening the capacity of AWTs through in-service professional development opportunities is the thrust of our work. This is because the teachers' conceptual understanding would directly impact the quality of the preschool programme they

Figure 16.3: *Journey of Sangareddy ECE initiative*

STUDY PHASE		INTERVENTION PHASE					EXPANSION PHASE	
Exploratory Study	Baseline Study	Centre Level Engagement Started	Teacher Capacity building through multi-modal approach				200 Anganwadi Centers • Spreading across 5 projects • Change in Sector meeting • Teacher Development Tracking • Center Development plan • Reaching all teachers in the district • Teacher Mela for capacity building Support for ECE expansion in Bangalore, Puducherry, Dhamtari	750 Anganwadi Centers • Focus on ensuring key Teaching Practices • Sector level hands on practice based workshops • Sector Meeting to all sectors of district • Need based center visits Support for ECE Teams - Expansion ECE Program in Bangalore, Mandya, Yadgir, Kalaburgi, Puducherry, Dhamtari, Udhamsigh Nagar
conducted in 270 Anganwadi centres and covered 45,000 household interviews	Is done for 157 centres from which 40 centres selected for intervention	Developmental Assessment tool for young children introduced	Workshops Sector Meetings Teachers Mela Teachers Seminar	Teacher Magazine ECCE Day Bala Mela Exposure Visit				
2012	2013	2014	2015	2016	2017	2018	2019	2020

Intensive engagement with ← 40 centers → ← 200 centers → 750 centers

Source: Sangareddy District Institute, Azim Premji Foundation. Used with permission

offer to children at AWCs. All efforts of capacity development of AWTs are guided by principles of 'Developmentally and Culturally Appropriate curriculum for young children'.

The in-service curriculum for in-service professional development is rooted in theoretical ideas of child development and early childhood education approaches, principles of adult learning, developing and transacting contextual curriculum in an experiential manner, learnings about personal effectiveness and efficacy, principles of assessment and material development for young children. We have developed the following documents over the past few years of our work in ECE. These inform the work we undertake with teachers through multi-modal engagement.

1. Curriculum for Anganwadi Centres of Sangareddy based on Telangana State Preschool curriculum
2. Curriculum for in-service capacity development of AWTs
3. A handbook for Anganwadi Teachers (this aids execution of preschool curriculum)
4. Developmental assessment of young children—a tool for ages three to five years

Multimodal Approach to Capacity Building

A competent Anganwadi Teacher who is sensitive to the needs of young children and is able to plan and implement developmentally and culturally appropriate curriculum, is crucial to executing a high quality ECE programme. Engaging with Anganwadi Teachers on the required aspects requires ongoing efforts that are systematically designed and situated in the larger context of their professional development. Our model leverages the existing ICDS structure and uses the platforms available to strengthen the Anganwadi Teachers' capabilities to offer ECCE programmes. Figure 16.4 shows the multimodal engagement and approach of work on the ground.

The model involves various kinds of engagements with Anganwadi Teachers. Each mode is presented below highlighting

Figure 16.4: *Multimodal engagement with ICDS system functionaries*

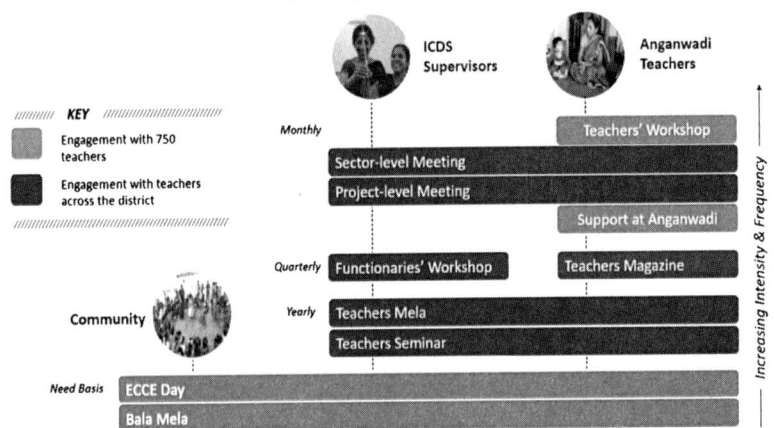

Source: Sangareddy District Institute, Azim Premji Foundation. Used with permission

the ECE content it focuses on, adult learning pedagogy used by us to work with teachers, and the frequency of the engagement.

a. Teacher Workshops

Content: The content is guided by the curriculum for in-service capacity development of early childhood educators for building holistic understanding of ECE content and pedagogy. Some illustrative topics covered are: importance of early years and early childhood education; domains of development and developmental milestones; how children learn and importance of play; classroom organisation and management; importance of TLM, making TLM and its usage; curricular planning—theme web and weekly activity planning; personal effectiveness (multi-tasking and time management); implementation of curriculum activities—sessions on music, movement, storytelling, discussions, conceptual activities, and so on.

Pedagogy: Discussion, demonstration, peer learning—sharing of experiences, use of videos, role play, etc.

Frequency: 12 days of workshops spanning across the year. Workshop is planned for a group of 15 to 40 teachers.

Figure 16.5: *Teacher's workshop*

Source: Azim Premji Foundation photo repository

b. Project-level Meetings

Content: Any important preschool concept. For instance, understanding use of assessment checklist, creating child profiles, demonstration of one or two pedagogical aspects; nature walks—the need, how to plan and conduct, how it helps children and is critical for a quality preschool programme.

Pedagogy: Orientation, demonstration

Frequency and Coverage: 150–300 teachers at a single gathering every month in five projects.

Figure 16.6: *Project meeting*

Source: Azim Premji Foundation photo repository

c. Sector-level Meetings

Content: Conceptual discussions for example importance of play, storytelling, and so on.

Pedagogy: Discussion and demonstration of curricular activities of the coming month that teachers can use in the anganwadi.

Frequency and Coverage: About 25+ teachers in each of the 40 sectors, over 750 teachers every month

Figure 16.7: *Sector meeting discussions on preschool curriculum*

Source: Azim Premji Foundation photo repository

d. Intervention at Anganwadi Centre

Purpose

1. Collaborative planning of curricular activities (weekly/ theme plan), demonstration of activities which are not familiar to the teachers or the children. The aim is to improve the quality of transaction of preschool education, duration and regularity.
2. Facilitate the use of available space in effective manner including material arrangement to create a more stimulating environment for holistic development of children (includes running blackboards, corners, circles, print rich environment etc.).
3. Development and use of low-cost or no-cost materials, effective use of available materials, increased access to materials for children. For instance, flash cards based on

Figure 16.8: *Observation during centre-level visits*

Source: Azim Premji Foundation photo repository

themes, fruit bibs, monsoon picture cards, puzzles, other available natural material in the surroundings, etc.
4. Providing support to teachers to help build a good relationship with parents and get basic support in ensuring regular attendance of children and running the centre (unused materials, ensuring basic amenities etc.). Display of children's work to the parents to build their confidence in Anganwadi Centre as a place of child development.
5. Providing support in 'good habit' formation—health and hygiene (brushing, handwash before and after eating, use of handkerchief, etc.).

How this Mode Helps Teachers: Teachers learn how to plan their work in advance so that they know what activities they need to do with children each day and what TLM they need to prepare and keep ready. The scaffolding during the on-site visits helps them fine-tune their pedagogical skills.

e. Anganwadi Teachers Seminar—A Platform for Peer Learning

Content: Anganwadi Teachers share their own successful and noteworthy practices with co-teachers and other functionaries, CDPO and Supervisors moderate the sessions.

Pedagogy: A seminar with careful selection of papers from the proposal entries received

Frequency and Coverage: About 400+ teachers once a year

How this Mode Helps Teachers: Presenting their work amidst peer is a huge boost to their morale, gaining acknowledgment for their work as teachers, learning from other teachers.

Figure 16.9: *Annual teacher seminar at Sangareddy*

Source: Azim Premji Foundation photo repository

f. Anganwadi Teachers' Mela

Content: Workshops on activities related to each domain of development.

Pedagogy: Four to eight concurrent workshops, each with a Teacher and three Foundation members facilitating curricular activities relating to a specific domain of child development. Mela provides opportunity to mobilise the large volume of the teachers on a single platform. Creates vibrancy and translates ideas into good practices, opportunity for discussing personal experiences which motivate teachers to take these ideas and implement in their classrooms.

Frequency and Coverage: One or two Teacher Melas in each project once a year covering all teachers in the district. About 150 to 200 teachers belonging to a specific project attend a Teacher Mela.

Figure 16.10: *Teachers engaged in experiential play during teachers mela*

Source: Azim Premji Foundation photo repository

g. Bala Mela

Content: Sensitising community on child development aspects.

Pedagogy: Both parents, children, other family members engage in preschool activities designed and facilitated by the Anganwadi Teacher and Foundation member. This Children's Mela offers an important opportunity for the teachers to strengthen their connection with the community.

Frequency and Coverage: Bala Mela is conducted on a need basis.

h. ECCE Day

Content: Importance of early years and preschool education, development of their own children as seen through Assessment Checklists, sharing daily progress of their children through profile bags, and so on. Performance by children on preschool activities such as songs or drama form the highlight of these sessions.

Pedagogy: Supporting teacher in planning, sharing, discussing, selecting videos and so on. ECCE Day has helped create a better connect between the Anganwadi Centres and community, and has resulted in an increase in the retention and regularity of children.

Frequency and Coverage: ECCE day events are conducted based on initiative of the AWT, on need basis.

i. Mobile Library

Content: A collection of 40 children's books from various publications are kept in Anganwadi Centre for one or two weeks for children to explore the books, after which the set is taken to another Anganwadi Centre. The teachers create various opportunities for the children to use the books. Foundation team collects observations regarding children's interest, books selection, their narration to other children and elders, on a periodic basis.

Figure 16.11: *Children reading books from the mobile library*

Source: Azim Premji Foundation photo repository

216 Chapter 16

j. Teachers' Magazine—'Toliadugulu' (First Steps)

Content: Themes covered so far are importance of early years, play and its importance, classroom organisation and community connect. This magazine has become a source of peer learning for the teachers.

Frequency and Coverage: Quarterly, four editions published and circulated to 1500+ Anganwadi teachers and all ICDS functionaries in the district.

k. Exposure Visits

Learning from similar contexts would enhance teacher motivation and creativity in executing their own preschool programme. Teachers visited Tara Mobile Crèche, CLR and Bharatiya Samaj Seva Kendra in a three-day exposure visit to Pune, Maharashtra.

Figure 16.12: *Teachers engaging with the magazine First Steps*

Source: Azim Premji Foundation photo repository

Our Learning and Insights from this Work

1. While the Anganwadi Teachers are not professionally qualified, a quality in-service programme can help them become better educators.

2. The ECE teacher's job is just as complex as that of a primary school teacher. AWTs should be treated as professionals, and this should reflect in their service conditions. There must be systematic effort to train them continuously.
3. Care needs to be given to work distribution at the AWC, such that non-ECE work, which while important, does not overwhelm ECE work.
4. Decent infrastructure continues to be a key concern. A proactive department and community support in enhancing infrastructure is a requirement.
5. An integrated effort to improve AWCs, which combines issues of infrastructure, curriculum and materials, community participation, professional development of AWTs, can lead to significant gains in the quality of preschool experience available to all children in our country.

Effects of our Work

Our experience and feedback from primary school teachers suggests that children who attend an Anganwadi Centre for more than a year adjust well to the primary school system. They display better social, language and cognitive skills, as compared to children in the same class who have joined without experience of a quality preschool experience at an Anganwadi Centre.

Some of the visible changes are:

- the average time the teachers engage in preschool activities has increased from 1 to 2.3 hours per day
- significant improvement was observed in components such as social, creative, language, fine and gross motor development with the overall scores increasing from 40.95% to 74.63% over the last three years. Figure 16.13 indicates the changes observed in Anganwadi Centres engaged intensively in terms of overall quality and duration of ECCE

Figure 16.13: *Overall impact on Anganwadi Centre's preschool programme quality*

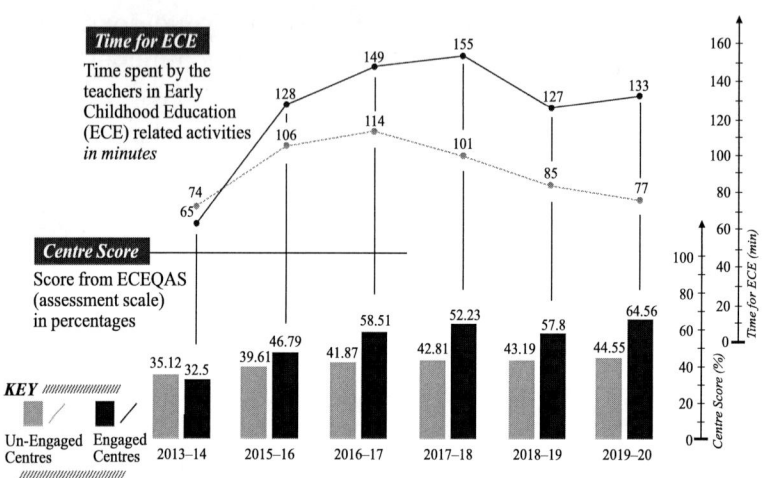

Source: Azim Premji Foundation

Another significant shift observed is the extent and nature of contribution made by the community towards the Anganwadi Centre. Several communities have begun providing learning aids such as books, building blocks, charts, stationery and so on. Gram Panchayats have begun taking active initiative in upgrading the basic physical infrastructure of the centres. Figure 16.14 shows the changes in physical environment of a few Anganwadi Centres. Such change is visible in several centres where the teacher offers a preschool curriculum.

Further, of the 36 Bala Melas that were conducted about 23 were fully supported and sponsored by the community.

While our work on the ground did not directly address many challenges listed in the earlier section, the model of engagement helped create local solutions that enabled the teachers, supervisory functionaries and community members to participate effectively, and contribute to making the Anganwadi Centre a vibrant learning centre.

Figure 16.14: *Infrastructure changes visible in Anganwadi Centres*

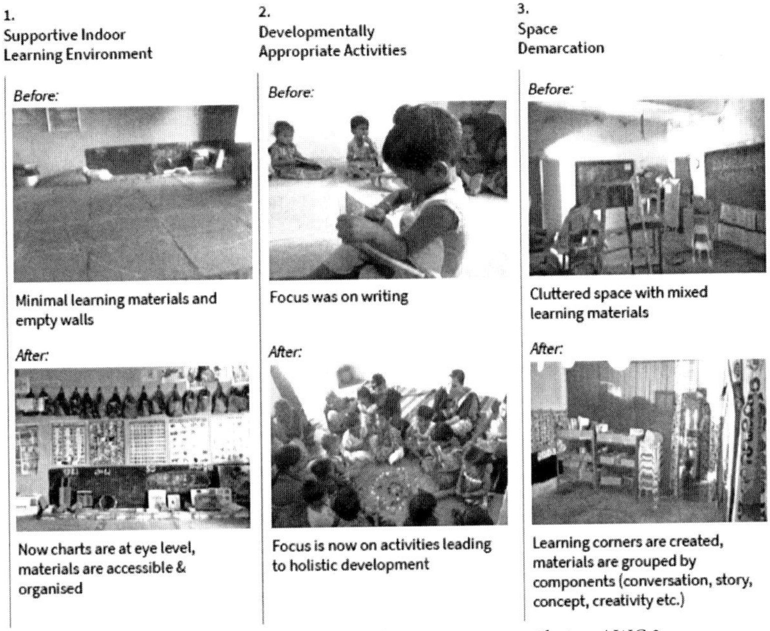

1. **Supportive Indoor Learning Environment**

Before: Minimal learning materials and empty walls

After: Now charts are at eye level, materials are accessible & organised

Photos: AWC 1

2. **Developmentally Appropriate Activities**

Before: Focus was on writing

After: Focus is now on activities leading to holistic development

Photos: AWC 2

3. **Space Demarcation**

Before: Cluttered space with mixed learning materials

After: Learning corners are created, materials are grouped by components (conversation, story, concept, creativity etc.)

Photos: AWC 3

Implications for Roll-out of National Education Policy—ECCE Teacher Preparation

The National Education Policy 2020 envisions that all early childhood educators are qualified professionals. The policy suggests that teachers without an undergraduate degree would need to undergo a one-year diploma programme, whereas teachers with an undergraduate degree would need to undergo a six-month certificate programme in ECCE. The qualification required to be appointed an Anganwadi Teachers is typically grade 10 and above. Over the next decade, there would be a massive requirement to adequately prepare all Anganwadi Teachers through various modes and help them become qualified ECCE professionals. Leveraging the existing ICDS implementation structure and in-service professional development platforms become extremely critical to achieve the vision of the policy. The various modes of engagement elucidated above and the potential of continuous enrichment and guidance to Anganwadi Teachers through these platforms are important to systematically explore and build multimodal engagement into the professional development programmes being planned for continuous professional development of ECCE teachers. The quality of the ECCE teacher's preparation is what will determine the quality of early learning programme she offers to children, thereby directly impacting the early learning and development of young children.

References

Azim Premji Foundation (2018). Good Practices and Overview—Early Childhood Education (ECE) Initiative Sangareddy, Telangana. Azim Premji Foundation, Bengaluru.

Centre for Early Childhood Education and Development (CECED). (2012). Early Childhood Education Quality Assessment Scale (ECEQAS). Ambedkar University: Delhi.

Early Childhood Education Initiative Sangareddy. (2014). Status of Early Childhood Education Services in Medak (Sangareddy) District. Azim Premji Foundation. Unpublished.

Early Childhood Education Initiative Sangareddy. (2018). Anganwadi teachers capacity development model for impactful early learning. Azim Premji Foundation: Sangareddy.

17
A Community Approach to Early Childhood Care and Education

Mary Punnoose and Shikha Kumari

The first six years of a child's life are globally acknowledged to be the most critical years for lifelong development since the pace of development in these years is extremely rapid. Seeing its extreme importance through recent research and development in the area of child development and education, it has been universally recognised that learning in early years is as important as learning in formal years of schooling. In this regard, Early Childhood Care and Education (ECCE) programmes have been implemented worldwide through various agencies to help parents, other care givers and professionals to provide stimulating and enriched learning experiences to young children during their early years.

The Need for ECCE: A Theoretical Framework

There has been considerable research and subsequent literature on childhood and education in the western as well as Indian context. Since the last few decades, a new era of developmental psychology has also advanced through lots of important research and discoveries in the field of child development. Famous psychologists like Piaget, Vygotsky and Bronfenbrenner have talked about different theories on child development. Piaget (1896–1980) proposed a theory based on constructivist approach to learning according to which a child constructs his/her/their own knowledge through interaction with the environment. Nature is the child's innateness to learn and explore, and nurture is all the experiences that the child learns from. He argued that children do not discover the world but rather actively construct an understanding of the world on the basis of their experiences with it. He also talked about age-specific stages of cognitive development—sensorimotor, preoperational, concrete operational, and formal operational–arguing that all children go through these basic stages and their development can be speeded up by variations in the environment (formal schooling, nurturing home environment) (Lightfoot, Cole, & Cole, 2008, pp. 19–21).

Vygotsky (1896–1934) proposed a sociocultural theory of learning emphasising that culture shapes interaction between the child and environment. He also highlighted the importance of interactions of adults/older peers in achieving the learning potential of a child (Lightfoot, Cole, & Cole, 2008, pp. 21–22). While these theories consider the child as active learner and culture as the enabler of learning, Bronfenbrenner provided another perspective on child development—an ecological perspective, stating that in order to understand human development, one must consider the entire ecological system in which the growth occurs—microsystems like the family, community, school and macrosystems like culture, agencies, media, policies, etc. (Bronfenbrenner, 1994, pp. 37–42).

All these theories suggest that the child should be considered an active learner and the environment, be it family, the community or the school, should all work in harmony to let children learn and develop to reach their potential. The pioneer agencies in the field of ECCE like the National Association for the Education of Young Children also acknowledge the same through a few guiding principles for ECCE (NAEYC, 2009).

Domains of children's development (physical, social, emotional and cognitive) are closely related. Development in one domain influences and is influenced by development in other domains.

1. Development occurs in a relatively orderly sequence, with later abilities, skills and knowledge building on those already acquired.

2. Development proceeds at varying rates from child to child as well as unevenly within different areas of each child's functioning.
3. Early experiences have both cumulative and delayed effects on individual children's development; optimal periods exist for certain types of development and learning.
4. Development and learning occur in and are influenced by multiple social and cultural contexts.
5. Children are active learners, drawing on direct physical and social experience as well as culturally transmitted knowledge to construct their own understandings of the world around them.
6. Development and learning result from interaction of biological maturation and the environment, which includes both the physical and social worlds that children live in.
7. Play is an important vehicle for children's social, emotional and cognitive development, and is also a reflection of their development.
8. Development advances when children have opportunities to practice newly acquired skills as well as when they experience a challenge just beyond the level of their present mastery.
9. Children develop and learn best in the context of a community where they are safe and valued, their physical needs are met, and they feel psychologically secure.

Appreciating this global orientation in the area of child development and education, the Indian education system has also tried to bring in reforms into the system at policy level. The National Curricular Framework and the National Policy on ECCE (2014) seem to be based on the above principles too.

Based on the above theoretical foundation as well as global and national recommendations, Prajayatna has devised a comprehensive approach to ensure quality ECCE through strengthening the existing structures in the system and empowering ecosystems around the child—parents, community and institutions like schools and preschools.

ECCE in the Indian context: Integrated Child Development Services (ICDS)

Launched on 2 October 1975, the ICDS scheme aimed to give Indian children a quality and healthy childhood to start with. It was and still is the world's biggest government scheme centred on young children.

The ICDS scheme covers an umbrella of services for the targeted beneficiaries—children 0-6 years, adolescent girls, and lactating and pregnant mothers. The ICDS built Anganwadi Centres as the common platform to provide these services to the beneficiaries.

These Anganwadi Centres are primarily considered as feeding centres rather than spaces for learning. This may be mainly because of lack of awareness of the community on importance of ECCE or lack of competencies of the Anganwadi Teachers in the field of ECCE. There is a lacuna seen in the Anganwadi Workers (teachers) to be able to address the developmental needs of the children as no effective training is provided to the teachers. Also, a lack of accountability, ownership as well as monitoring is visible in the overall management of the anganwadi system. All these gaps have resulted in the poor access to the anganwadi services by a majority of younger children across the country. It has led to not only early health issues but also low learning levels amongst children, leading to an increase in the drop out/irregularity of such children further at the school level. These are the symptoms of a 'systemic' problem and it needs to be addressed on a priority basis.

Prajayatna's Evolution and Strategy

Prajayatna grew out of a decade of experience with the issue of child labour that highlighted the need to address the 'system' rather than the 'symptom' in the education scenario in Karnataka. Prajayatna's key approaches towards reforming the education system is institutionalising processes of community ownership and developing a capability-based approach to learning.

It has been working for years to raise the collective effort of the community in the ownership of education. It has tried to bring in systemic reform in education over more than a decade. Following the community oriented systemic approach over the years, it has adopted few specific strategies in ECCE:

- Learning—classroom management: Experiential learning techniques to develop the cognitive, motor, and social skills
- Empowering teachers: teacher training, capacity building, collaboration and giving handholding support
- Community ownership: Strengthening existing community structures, community, parents, local self-government like Gram Panchayat
- Strengthening support system: Monitoring through government supervisors, project officers, training centres, etc.

Figure 17.1: *Prajayatna's strategy for ECCE*

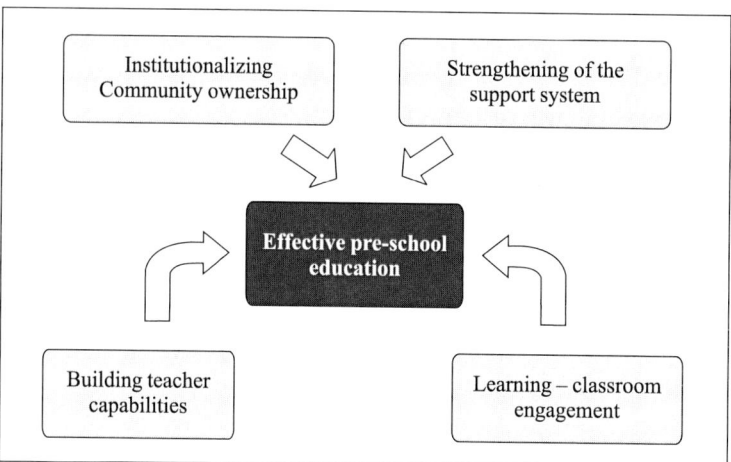

A. **Transforming Classroom—Learning Environment: An Integrated approach (Prajayatna, 2019)**

i. **Primary guiding principles of the programme**
- Early childhood is the most important stage of life as it lays the foundation for all domains of development. Therefore, the ECE programme caters to all areas of development—physical, motor, socio-emotional, language, cognition, creativity and aesthetic sense.
- Development across domains and the skills therein are a continuum and there are various stages of development. Every child will progress through this continuum at his/her own pace.
- All learning has to be contextualised in the child's real-time environment and surroundings.
- Every child learns differently and at different speeds, and classroom practices have to cater to these differences.
- Children learn through activity and usage of their senses.
- All learning and knowledge should be application-oriented for the child, and not dependent upon rote memorisation.
- A non-threatening and stimulating environment is conducive to learning and supports the children to better express themselves.
- Understanding and relating to a child is essential for learning; the teacher's engagement with the child begins only after the child has had time to adjust to the new surroundings.
- Assessments are integrated into the learning process.
- Learning happens everywhere and the teacher plays the role of a facilitator.

ii. **The ECCE Curriculum**

Prajayatna's ECCE curriculum has been designed in convergence with the National Policy on ECCE (2014). Over years of experience and research, the organisation has developed an ability-based framework, called the Learning Ability Framework. According to this framework, all children follow the various aspects in the curriculum through a sequence of four stages, thus catering to a multi-age and multilevel teaching process. Children are involved in the appropriate activities based on their stage of development in the sequence rather than their age. As children pass through each stage, their capabilities evolve as do the complexities of skill areas.

The four stages in the child's development of skill area/aspect are:

1. *Evolving:* explores all the materials and experiences that are provided. The exploration may be tentative and without a stated or a conscious purpose initially
2. *Interested:* follows simple instructions and completes the given tasks under adult supervision
3. *Involved:* understands complex instructions and is able to appreciate basic concepts presented, requires adult support
4. *Self-directed:* appreciates the concepts presented and applies them to real-life problems and situations independently

Based on this framework, the ECCE curriculum has been developed which is child-centric and holistic. It caters to all areas of development and provides learning opportunities for social, emotional, cognitive and language development.

For the children of 3–6 years, the ECCE curriculum aims to develop the following basic competencies:

- ability to perform tasks independently and complete tasks
- ability to work in a group
- ability to use material and tools
- ability to regulate self and emotions
- identify, name and understand basic concepts
- oral language and communication
- pre-numeracy and number sense and basic operations

- pre-reading skills and reading
- pre-writing skills and writing

The curriculum contents cover all areas of developmental domains, skill development and knowledge enhancement. The skill areas and the concept knowledge are addressed sequentially and set the prerequisite for the advanced levels. Thus, these will progress from

- simple to complex
- known to the unknown
- concrete to representational (that is, real object to the image)

iii. The Learning Cycle

The children go through a learning cycle which comprises:

- ***Exposure:*** A significant part of the teacher's role is to give the child sufficient exposure to new things. This includes setting up context, quoting examples, introduction of topic, enabling the child to share about her/his knowledge concerning the introduced topic, etc.
- ***Experience:*** This involves engaging children with hands-on materials or engaging them in particular activity so that they get direct experience through deeper understanding.
- ***Practice:*** As practice is the only way to become proficient in a new skill or behaviour it is essential to engage children in practice activity using different means of reinforcement.
- ***Evaluation:*** It helps in understanding the progress made by the child in the context of learning objectives and set learning outcomes. The evaluation must serve as feedback mechanism, to enable child and teacher to take necessary steps to learn further.

iv. Concept (Theme)-based Method

A concept or theme provides the content and a framework for organising the learning activities and integrating different areas of the curriculum. Through a broad range of subject matter, provided by the selection of the appropriate theme, a variety of experiences and active involvement, children can develop skills as well as learn factual information about the subject matter being studied and understand the concept in its entirety. It also ensures that all the activities are linked and coherent and thus not approached in a fragmented manner.

The themes are carefully selected with the primary criterion being that they should be relevant to the child's context and situation. The activities of the anganwadi are centred around a theme each fortnight/month. Once the themes are decided, teachers map out the learning outcomes consisting of both the information and skills to be addressed based upon the Learning Ability Framework. Then activities and experiences are selected to cover different areas of the curriculum. The theme-based method along with the Learning Ability Framework can guide the teacher's lesson plan. Since this happens collectively at the sector level through the Teacher Collectives, this method ensures contextualisation and provides scope for adaptation that a fixed and rigid curriculum may not provide.

v. The Learning Process

The curriculum is transacted through a step-by-step process that involves teachers. Teachers come together through collective meetings in which they together identify what children need to learn and how they will learn. A Prajayatna team member facilitates the discussion and helps the teachers in planning and sharing ideas.

1. ***Concept identification:*** Concepts based on child's immediate environment are identified, keeping in mind the age and ability of the children.
2. ***Concept mapping:*** Concepts are mapped in teachers' collective meetings and learning outcomes are identified for children. The outcomes also include pre-literacy and pre-numeracy skills.
3. ***Concept expansion:*** Based on the learning outcomes, activities are designed and monthly lesson plans are prepared accordingly.

4. ***Classroom transaction:*** The teacher uses a lesson plan and both group-based activities (like conversation, storytelling, rhymes) and individual activities (like early literacy and numeracy activities, creative activities) are arranged. The teacher uses ability-based grouping to help each child learn at their level.
5. ***Assessment:*** The assessment is continuous and comprehensive, tracking and documenting children's milestones, progress, work and classroom engagements. The stage of development of the child is mapped in the assessment matrix—Learning Ability Framework—which helps the teacher to support further learning of the child. It is consolidated and documented twice a year and shared with the parents as well.

Baseline, Midline and End line assessments are also taken to statistically compare and assess the effectiveness of the ECCE programme.

B. Teachers Empowerment—A Decentralised Approach

Prajayatna's focus has been on building on the teacher's skills and capabilities to create an environment which is conducive for the development of the children. This involves understanding and working with children to develop their abilities, working with the communities to ensure the needs of the children are met, and supporting teachers in the classroom (onsite support) to give inputs and feedback which in turn build their capacities. Teachers facilitate and engage the children through various activities ensuring development of abilities in all domains. Thereby, concept-based classroom transactions are mapped by the teacher based on contextual experiences. The classroom offers each child a space to learn experientially, through the use of materials (based on need), at their own pace and level of exposure.

The teachers are categorised using the teachers' ability framework, and based on their needs, onsite support is provided after discussion at Collective meetings.

A Community Approach to Early Childhood Care and Education 231

Figure 17.2: *Sample of concept mapping*

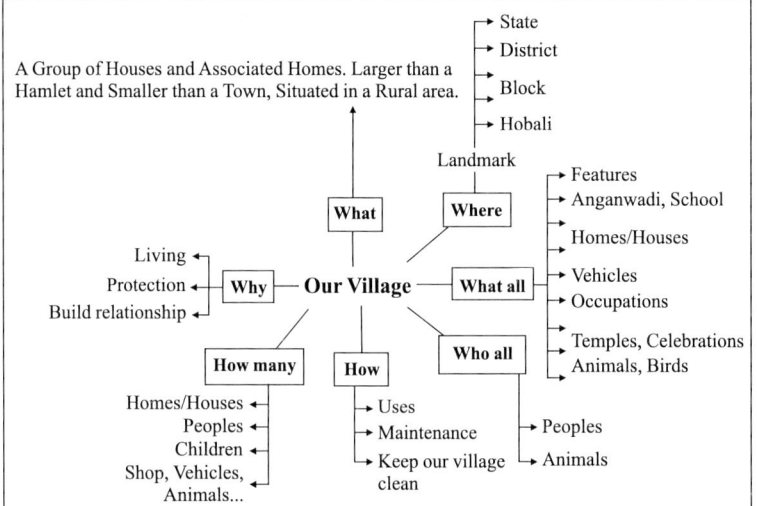

Figure 17.3: *Example of learning outcomes derived for the concept 'our village'*

Concept: Our Village	Learning Outcomes
\multicolumn{2}{c}{Ability + Content = Learning Outcomes}	

Ability + Content = Learning Outcomes

- Able to understand the village belongs to particular GP, Hobli, Taluk/Block, district and State
- Able to tell type of houses in the village
- Able to tell the facilities available in the village and their uses—school for learning, hospital when sick etc.
- Able to name occupations that people in the village are engaged in
- Able to tell the landmark to reach their home
- Able to speak at least three sentences about the village
- Able to differentiate between clean and dirty
- Able to tell at least two things about keeping their village clean
- Learn at least 5–8 letters connected to the concept. Ex: B, U, S – C, A, R
- Able to count up to 5
- Able to identify and name different occupations and what tools they use (carpenter and saw, farmer and hoe, etc.
- Able to draw and colour houses and different institutions like school, AWC
- Able to use the concept of far-near in terms of their neighbours

Teacher Collectives. These are monthly meetings with the teachers which are conducted at the sector level and facilitated by Prajayatna. Annually eight or nine meetings are held on the dates designated by the Department of Women and Child Development. Each sector's Anganwadi Teachers and Supervisors participate in this meeting. This process uses brainstorming, large group interactive discussions and small group discussions and presentations. It is a day-long process and the main objectives of the Collective are:

- Reviewing the progress of the curriculum in the past month
- Refreshing knowledge regarding ECCE (introduction of new aspects related to ECCE to enhance conceptual understanding)
- Identifying the concept/s for the forthcoming month
- Development of the concept map by large group
- Expansion of the concept to their sub-components
- Small group activity of preparing and sharing the following for each concept:

    Expansion of the concept – Suitable activities for the concept – Materials required for activities – Preparation of the daily lesson plans for the coming month

Apart from the capacity building sessions, teachers' empowerment also happens through strengthening the existing monitoring systems through:

- Monthly meetings with supervisors to ensure that their capabilities are enhanced as to support the teachers
- Enhance understanding of their role in improving the quality of the anganwadi
- Ways of supporting the teachers
- Documenting their feedback

C. Building Community Structures

Prajayatna's ECCE programme also works with the parents and other stakeholders as it is understood that they play a pivotal role in the development of the children as well as in the proper functioning of the Anganwadi Centres. They are engaged with in the following manner:

a. **Anganwadi Level Community Meetings:** Anganwadi Level Monitoring and Support Committees (ALMSC) are community level committees mandated by the government; the committee comprises significant members of the community and parents of children attending the anganwadi. Its main responsibility is oversight and providing resources, guidance and support to the anganwadi. They are meant to meet every month and discuss all issues related to the anganwadi, such as facilities, infrastructure at the anganwadi, ensuring the delivery of all the duties and responsibilities of all the stakeholders, guiding the teacher and providing support for all areas of functioning including health, immunisation, nutrition and education.

    The Anganwadi Level Community Meeting is a centre-level democratic process in which the members of the ALMSC, mothers, Anganwadi Teachers, helpers, local community representatives, School Management Committee, school teachers, local elected representatives, local youth groups and organisations and individuals interested in education, come together on a common platform to discuss the need for quality early childhood care and education.

    This meeting enables the community to develop its own perspective by making them understand the importance of ECCE, the objectives behind establishment of the anganwadis, identifying the issues, taking responsibility for solving the identified issues, preparation and implementation of the action plan.

b. **Gram Panchayat and ALMSC/BVS network meetings:** Panchayat Raj institutions serve as local government to the people at the grassroots. Because they are easily accessible to the community, they are more likely to be able to fulfil the requirements of the community located in their vicinity. Quality ECCE being the most important requirements of children aged below 6 in the community, the Gram Panchayat has a major stake in ensuring that children within its purview are not deprived of this facility. Thus it is very important to involve Gram Panchayats in the development of their anganwadis.

   The objective of the meeting is to bring both the structures together and work for the development and better governance of the anganwadis.

c. **Parent Meetings:** Prajayatna conducts parent meetings at the anganwadi once every three months. The purpose behind these meetings is to actively and consciously involve the parents in child care and early education. The focus remains on discussions with parents on the areas of intervention that can be conducted at home in the areas of health and nutrition, immunisation, early learning, informal evaluation of the child's progress over the course of the year etc. These meetings are facilitated with the use of flip cards and use the method of interactive discussions. The facilitators use the cards as aids for initiating discussions and as illustrations to support the discussions. The cards address different ways by which parents can get engaged in the child's learning process.

D. The Impact

Effective Teacher Empowerment in different levels—teachers, supervisors and CDPO's, constant onsite support and building the community structure has led to:

- Enhanced attendance of children in the centres—parents bring their children to the centres, ensure materials for the children
- Teachers are engaged with the children in their learning process
- Improved timings and attendance of the teachers
- Meaningful teachers collective meetings which have been platforms for the teachers to enhance their capabilities
- Children's learning is documented and tracked
- Children are equipped when they are enrolled in school—feedback of school teachers
- Gram Panchayats are involved in the functioning of the centres—resource allocation and mobilisation (in five years raised more than Rs. 1 Crore for 200 anganwadis of which more than 90% was from the GPs)
- ALMSC actively engaged in the management of the Centres

The Early Child Care and Education approach of Prajayatna has impacted about 1305 Anganwadi Centres and 20,000 children in Karnataka and Jharkhand. Through its work, Prajayatna is helping several stakeholders in ensuring quality learning experiences to thousands of young children in their foundational stages of life.

Conclusion

The National Education Policy 2020, has flagged the importance of Early Childhood Care and Education. It calls for universalisation of ECCE for which the anganwadis need to be strengthened with infrastructure and facilities along with trained teachers. This is a long overdue decision and a welcome step and needs to be prioritised during the implementation of the NEP. It is hoped that this will lead to the formalisation of the anganwadi. With the thrust on foundational literacy and numeracy, the importance of ECCE gains more prominence. Yet, care needs to be taken to see that the basic tenets of ECCE are not ignored in the rush to integrate the anganwadi with the schools. The danger of the anganwadi / preschool becoming a downward extension of the school needs to be avoided at all costs.

The lack of mention of the role of the community and the family is a drawback in the policy along with the lack of mention of any community structures to support the functioning of these centres. Effective early childhood care and education settings see the child in the context of the family, and the family in the context of the wider community. The active involvement of the community will ensure proper functioning as well as lead to an active and dynamic space of learning which develops and grows according to the changing needs of the community.

There is a need for a paradigm shift in the way ECCE is viewed in the country from that of preparing the child for school to that of developing a strong foundation for life. For this, there is a need for the formation of a curricular framework which then allows for implementation according to the local context. Training of teachers and a continuous process for their empowerment needs to be institutionalised. The need to make the community, the primary stakeholders, as partners in the learning as well as the decision-making process needs to be incorporated as well. Many of these issues have been mentioned in the NEP and should be taken up on priority. All this calls for a systemic change which needs to be made keeping the needs and interest of the children at heart, as in the words of Nelson Mandela, 'There can be no keener revelation of a society's soul than the way in which it treats its children.'

References

Lightfoot, C., Cole, M., & Cole, S. R. (2008). *The development of children*. Worth Publisher.

Bronfenbrenner, U. (1994). Ecological models of development. In M. C. M. Gauvain, *Readings on development of children* (pp. 37–42). International Encyclopaedia of Education.

NAEYC. (2009). *Developmentally Appropriate practice in early childhood programmes serving children from birth through age 8.*

Prajayatna. (2019). *Early childhood care and education—Process guide.* Prajayatna.

18

Ensuring Quality through Teacher Appraisals and In-Service Education

GAURAVI JADHAV, VALENTINE BORGES
and ELIZABETH MEHTA

In developing countries, poor learning outcomes could be attributed to factors such as the socioeconomic background of students and paucity of quality resources but also to poor quality of teaching. In fact, teaching quality at school level is considered to be the most important variable that influences learning outcomes (Scheerens, 2000). It is difficult to define quality teaching because schools have diverse teacher and learner populations. However, a competent teacher should have good subject knowledge, pedagogical skills and good connect with the learner community besides being a diligent worker. This would help bridge the gap between the curricula or textbook content and the learner society. The constructivist pedagogy expects teachers to facilitate active learning by *constantly* enriching the curriculum of its learner community. This not only calls for certain key attributes among teaching professionals as an essential professional requisite but also necessitates timely upgradation.

Need for Teacher Appraisal

Schools that wish to improve learning outcomes need to effectively monitor their teaching faculty. Francis de Clercq (2008) describes two kinds of monitoring practices: the traditional bureaucratic type and the non-orthodox professional type. The orthodox bureaucratic approach aims to ensure a certain level of professional conduct of the teaching faculty in terms of lesson planning, depth and delivery of curricula, and other professional competence that the school management may expect from its teaching staff. While this type of monitoring is done either by supervisors within the school management or by a third-party and is often a one-time event, the non-orthodox type refers to peer-monitoring that focuses less on compliance of rules or expectations of the management and is more self-driven, flexible and offers context-specific evaluation.

School managements constantly strive for greater accountability and control over their teaching staff. The appraisals help them identify their strengths and weaknesses, while enabling them to design professional development endeavours aimed at improving the school's standards (Bartlett, 2000). De Clercq (2008) broadly classifies the appraisal systems as development and performance oriented. While the former is pinned on the understanding that teachers aspire to improve their professional attributes by reflecting together on the areas that they need to work on to perform better, creating accountability is the key objective of the latter. Hence teachers need to markedly work on certain critical attributes that would ensure their confirmation, promotion, or dismissal from the institution (Monyatsi, Steyn, & Kamper, 2006).

De Clercq (2008) emphasises that for any appraisal system to serve its intended purpose, it is necessary for it to be conducted in a collegial and trusting manner. The appraisal system should endeavour to work on newer ideas and contemporary practices in the teaching profession that would not only improve the school's teaching community (rather than single out teachers) but in turn improve the teaching quality of the entire school. To accomplish this, an appraisal system cannot be one-time; rather it needs to be continual with frequent classroom visits, with all stakeholders (management and teachers) genuinely engaging in fruitful dialogue and, more importantly, giving regular constructive feedback (Marshall, 2012). Finally, the school management should convince teachers as prime stakeholders in the system, that monitoring and appraisals are intended to help develop training programmes and workshops that work on their beliefs and attitudes, which in turn would raise the standard of the teaching and consequently impact the learning community in the long term (de Clercq, 2008).

Developmental Appraisal for Preschool Teachers

Muktangan mentors seven English-medium Municipal Corporation schools in Mumbai. Each of these has a preschool, with about 600 students in total. At Muktangan the process of teacher appraisal is more of a developmental tool than one to manage rewards and recognition. Hence, the performance appraisal is integrated with development appraisal. While the performance appraisal meticulously monitors the teaching staff's past performance, the developmental appraisal process focuses on reinforcing professional competence in teachers to improve their future performance like a feedback mechanism. This process is unlike a third-party assessment system which is one-time with little contact and communication between the appraiser and the appraised. At Muktangan the appraisers (ECCE senior faculty) spend adequate time with teams/subordinates to ensure quality appraisal, while the process is carried out at three critical time-points each year, namely baseline (commencement of the academic year), midline (after first semester) and endline (end of the second semester). Each event provides vital information to the management and senior faculty to plan professional development sessions at these critical points.

This study assesses the effectiveness of Muktangan's appraisal tool for use in enhancing the ECCE teacher performance as an integrated aspect of the organisation's developmental appraisal system.

Material and Methods

The Tool

The developmental appraisal tool for preschool teachers is a pre-validated tool and was revised in the academic year 2015–16 and comprises 20 attributes classified into two separate insolvent categories, judged under critical attributes (CA) and key performance in professional area (KPA). The CA encompasses skill sets like punctuality, teamwork, communication skills and others that the school management deems essential in a teacher in the context of a high-performance working professional, that is, skill sets each trained professional should possess for their own and the organisation's developmental aspirations. The KPA category encompasses skill sets such as content knowledge, clarity in academic communication, appropriate use of subject-related resources and others pertaining specifically to the ECCE teaching profession, that is, skills the ECCE teacher should aim to improvise on to facilitate the organisation's vision of an empowered teaching community for ECCE. Each of the 20 attributes is scored against 12 points ranging from 0, 1–, 1, 1+ up to 4, with zero indicating one and four indicating 12 points. Nevertheless, each of the 20 attributes is separate, non-negotiable and imperative for strengthening the ECCE teaching community at Muktangan.

The Process

Prior to administering the tool, the ECCE coordinator and senior ECCE facilitators conducted workshops to train the teacher community and department leaders on how the tool is to be used while reiterating the concept and need for continuous appraisal. The tool was administered at three critical time-points in the year, namely baseline (commencement of the academic year), midline (after the first semester) and endline (at the end of the second semester). At each time-point, the teachers (appraisees) scored themselves, blinded to the scores given by the senior faculty (appraisers) who were also blinded to how the appraisees rated themselves. This was followed by a one-on-one discussion between the two to understand and communicate each one's rationale leading to the scores. Based on the baseline ratings, the teachers selected two professional development goals they intended to work on in the current semester. As the year progressed the preschool faculty decided on certain time intervals to observe teachers at different sessions of classroom interaction and recorded key observations in a teacher observation book. Additionally, the ECCE faculty reminded them of their goals whilst providing essential feedback post-observation sessions. Besides this, the senior ECCE coordinator would also document her observations and share her feedback with the preschool faculty, thus providing inputs for subsequent appraisal time points.

Data Analysis

Scores given by the appraiser and the appraisee were statistically analysed at the end of the study. Data analysis was carried out to check for an association between the two raters for each of the attributes using the chi-square test. The degree of inter-rater agreement was denoted by Fisher Exact Test, with F value <0.05 considered significant while kappa analysis was carried out for assessing the degree of inter-rater reliability.

Results and Discussion

The study assesses the usefulness of the appraisal tool in the integrated developmental appraisal system by analyzing scores of 47 preschool teachers at Muktangan. The appraisal tool was administered across seven Muktangan-mentored preschools at three critical time points and its qualitative outcome provided inputs for consequent professional development workshops. The process is illustrated in Fig. 18.1. Of the study participants, most (85%) were those with five years or lesser tenure as preschool teachers, while 35% among these had completed a year as ECCE teachers. The longest tenure was seven years represented by a single teacher and over 10% had completed six years of teaching. This makes it an ideal study sample as teacher attrition in the first five years of service worldwide is observed to range from 5% to 50% (Lindqvist, Nordänger, & Carlsson, 2014; Schaefer, Long, & Clandinin, 2012). Reasons for teacher attrition have been well-reviewed by Schaefer et al., (2012) who highlight the need for teacher education and a conducive school environment to sustain and retain teachers in their early tenure. While several factors influence teacher sustainability, providing professional learning opportunities to in-service teachers is particularly important for retaining teachers (Oke, Ajagbe, Ogbari, Adeyeye, 2016). The developmental appraisal tool in its present form provides insights into areas of focus for planning professional development sessions. Moreover, it is seen that self-appraisal is among the best ways of meeting an individual's professional development needs (Keitseng, 1999).

Figure 18.1: *Developmental appraisal system flowchart indicating a cyclic pattern of appraisal and reinforcement through professional development workshops at critical time points along the academic timeline*

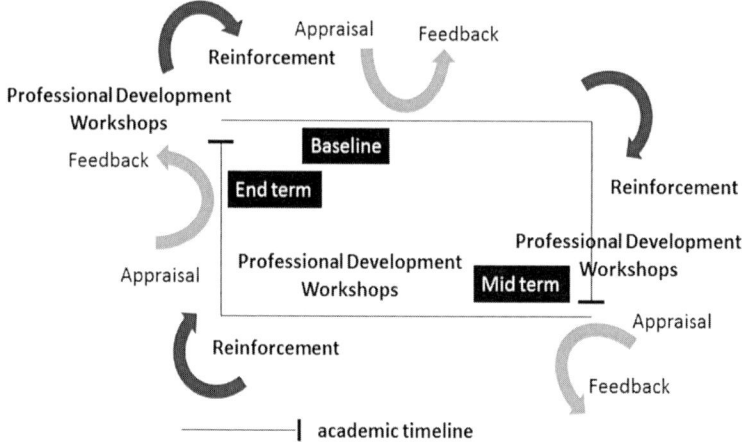

A strong association was observed between the scores assigned by the two raters (P < 0.0001) with κ statistic showing strong relation (contingency coefficient = 0.8753, 0.877 and 0.8741 at baseline, midline and endline respectively) and strong agreement (Fisher's Exact Test < 0.0001) between assessor's (supervisor's) and assessee's (teacher's self-assessed) scores with fair inter-rater reliability (κ = 0.5+) at each critical time point. These results verify the tool's reliability in assessing the key attributes that are required in teachers for quality in ECCE. The κ statistic (Table 18.1) for both sets of attributes show fair inter-rater reliability at each time point and hence asserts that school management can rely on the scores to plan professional development sessions focusing on an area of concern for the majority of the teacher community. Overall, these results have significant implications in improving the process of ECCE teacher performance appraisal at Muktangan. The results indicate that greater engagement between the two raters (assessor and the assessed) will help enhance the inter-rater reliability and strengthen the teacher professional development programme by planning more relevant content and need-based mentoring to improve the overall quality of Muktangan's ECCE programme. It must be noted that in the past four academic years (2012–13 to 2015–2016) among the newly appointed preschool teachers,

Table 18.1: *Comparison of baseline, midline and endline appraisal data*

	Baseline	Midline	Endline
Overall			
Chi-square	$P < 0.0001$	$P < 0.0001$	$P < 0.0001$
Contingency coefficient	0.8753	0.8770	0.8741
Fisher Exact Test	$P < 0.0001$	$P < 0.0001$	$P < 0.0001$
Kappa coefficient	0.5166	0.5134	0.5009
Critical Attributes			
Chi-square	$P < 0.0001$	$P < 0.0001$	$P < 0.0001$
Contingency coefficient	0.8714	0.8862	0.8872
Fisher Exact Test	$P < 0.0001$	$P < 0.0001$	$P < 0.0001$
Kappa coefficient	0.5427	0.5145	0.5350
Key Performance in Professional Areas			
Chi-square	$P < 0.0001$	$P < 0.0001$	$P < 0.0001$
Contingency coefficient	0.8690	0.8806	0.8799
Fisher Exact Test	$P < 0.0001$	$P < 0.0001$	$P < 0.0001$
Kappa coefficient	0.5	0.5	0.5

Muktangan has seen an attrition rate of less than 15%, in the range of 0–6.5 % of total ECCE teachers in these years. This reiterates the efficacy of the developmental appraisal system.

Conclusion

The National ECCE Policy (2013), National Focus Group (2006) position paper and the National Curriculum Framework (2005) position paper on ECCE in India, emphasise the importance of adequately trained workforce and quality in teacher education. However, quality in ECCE has been plagued by shortcomings in understanding and implementing these policies. Muktangan recognises the need for a comprehensive pre-service and in-service teacher education for the early years and has developed a 12-point Likert scale tool to evaluate teacher performance based on 20 diverse attributes categorised under critical attributes and key performance in professional areas that take into account observations by both assessor and the assessee. The tool is dependent on inter-rater reliability to provide crucial inputs to improve classroom deliverance, and reduce teacher attrition, thus ensuring programme sustainability. The developmental appraisal process as a whole, with active appraiser and appraisee engagement, will prove key to the success of Muktangan's ECCE programme and in developing Muktangan into a sustainable learning model.

The Integrated Child Development Services (ICDS) scheme delivers non-formal early years education to over 150 million children in the age group of zero to six years in India. The ICDS team comprises Anganwadi Workers, helpers, Supervisors, Child Development Officers and District Programme Officers. For effective implementation of services, supervisors need to work closely with the Anganwadi Workers and helpers ensuring quality in the delivery of services to the stakeholders. A developmental appraisal system that covers all non-negotiable elements of the ICDS scheme could serve as a quality assurance mechanism. This will ensure efficient and prompt interaction between supervisors and workers and an efficient reporting system for the concerned officers.

National Education Policy: Scope for Quality Improvement Through Professional Development

The secret to successful attainment of school readiness is attributed to school infrastructure, curriculum and to trained teachers. Teachers form an integral part of the social learning environment (Shaari & Ahmad, 2016). Hence, just as children's behaviour and development is influenced by the physical learning environment (Barbosa et al., 2016), the role of trained, proficient preschool teachers should not be overlooked in a preschool programme. Although there is no clarity on the continuity of the ICDS (that has an extensive network and grassroots connectivity along the length and breadth of the country), section 1.6. of the NEP mandates that every *balavatika* should have an ECCE-qualified teacher (MHRD, 2020) and continues to use the terms anganwadis and Anganwadi Workers that are an outcome of the ICDS.

It is now universally acknowledged that students attending high-quality formal preschool programmes benefit more than those who do not. Among the factors that are instrumental in influencing long-term benefits of formal preschooling is a high preschool staff-per-child ratio and the preferential recruitment of formally trained staff (Bauchmüller et al., 2014). In this context, the NEP makes every attempt to ensure that the existing foundational years staff, that is, the Anganwadi Worker/preschool teacher, is entitled to professional growth either through a six-month certificate programme or a year-long diploma. In section 1.7 the policy states further that the training body constituted would be expected to adapt to more contemporary methods such as digital or distance mode using DTH channels and smartphones providing last-mile connectivity ensuring every preschool staff is trained.

ECCE teachers in India are predominantly engaged in routine duties related to supplementary nutrition, the formation of habits of hygiene and eating, and sharing, with play-related activities forming an important part of education. While their knowledge of how to help children develop cognitive abilities, foundational literacy and numeracy is limited, activities related to the development of these skills are seldom discussed and they do not seem proficient in integrating such activities as part of their daily routine at the ECCE centre. While the results are better in centres where teachers are trained (usually adopting the P-P-P model), those that do not have this training seem to have little knowledge of the developmental benefits that these interventions have on the child (Anand & Mckenney, 2015).

A preschool programme is probably only as good as its teachers. Teacher training alone cannot ensure quality and there is sufficient evidence to mandate that ongoing support is necessary to ensure optimal transfer of knowledge and skills to practice (Dhamotharan & Loh, 2019; Elek & Page, 2019). Continual coaching or professional development is known to improve teacher instruction and hence improve learning outcomes by ensuring that developmentally appropriate activities and practices are followed that positively impact child development (Borko, 2004; Fukkink & Lont, 2007; Pianta et al., 2008). This concern is addressed in section 2.6. of the NEP, while section 2.7. states 'all viable methods will be explored to support teachers in the mission of attaining universal foundational literacy and numeracy' probably by state governments. This section also makes provisions of the need for and the possibility of peer-tutoring by volunteers from the local community and beyond (MHRD, 2020). This is probably an indirect reference to the scope of not-for-profit organisations engaged in the field of teacher education to contribute towards the national mission and vision.

Teacher attrition is also a growing concern at all levels. Teachers with higher education credentials often think that these would eventually lead to career progression. Besides work stress and relocation, career stagnation is also a leading cause for teacher attrition. While some teachers consider continuing in the same profession because they do not have higher qualifications leading them to feel they have fewer appealing options, there are others who consider more lucrative opportunities owing to their better educational competence and proficiency. This aspiration is responsible for higher teacher turnover rates (Bullough et al., 2012; Guarino et al., 2006; Kwon et al., 2020; Wells, 2015) evident in private centres in India. Often among ECCE teachers, progression to teaching higher grades is seen as career progression (Kwon et al., 2020). To address this concern on the dilemma of career progression and the challenge of teacher turnover, section 5.17 of the NEP provides scope for a robust merit-based framework of tenure, promotion and salary structure to be emulated, with multiple levels within each teacher stage, that incentivises and recognises teachers who consistently outperform their expectations (MHRD, 2020). One must acknowledge that the scope and aspiration for career progression and the scar of retention that often maligns the functioning of a programme can only be addressed through meticulous development appraisal or monitoring-and-feedback system. However, the NEP falls short of addressing this and neither mentions the scope for such monitoring mechanisms, apart from defining the scope of an accrediting body or State School Standards Authority (in section 8), limiting it to auditing the physical and social learning environment. Muktangan's developmental appraisal system could provide meaningful insights and facilitate effective communication of expectations and challenges between administrators and preschool teachers that could have significant implications in improving the teaching quality and reducing teacher attrition in preschools.

References

Anand, G., & Mckenney, S. (2015). Professional development needs: Early childhood teachers in public child care centres. *Staff and educational development international*, *19*(2/3), 85–104.

Barbosa, S. C., Coledam, D. H. C., Stabelini Neto, A., Elias, R. G. M., & de Oliveira, A. R. (2016). School environment, sedentary behavior and physical activity in preschool children. *Revista Paulista de Pediatria (English Edition)*, *34*(3), 301–308. https://doi.org/10.1016/j.rppede.2016.02.003.

Barlett, S. (2000). The development of teacher appraisal: A recent history. *British Journal of Education Studies,* *48*(1), 24–37. https://doi.org/10.1111/1467-8527.00131.

Bauchmüller, R., Gørtz, M., & Rasmussen, A. W. (2014). Long-run benefits from universal high-quality preschooling. *Early Childhood Research Quarterly*, *29*(4), 457–470. https://doi.org/10.1016/j.ecresq.2014.05.009.

Borko, H. (2004). Professional development and teacher learning: Mapping the terrain. *Educational Researcher*, *33*(8), 3–15.

Bullough, R. V., Hall-Kenyon, K. M., & MacKay, K. L. (2012). Head start teacher well-being: Implications for policy and practice. *Early Childhood Education Journal*, *40*(6), 323–331. https://doi.org/10.1007/s10643-012-0535-8.

Clercq, F. (2008). Teacher quality, appraisal and development: The flaws in the IQMS. *Perspectives in Education, 26*(1), 7–18. https://www.researchgate.net/publication/289284692_Teacher_quality_appraisal_and_development_The_flaws_in_the_IQMS.

Dhamotharan, D. M. D., & Loh, C. (2019). Continuing professional development for ecce teachers in selected states in Malaysia: What teachers and operators say. *Advances in social sciences research journal*. https://doi.org/10.14738/assrj.64.6471.

Elek, C., & Page, J. (2019). Critical features of effective coaching for early childhood educators: A review of empirical research literature. *Professional development in education*, *45*(4), 567–585. https://doi.org/10.1080/19415257.2018.1452781.

Fukkink, R. G., & Lont, A. (2007). Does training matter? A meta-analysis and review of caregiver training studies. *Early childhood research quarterly*, *22*(3), 294–311. https://doi.org/10.1016/j.ecresq.2007.04.005.

Guarino, C. M., Santibañez, L., & Daley, G. A. (2006). Teacher recruitment and retention: A review of the recent empirical literature. *Review of Educational Research*, *76*(2), 173–208. https://doi.org/10.3102/00346543076002173.

Keitseng, A. (1999). Self-appraisal: a step towards meeting individual's professional development needs for Botswana secondary school teachers. *Journal of In- Service Education,* *25*(1), 23–37. https://doi.org/10.1080/13674589900200066.

Kwon, K. A., Malek, A., Horm, D., & Castle, S. (2020). Turnover and retention of infant-toddler teachers: Reasons, consequences, and implications for practice and policy. *Children and Youth Services Review, 115*, 105061. https://doi.org/10.1016/j.childyouth.2020.105061.

Lindqvist, P., Nordanger, U., & Carlsson, R. (2014). Teacher attrition the first five years: A multifaceted image. *Teaching and Teacher Education, 40*, 94–103. https://doi.org/10.1080/13674589900200066.

Marshall, K. (2012). Teacher Evaluation: What's Fair? What's Effective? Fine tuning teachers evaluation. *Educational leadership, 70(3)*, 50–53. https://marshallmemo.com/articles/Ed-Leadership-Nov-2012.pdf.

Ministry of Human Resource Development. (2020). National education policy. *Government of India*. https://innovateindia.mygov.in/wp-content/uploads/2020/08/NEP_Final_English_0.pdf.

Monyatsi, P., Steyn, T., & Kamper, G. (2006). Teacher perceptions of the effectiveness of teacher appraisal in Botswana. *South African Journal of Education, 26(3)*, 427–441. DOI: 10.4314/saje.v26i3.25080 https://files.eric.ed.gov/fulltext/EJ1150398.pdf.

National Council of Educational Research and Training. (2005). National curriculum framework. http://www.ncert.nic.in/rightside/links/pdf/framework/english/nf2005.pdf.

National Council of Educational Research and Training (2006). Position paper on early childhood education. http://www.ncert.nic.in/new_ncert/ncert/rightside/links/pdf/focus_group/early_childhood_education.pdf.

Oke, D., Ajagbe, M., Ogbari, M., & Adeyeye, J. (2016). Teacher retention and attrition: a review of the literature. *Mediterranean Journal of Social Sciences, 7*(2 (S1), 371–378. DOI: 10.5901/mjss.2016.v7n2s1p371.

Pianta, R. C., Mashburn, A. J., Downer, J. T., Hamre, B. K., & Justice, L. (2008). Effects of web-mediated professional development resources on teacher–child interactions in pre-kindergarten classrooms. *Early Childhood Research Quarterly, 23(4)*, 431–451. https://doi.org/10.1016/j.ecresq.2008.02.001.

Schaefe, L., Long, J., & Clandinin, D. (2012). Questioning the research on early career teacher attrition and retention. *Alberta Journal of Educational Research, 58(1)*, 106–121. Retrieved from- https://pdfs.semanticscholar.org/0e11/56c8ec5fc29d4836e1965e69c120c99c3e4a.pdf?_ga=2.77981076.1286737716.1566242944-780503365.1566242944.

Scheerens, J. (2000). *Improving school effectiveness.* (Fundamentals of Educational Planning; No. 68). Paris, France: Unesco International

Institute for Educational Planning. ISBN (Print) 9280312049. https://ris.utwente.nl/ws/portalfiles/portal/5154343/Improving-122424e.pdf.

Shaari, M. F., & Ahmad, S. S. (2016). Physical learning environment: Impact on children school readiness in Malaysian preschools. *Procedia—Social and Behavioral Sciences, 222*, 9–18. https://doi.org/10.1016/j.sbspro.2016.05.164.

Wells, M. B. (2015). Predicting preschool teacher retention and turnover in newly hired Head Start teachers across the first half of the school year. *Early Childhood Research Quarterly, 30*, 152–159. https://doi.org/10.1016/j.ecresq.2014.10.003.

19

In-service Programme for Teacher Educators for Early Years Education

JIGISHA SHASTRI and KINNARI PANDYA

The Azim Premji Foundation initiated work in the area of Early Childhood Education (ECE) in Sangareddy (erstwhile Medak) District of Telangana with the anganwadis of the Integrated Child Development Services Scheme (ICDS). The aim of the initiative was to understand the ICDS system and enable the system to transform the anganwadis into 'vibrant learning centres', a goal articulated in the National Early Childhood Care and Education Policy 2013.

It has been well recognised that the teacher is the fulcrum of a quality early childhood education programme. A teacher of young children should be knowledgeable about child development, growth and learning, should be aware and be able to put into practice an appropriate pedagogical programme. Besides knowledge, the ECE teacher should also have the skills to interact and engage with young children and implement a developmentally and culturally appropriate programme. The ECE teacher should be sensitive to children's needs, be a patient observer, curious, warm and approachable. To become teachers with such holistic attributes, it is imperative to receive appropriate training, be it pre-service or in-service.

The Integrated Child Development Services scheme with its massive mandate to promote holistic child development and reach the poorest of the poor, is run by Anganwadi Workers (AWWs), now being referred to as Anganwadi Teachers (AWTs). The AWTs have the minimum pre-service qualification–grade level 8 and a brief induction training for a complex role they are required to perform as early childhood care-givers and educators. For them to be effective in their roles as a teacher, a critical link is that of a teacher trainer and teacher educator who would help in building the AWTs capabilities in-service. For the Azim Premji Foundation to be able to contribute effectively to the ICDS system, and its goal to promote children's psycho-social development and work with AWTs, the Foundation had to prepare a strong internal team of key resource persons in the area of Early Childhood Education. This internal team would, in turn, train, demonstrate and handhold the AWT in implementing a developmentally appropriate, play-based, early childhood education programme.

This paper articulates the nature of such an in-service capacity development programme offered to teacher trainers/educators from varied backgrounds, and the stages of their development as teacher trainers/educators.

Development of Teacher Educators—The In-service Journey

Teachers need to know what they have to teach children, and how. Similarly, teacher trainers need to know what teachers would need to practice in their classrooms, and theoretical ideas and skills of working with adult learners, the teachers.

Figure 19.1: *Common attributes of programme for children, teachers and trainers*

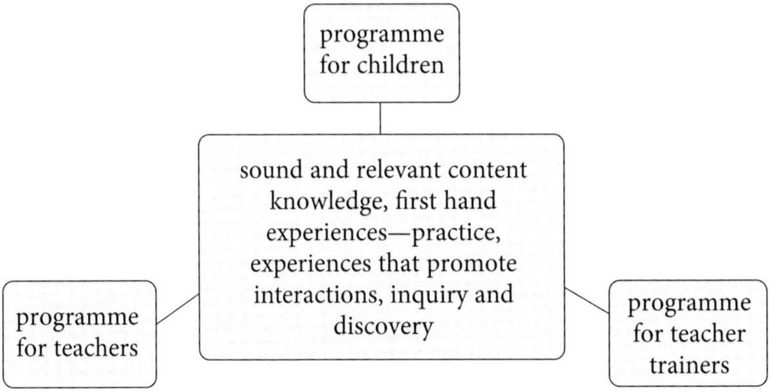

```
                    ┌──────────────┐
                    │  programme   │
                    │ for children │
                    └──────┬───────┘
                           │
    ┌──────────────┐  ┌────┴─────────────────┐  ┌──────────────┐
    │              │  │ sound and relevant   │  │              │
    │              │  │ content knowledge,   │  │              │
    │  programme   ├──┤ first hand           ├──┤  programme   │
    │ for teachers │  │ experiences—practice,│  │ for teacher  │
    │              │  │ experiences that     │  │   trainers   │
    │              │  │ promote interactions,│  │              │
    │              │  │ inquiry and discovery│  │              │
    └──────────────┘  └──────────────────────┘  └──────────────┘
```

A quality early childhood programme provides a vibrant and stimulating environment for children to learn from, an interactive approach to teaching and learning, with firsthand experiences and inquiry-based experiences. The programme should cater to the individual needs of children and respect the differences. For such a programme to exist, the teachers of young children should go through a similar capacity building programme; a training programme that focusses on knowledge building, putting knowledge into practice through firsthand experiences, where teachers themselves learn to be inquirers and discoverers. These attributes should be present in the programme for teacher trainers as well.

The need for reaching children of 3–6 years age group at their level, offering a programme suitable to each child's needs and developmental potential, requires a teacher to possess several skills and knowledge about theories of working with children. The core principles, concepts and pedagogic practices that a teacher would need to use in the classroom, is what teacher trainers should be well-versed with and able to mentor a teacher to perform. The knowledge of how children learn, and for teachers to learn the way children learn, is what would make a teacher an adult learner, who sets aside her 'adult' persona, and plans and engages with children in play-activity-based curricular practices. Figure 19.1 represents these common features of an early childhood programme, that ought to be consistent in training teacher trainers and teacher educators, as well as the curriculum for children.

What We Set Out to Achieve

The key aim was to 'develop a team of teacher trainers that will be able to provide quality Early Childhood Education intervention in the ICDS Anganwadi Centres'.

- Build an indepth understanding about ECE—the principles, practices and domain

- Develop capacity for training, mentoring the system functionaries—the pedagogic practices and skills to work as 'teacher trainers' and 'mentors'
- Enhance skills to plan, implement, and assess a quality ECE programme
- Enable reflective practice and action research

Participants—The In-service Teacher Educator Team

The 16-member team consisted of young men and women with a postgraduate degree in Social Sciences and two team leaders. These members had varied pre-service educational qualifications—Masters in Education, Social Work, Business Management, Diploma in Early Childhood Education, and Research. Of the whole team, only one person had some prior experience of working with young children.

The aim of the trainer programme was to enable this group of participants to become ECE teacher trainers. In the following sections, we highlight the stages of professional development this team of participants underwent and the overall mentoring plan that enabled the development of teacher trainers.

Stages of In-service (Teacher) Professional Development

Learning in any form is sequential and individuals move through a process of not knowing to knowing, extending and expanding their understanding of concepts and putting their learning into practise. According to Katz (2009), teachers in the growth of their professional competence go through developmental sequences or stages. Each of these stages, according to Katz, also have very specific training needs. The Stages of Development and Training Needs of Preschool Teachers by Katz (2009) is described below in brief.

1. **The Survival Stage:** This is the first stage where the main concern of new teachers is whether they will be able to survive the daily challenges that they encounter. This lasts

for the first three months to one year of a teacher's practice. During this stage, the teacher needs support and guidance. They need direct help with specific skills and insights into children and their behaviour, managing the classroom, and so on. Teachers need constant training from a person, a mentor who knows them and their context.

2. *The Consolidation Stage:* This is the second stage. This begins around the end of the first year. The teacher has survived the first stage and is now interested in understanding individual children and helping them. On-site training is still very valuable, with the mentor observing the teacher in action and providing direct suggestions as well as together exploring an individual case. Rapport between the mentor and the teachers is key for extended give and take conversations between them.

3. *The Renewal Stage:* This is where the teacher herself looks for renewal, being tired of the routine and wanting to learn and practice something different. Teachers at this stage should have opportunities to interact with other colleagues in the field, attend workshops and seminars, attend other programmes, and read professional magazines and journals. The teacher should at this stage seek to expand her horizon as a practising teacher, a professional.

4. *The Maturity Stage:* This is the fourth stage of professional development. By this stage the teacher is comfortable with herself and feels confident about her own competence. Teachers at this stage benefit from participating in seminars and conferences, work towards an advanced degree, and read on larger issues related to education and children.

In-service Capacity Building Plan for Teacher Educators

The programme for professional development of ECE teacher trainers broadly corresponds to the stages of professional development by Katz (2009) described above. The mentoring programme by Azim Premji University faculty was phased and involved multiple modes of training the trainers. The following section describes the phases of capacity development, and the various stages that the trainee trainers have passed through over the last few years of their journey as ECE professionals.

Phase I: Introduction to the ECE Domain

The aim was to gain knowledge about children, development, learning and early childhood education principles and perspectives. This was achieved through face-to-face, intensive, interactive training. It included class discussions, reflective exercises, use of audiovisual aids and some practicum workshops through simulation of young children's classrooms.

The training took place over a period of six months wherein participants were gradually immersed into the field of young children and early childhood education. The topics covered were importance of early years and early childhood education, understanding children, their growth and development, play, process of learning in children, developmentally appropriate curriculum and its features, and assessment of young children. The components of an ECE programme (indoor/outdoor play, music, movement and songs, stories, readiness activities, creative activities, conversation, learning corners) were handled through interactive workshops. Trainees sang and danced like children, organised spaces into learning corners, engaged with materials, participated in art and craft activities. This gave them an insight into children, their behaviour, questions that arise when children interact with each other and materials, organising classrooms and activities, and so on. The hands-on experiences also gave them an opportunity to understand dilemmas and issues that teachers face while engaging children in classrooms. In each of the workshops, an attempt was made to link theoretical ideas learnt and actual actions and practices.

During this stage the team was continuously supported with training in both theory and skill development. Rigorous and continuous interaction took place between the faculty and the teacher trainers/participants; face-to-face as well as through group emails. This was also a period of rapport building between the mentors and the team, that strengthened the relationship that still continues seven years later.

Stage 1: Survival Stage. The trainee trainers on the other hand were discovering a new domain of work and professional engagement. Several of the participants in the programme were male and had to navigate their identity as 'ECE professionals' in an otherwise female community of practitioners, and AWTs. They underwent the programme discovering newer content knowledge, becoming child-like, rediscovering themselves as individuals and as a team of ECE professionals dedicated to the cause of young children and their development.

Phase II: Immersion in the ECE Domain

This phase dealt with linking theory and practice. The focus of this phase was on gaining in-depth understanding about children and learning and putting it into practice by working with children in the anganwadis. This involved visiting anganwadis, interacting with various cadre of ICDS personnel—the Project Officer, Child Development Programme Officer (CDPO), Supervisor, Anganwadi Teacher and Helper. This phase also involved the participants observing the mentors directly engage in taking workshops for the ICDS functionaries and being assistant facilitators.

Stage 1: Survival Stage in progress. This too was a critical continuation of the survival stage of teacher professional development. The trainee team had to build rapport with the various stakeholders of the ICDS scheme. During their visit to the Anganwadi Centres, they had to understand the context, and create their identity as ECE practitioners. They were expected to try out their newly learnt skills through the capacity development sessions. The challenge for the team on the ground was to engage young children meaningfully for some length of time. The nature of the intervention programme in the Anganwadi Centres required the participants to visit the centres in pairs. A systematic engagement was planned which began with being participant observers to practise telling stories, singing songs, and then as they gained confidence conducting activities and holding thematic conversations. This was a crucial phase involving lot of questions, reflection, learning new skills and therefore required intensive handholding of the participants. Participants shared written and oral observations, and in addition to face-to-face discussions, also engaged in discussions on email groups. Visiting the anganwadis in pairs provided psychological and practical support, and led to collaborative learning. The team members also practised the activities with each other before implementing it with children. Phase II was for a duration of six months.

Phase III: Strengthening Concepts and Gaining Mastery over the Domain and Practices

This phase aimed at helping the participants move towards independence. The team began to reflect on their own individual capacities, designing personal capacity building goals, and got involved in planning the programme, and supporting the AWTs in implementing it on field. Each pair of the participants was linked with specific AWTs whom they had to mentor. They brought forth issues and challenges with individual AWTS.

The team also participated in conducting brief training sessions. It is important to note here that like children, the teacher trainers also indicated individual differences. Therefore, though all of them had a common goal and agenda, they also followed their own individual pathway to learning. By now individual strengths and interests among the participants had also started emerging. Hence if one participant was comfortable in interacting with the ICDS personnel, another showed strength in conducting activities on field and a third in documenting the work. It is important to note that individual variations in people should be accepted and appreciated and a training programme should always make space to incorporate and encourage individual needs and interests of participants. By the end of the second year the team started functioning independently, building rapport with AWTs, being role models and supporting AWTs towards creating interactive vibrant learning centres.

Stage 2: Consolidation. In several ways, this phase corresponded with the second stage of teacher professional development. The team members were able to engage meaningfully with children during their visits to the Anganwadi Centre. They were further able to engage with the AWTs, build their trust and relationship with the community and ICDS functionaries.

The trainees were regularly observed on-site by the mentors, given feedback, and engaged in detailed reflection sessions that helped resolve their dilemmas and clarify theoretical underpinnings of their practices with teachers and children. As the process of on-site mentoring required, appropriate 'openings', case-based examples were used to discuss and clarify the concepts on developmentally and culturally appropriate curriculum and pedagogic practices.

> **At the end of Phase 3, we collected a few responses from the participants.**
>
> *Male member (MSW): Now I have confidence to become a good resource person for AWWs trainings and developing the materials and activities.*
>
> *Female member (MBA): The key areas in which we need to develop is 'planning with flexibility embedded'.*
>
> *Male member (MSW): I perceive my role to be a 'support to AWW in PSE transaction, materials preparation, capacity building. Also develop training modules, developing resource centre and be a resource person'.*
>
> *Female member (ECE Diploma): Most of the parents and community are not aware (of the importance) of ECE. Making them understand is very important to develop ECE.*
>
> *Female member (MAEd): Became more comfortable with teachers (AWWs) and overcoming fear of teacher's resistance.*

Phase IV: Independence and Expanding Circle-of-practice

(Ongoing period) In this phase the focus was on building capacity of the AWTs through the participants. They began functioning as teacher trainers, conducting workshops, participating in sector meetings with larger groups of AWTs, mentoring the AWTs to design a developmentally appropriate programme and implement it. They have been visiting quality ECE programmes across the country and exchanging learnings with them. Reading circles within groups encourages new learning, exchange of ideas.

Stage 3 and 4: Renewal and Maturity. Through the fourth phase of capacity development, the participants were visibly intrinsically invested in their role as early childhood trainers. They engaged in self and peer capacity development, participated and presented their work in conferences, organised seminars as peer learning platforms for AWTs and functionaries. They found renewed meaning in their role of ECE practitioners by seeing the tangible changes in the AWCs and AWTs with whom they had been working extensively.

The stage 4 of maturity in professional development is a continuing phase for this team of trainee trainers—now expert teachers themselves. They have become mentors of their newer colleagues, and play the role of master resource persons for AWTs within Telangana and other states where the Foundation is expanding its work in Early Childhood Education domain.

Table 19.1 summarises the overall capacity development plan and stages of professional development for Trainee Trainers.

Teacher Educator Team's Status Today

This process has created a strong capable team of reflective, knowledgeable and sensitive trainers and practitioners. They have a good theoretical understanding of early childhood education and developmentally and culturally appropriate practice and curriculum. Over the last seven years of continuous engagement

Table 19.1: *Framework for in-service capacity building plan for teacher educators*

	Phase I *Introduction to the ECE domain*	Phase II *Immersion in the domain*	Phase III *Strengthening and mastery of concepts and skills*	Phase IV *Independence and expanding circle-of-practice*
Stages of Teacher Professional Development (Katz, 2009)	Survival Stage		Consolidation Stage	Renewal and Maturity Stage
Objective	ECE theoretical concepts	Linkages between theory and practice on field	Reflecting on one's own capacities	Helping the AWW to function independently
Duration	First six months	Next six months Year 1	Year 2	Year 3 onwards
Aspects of capacity building	Theoretical understanding of ECE Exposure to other quality ECE programmes	Exposure to ECE programmes of anganwadis Interacting with ICDS personnel, planning Implementing activities for children	Planning and implementing developmentally appropriate curriculum Serving as role models Supporting Anganwadi Workers in planning and implementing DAP Conducting training programmes	Team to support the AWWs to be fully functional independent ECE workers

Mode of Capacity Building	Face to face workshops Email discussion groups Guided face to face discussions based on readings On-site observation and practice Attending other ECE programmes Reflective discussions		
Role of ECE Mentors (Early Childhood Faculty from Azim Premji University)	Facilitating workshops Constant feedback and facilitation of email discussions Observing and giving feedback on plans, engagement with AWWs and children Support and guidance on site	Fostering reflective practice: About one's own role as an ECE professional and on field mentor of the AWW For developing and implementing quality ECE programme	Constant mentoring to reach independent and expert level for ECE domain
Outcome	Theoretical grasp over developmentally appropriate curriculum and practice	Confidently planning and implementing, theoretically sound developmentally appropriate single activities	Beginning to be reflective practitioners Motivating and encouraging AWWs to participate	Mentor AWWs to take ownership of and offer quality ECE program

(*Contd.*)

Table 19.1: (Contd.)

	Phase I Introduction to the ECE domain	Phase II Immersion in the domain	Phase III Strengthening and mastery of concepts and skills	Phase IV Independence and expanding circle-of-practice
Stages of Teacher Professional Development (Katz, 2009)	Survival Stage		Consolidation Stage	Renewal and Maturity Stage
			Beginning to plan and conduct weekly programmes independently	
Final Outcome	A fully capacitated team to work as mentors for ECE programmes, that is curriculum developers and implementers, action researchers, trainers, and advocates of ECE			

with the team, and currently sporadic indirect mentoring, the team has matured to the level of advanced trainers and facilitators. Most members of the participant trainees are able to plan an appropriate ECE programme as well as guide the AWT in doing so. They have become mentors, training others, handholding on field, curriculum developers and strong advocates of Early Childhood Education. They independently conduct workshops for groups of AWTs, mentor them in small groups at the Foundation centre, serve as resource persons for trainings conducted by the state government and AWW Training Institute. On a regular basis the team members participate as resource persons in sector and project meetings, hold seminars for AWTs (the AWTs are mentored by the team to present their work). The team members also mentor new members who join the group, and conduct training programmes for other teams of the Foundation to prepare and support them to begin early childhood education related work their own districts.

Mentoring the Team—Our Reflections

The mentors of the team were Early Childhood Education Faculty from the Azim Premji University with significant experience in the field of ECE. The role of mentoring the team was a satisfying and challenging process. The challenge lay in building capacities of non-ECE persons to transform themselves into becoming expert teacher trainers. As university faculty usually involved in working with pre-service professionals, this opportunity to work with in-service trainees was unique. The critical component of the capacity building programme lay in identifying the core-theory and skill set required for in-service personnel and finding the right balance in developing and showcasing practices that are theoretically rooted.

Both on-site and off-site support was provided, maintaining a continuous connection, and encouraging open communication. This process of mentoring was and is a continuous process of development. The involvement of the mentors was in entirety—

from planning the workshop, identifying each specific reading to conducting workshops, field visits with the team members. The visits led to specific observations which were then discussed and reflected upon with individuals and the whole group. The mentoring also involved becoming role models in the field, demonstrating activities, engaging with children and AWTs. Each lesson plan of engagement developed by each team member was given feedback and an attempt was made to answer each and every query raised by them.

The unique opportunity available in this programme was the continuous on-site engagement. The constant engagement on field with children and teachers brought the theoretical ideas in the specific workshops to life and built a rich interplay of implementing ideas in their daily work and improvising their own practice. This direct engagement on-site also resulted in observing changes in Anganwadi Centres where the participants were contributing. The pace of learning among participants was therefore evidently higher than a capacity development programme that would be primarily theoretical with fewer opportunities for practice and experiencing the changes in the Anganwadi Centres. Learning and practising learning went hand-in-hand here—an ideal requirement for developing teachers and educators.

The stages of professional development for teaching professionals are more or less similar and common to the range of professionals involved in practice—be it teachers or teacher trainers in the early education field—as are the core theoretical and pedagogical principles for early childhood practice. The key lies in the quality of experiences and mentoring available to both teachers and teacher trainers to move from novice to expert or survival to mature stages of professional development.

Relevance of This Approach in the Context of National Education Policy 2020

The National Education Policy 2020, has brought Early Childhood Care and Education (ECCE) domain to the forefront of quality schooling in India. With its emphasis on early childhood education, and mainstreaming of 3 to 6 years of ECCE, there is an anticipation of increased quality early childhood education programme and as a result of it increase in the demand for good teachers. Organisations working in the sector, and schools will also have to gear up to strengthen capacities of their existing teachers. The above model of preparing high-quality ECE teacher trainers through rigorous in-service programmes for trainers can serve as an example of mentoring people with an interest in early years, and opportunity for continuous field engagement. Multimodal programmes with support from university departments can be designed to enhance the skills of existing in-service teacher trainers such as the SCERT and DIET functionaries, supervisors and CDPOs and fresh candidates, and leading them to become quality trainers of early years teachers as well as advocates for early childhood education.

REFERENCES

Katz, L. G. (2009). The challenges and dilemmas of educating early childhood teachers. In A. Gibbons and C. Gibbs (Eds). *Conversations on Early Childhood Teacher Education*. World Forum Foundation.

Ministry of Women and Child Development. (2013). *National early childhood care and education (ECCE) policy, 2013.*

Ministry of Human Resource Development. (2020). *National education policy 2020.*

Section 4

Resources for Early Childhood Educators

20

ECD Toolkits for Quality Early Years Education

GAURAVI JADHAV and JUMANA RAMPURAWALA

Muktangan Education Trust is a non-government organisation doing pioneering work in the field of preschool and school education since 2003. Muktangan works with economically marginalised urban communities in Mumbai through the hub-and-spoke model by providing quality teacher training to community members at the teacher training centre (the hub) and teachers (the spokes) in turn teach children from the same community at English-medium public schools from preschool to standard ten. Muktangan has mentored over 800 such change-agents who have shaped the lives of over 5000 children in 16 years.

Muktangan also reaches out to the local self-government mentored schools that is, anganwadis (AWs) and Zilla Parishad (ZP) schools in rural Maharashtra by facilitating knowledge transfer for capacity building of facilitators from partnering NGOs, who in turn work with Anganwadi Workers (AWW) and ZP school teachers. Through local partners Muktangan has reached out to over 50 NGO teacher educators (facilitators), 250 AWW and their helpers and 200 ZP school teachers, impacting over 7000 children in preschool and elementary years of learning, in less than five years.

Muktangan's early years education programme seeks to offer each child a developmentally appropriate curriculum. It is based on the premise that children are natural seekers of information and construct their own understanding and knowledge through play or play-based activities. They attempt to make sense of their world continuously, each in their own way and at their own pace. The job of the adult is to observe each child in their individual process of learning and to provide a learning environment where children can self-construct their further understanding based on these non-judgmental observations, not just teach what they believe the child needs to know.

In keeping with their vision, Muktangan is now creating and providing toolkits for educators and parents to easily and effectively replicate their unique processes with children and to advocate positive, systemic change in the implementation of education within the mainstream.

Investment in Early Years

Play, as established through multiple researches, contributes to the overall wellbeing and development of young children. Through structured play-based activities children learn important aspects of school readiness, peer interactions, using materials in creative ways and experience a joyful childhood in the process (Kroeker, 2017). It is known that greater investments in quality early childhood programmes can lead to higher return on investment in the nation's economy and workforce development (Heckman, n.d.). Although financial returns from early years investment are not evident in the short term, cognitive, social and behavioural development is realised in short or medium term.

Need for a Toolkit

In India, though the ICDS scheme has existed since 1975, its reach has been limited to addressing health and nutrition in young children and expectant mothers (PIB, Nov 2017). Several non-governmental initiatives advocating innovative early childhood education practices operate in pockets and cannot possibly cover the vast population of young *underserved* children. In the majority of playschools in the private sector, preschool is regarded as a downward extension of primary school, emphasising more on

Figure 20.1: *Children engaged in free play activity*

Copyright © Muktangan Education Trust. All rights reserved. Reproduced with permission

formal reading and writing and less on play. In existing educational practice there is a lack of understanding of what is developmentally appropriate for young children as also adequate training in this regard (Vasal, 2007). As a result, a preschool teacher or AWW ends up teaching what a child is required to master in formal school or nothing at all. The Muktangan tool kits will help in addressing these lacunae.

In India the space of early childhood care and education got new energy with the National ECCE policy coming in 2013. Recently the NCERT too has spelt out guidelines for quality early years education (2018) and the preschool curriculum (2019). The NEP 2020 also mentions the need for easy to use resources for early years practitioners. Muktangan ECD toolkits complement their spirit to a great extent.

The toolkits are designed to contain developmentally appropriate processes to be implemented through a daily routine based on children's needs and interests. It is user-friendly and multilingual for use in the rural and urban contexts. It aims to address the need for quality in ECCE. Our aim is to make it replicable and scalable to eventually benefit the masses.

Process-based Daily Routine Toolkits

Figure 20.2: *Teacher demonstrating show and tell process*

Copyright © Muktangan Education Trust. All rights reserved. Reproduced with permission

A consistent daily routine is very important for young children. Consistent routines help ease the transition from home to school, they also help children predict what to expect each day and give them a sense of security.

Our toolkits are process-based and explain to the user as to what process needs to be done and why. It can be easily adapted and fitted into the class routine. The processes are not fixed timetables where subject teaching is done, it is not rigid in its content and gives the user flexibility to adapt and use their creativity in giving the best education to their children.

The Muktangan recommended daily routine components are developmentally appropriate and planned in a purposeful manner to support the holistic development of the learner and is the recommended tool to implement the ECD curriculum.

The following components of daily routine are presented as appropriate to be followed consistently in early years:

- *Greet and Meet* – promotes personal socio-emotional development

- *Show and Tell* – promotes language development
- *Outdoor Play* – promotes physical-motor development
- *Story Circle* – promotes language, literacy and moral development
- *Constructive Play* – promotes cognitive and aesthetic development
- *Concept Circle* – promotes conceptual development
- *Meal Circle* – promotes physical and social development

Salient Features of the Toolkits:

- The toolkits are available for each of the above processes and also as a set in three languages: Hindi, Marathi and English.
- Each toolkit handbook outlines the kind of planning and preparation teachers need at the beginning of the year and for each week/day. The reason for each of the steps is also clearly spelled out so that teachers have a goal when they work with children.
- These step-by-step processes are demonstrated in the videos.
- The toolkit has a balance of child and teacher initiated activities.
- Parent engagement strategies are also suggested.
- It also has simple *do it yourself* assignments that help teachers enrich their classroom and teaching experiences by creating no-/low-cost teaching-learning material.
- The *monitoring tool* provided at the end of the toolkit helps the teacher/user track changes.
- As required, there are addendums like audio files, song book, game book, printables' and so on for different toolkits.
- Orientation training for the toolkit is also offered for those interested.

The toolkits thus demonstrate a way to *put in action* the early years curriculum. The tone is not prescriptive and gives the user scope to reflect on the processes. Presented below are some key content from our toolkit documents which you could apply in your settings. Before understanding the activities let's look at the context of the activities in the toolkits.

Philosophy behind the Toolkit

The processes of toolkits are based on the philosophy of active-constructivism (see Figure 20.3) whereby children are facilitated by an adult to develop twenty-first century skills.

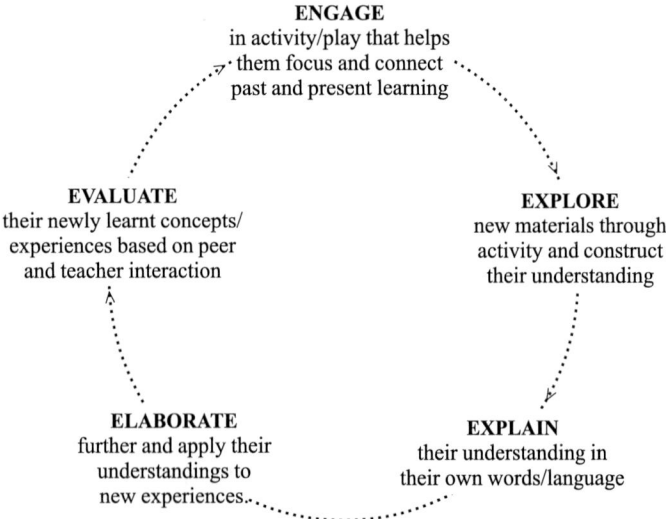

Fig. 20.3: *Five E's of active-constructivism that help develop twenty-first century skills*

ENGAGE in activity/play that helps them focus and connect past and present learning

EXPLORE new materials through activity and construct their understanding

EXPLAIN their understanding in their own words/language

ELABORATE further and apply their understandings to new experiences

EVALUATE their newly learnt concepts/experiences based on peer and teacher interaction

Our processes build skills that prepare children to adapt, excel and contribute to our ever-changing global environment. These skills are:

- Creativity and innovation
- Critical thinking and problem solving
- Collaboration

- Confidence
- Communication

Instructions to the User

In order to ensure that users get the maximum benefit from the tool kit there are certain conditions that the user needs to fulfil. Even if there are constraints of the teacher/preschool, the toolkit contents will be useful for all.

- Maintain an appropriate teacher-child ratio: In accordance with the government's National ECCE policy, the maximum adult to child ratio should not be more than 1:20 (3 to 6 years) and 1:10 (below 3 years)
- View accompanying video/audio files: Users need to view and listen to the accompanying video/audio files, which are a part of the toolkit
- Planning and organisation by the teacher: The teacher should plan activities and organise material required well in advance before conducting the outlined processes
- Parental involvement: For the success of any ECD process, it is imperative to involve parents through meetings or direct participation in classroom activities, to make them aware of the benefits of these processes. Some tool kit processes may require more direct involvement with parents

Overview of Three Toolkit Contents

1. Greet and Meet toolkit

This is the very first process to be implemented in the daily routine for children. The process takes 15 to 20 minutes. The children and teachers come together in a circle, greet each other cheerfully and sing songs to welcome each other at the start of the day. This process helps with the personal socio-emotional and twenty-first century skill development of the learner.

Figure 20.4: *Greet and Meet toolkit contents*

This Tool Kit contains: Handbook, Video, Song Book, Audio Files and Printables

01	Introduction
02	Philosophy of the Took Kit
03	The Daily Routine
04	Note to the User
05	Chapter 1. Importance of Greet and Meet
06	Chapter 2. Greet and Meet process guide
07	Chapter 3. Introducing a new song
08	Chapter 4. Do-it-yourself assignments
09	Chapter 5. Tracking Tool Kit Progress

Copyright © Muktangan Education Trust. All rights reserved. Reproduced with permission

As evident from Figure 20.5, the toolkit handbook explains the Greet and Meet processes in detail.

Figure 20.5: *Greet and Meet Process*

Process A	Teacher greets the children cheerfully
Process B	Children mark attendance using name tags.
Process C	Teacher and children sing songs or play musical instruments together
Process D	Children use charts to identify the current day, current month and weather
Process E	Teacher and children sing the Transition song

Copyright © Muktangan Education Trust. All rights reserved. Reproduced with permission

These are five processes outlined in the Greet and Meet toolkit. Given below is the first process which you can try with children/students in your classroom.

Process A: Teacher greets the children cheerfully.
Duration: approximately 2–3 minutes
Why is greeting cheerfully, important?

- Creates a secure, friendly environment
- Supports and eases social, emotional and academic learning
- Inculcates social etiquette
- Enhances the mood of the classroom and energises the child for the learning ahead
- Develops twenty-first century skills: confidence, communication

How does the teacher greet the children?

The teacher must plan to cheerfully greet the children in any of the following ways:

- Greet every child with a cheerful smile and a hug
- Use the greeting word of different languages spoken by the children such as *namaste, namaskaram, vanakkam, suswagatam*
- Use different and innovative ways to invite the child into the classroom, such as asking the child to enter the class:
  o Hopping
  o Jumping through a hula hoop
  o Jumping through shapes made of rope on the floor
  o Skipping
  o Twisting and shaking the body
  o Clapping
  o Giving the teacher a high five
  o Sticking a picture of an animal on the wall outside the door, and children stamp the picture with their thumb print

Note: After a few days, the teacher may ask children to suggest their own ideas of how they would like to enter the classroom.

The following is a do-it-yourself activity from the Greet and Meet toolkit:

Display charts: Days of the week chart

Requirements
- Chart paper
- Sketch pens, markers
- Adhesive tape
- Transparent plastic sheet

Procedure
1. Identify an activity to associate with each day of the week, for example, Monday—coming to school, Tuesday—a particular snack, Sunday—home, etc.
2. Divide the chart into 2 rows and 7 columns.
3. Draw pictures related to the day's activity, in each column of the first row.
4. In the bottom row, write clearly the names of the days of the week.
5. The names of the days of the week should be written on the chart in the languages required.
6. Wrap/cover the entire chart with plastic for durability.

Figure 20.6 shows a sample of such a chart.

Figure 20.6: *Days of the week chart*

Copyright © Muktangan Education Trust. All rights reserved. Reproduced with permission

How is the chart used?

Grasping the concept of time is difficult for a pre-schooler. Such abstract ideas need to be re-visited repeatedly to make them familiar to young children. The days of the week chart help children mark the current day. This chart should be placed where every child in the classroom can see it.

The teacher points to the day of the week in the chart and children identify the current day of the week. Teacher may also ask what day it was yesterday, or what day it will be tomorrow.

Apart from the handbook there is also songbook and song chart—a sample of it is given below. Particularly for English songs, there is transliteration as well so that it teachers can use them effectively. The tunes for the songs are available in the audio file.

Figure 20.7: Sample of a song from toolkit

>Form a circle
>Big and round
>Let us form a circle
>Round and round
>Stand in a circle

2. Show and Tell toolkit

This process can be done immediately after Greet and Meet. In Show and Tell the teacher or children bring to the classroom, objects of daily use which interest them, and share their experiences regarding the object in a group. This helps develop language and literacy skills and confidence to present their own object in class. This process takes approximately 20 minutes. This process is mainly child led, but teacher may lead it too, particularly to show children how to begin, or if children are shy.

The Show and Tell toolkit also offers plan and activity details for involving parents to understand the process. Additional resources for teachers in the appendices are also there.

Figure 20.8: *Show and Tell process*

The processes listed below need to be followed for both the Teacher's Show and Tell and the Children's Show and Tell.

Process A	Teacher introduces the object
Process B	Children explore the object
Process C	Teacher encourages children to share experiences about the object
Process D	Teacher and children sing the Transition song

Copyright © Muktangan Education Trust. All rights reserved. Reproduced with permission

These processes are given in detail in the handbook. We share one process below:

Process A: Teacher introduces the object
Duration: approximately 2–3 minutes

Introduction of the object is done in two parts:

a. The object is introduced enthusiastically.

Figure 20.9: *Teacher conducting Show and Tell*

Copyright © Muktangan Education Trust. All rights reserved. Reproduced with permission

Why introduce the object enthusiastically?

- Children learn better when they are engaged and excited to learn.
- Piques the child's curiosity and gets him/her excited to learn.
- Develops twenty-first century skills: creativity, communication.

How to introduce the object enthusiastically?

- The teacher sings the transition song so all children are signaled to seat themselves in a small circle (if there are two teachers in the class then each will sit separately with small groups).
- Teacher must ensure that the covered Show and Tell tray, slate and chalk are close by.
- Before uncovering the tray, the teacher asks the children to guess what the object in the tray may be, creating excitement and wonder.
- The teacher then dramatically uncovers the tray, removes one object, and shows it to the children.
- In Children's Show and Tell, the teacher invites the child who brought the object to sit next to her/him, and name the object he/she has brought.

b. The name of the object is introduced in writing

   Why introduce the name of the object in writing?

   - Writing the name helps children with object–word association, which develops language and literacy skills.
   - Develops twenty-first century skills: communication, confidence.

   How to introduce the name of the object in writing?

   - After children name the object in their chosen language, the teacher writes the name on the slate, in the language of instruction.

- Teacher points to the written word, reads it loudly and clearly, and makes the children repeat after her.

3. **Outdoor play toolkit**

Figure 20.10: *Cover Page of Outdoor Play Toolkit Document (in Marathi)*

Copyright © Muktangan Education Trust. All rights reserved. Reproduced with permission

Play is the most important component of the preschool curriculum and something that must happen every day in the preschool routine. This toolkit particularly focuses on outdoor play which is very important for physical-motor skills development of children.

Planning for different outdoor play involves activities that could cater to all or most of the skills. These are mentioned in detail in the handbook. It is recommended that outdoor play must be conducted for 20 to 30 minutes, preferably before snack or lunch time.

Following is an excerpt from the Outdoor Play Process Guide.

Making the outdoor area or designated play space safe and free of hazards:

Why make the outdoor area or designated play space safe and free of hazards?

Making the outdoor area or designated play space safe and free of hazards is essential to prevent injury/accidents among children.

How can the teacher make the outdoor area or designated play space safe and free of hazards?

If the designated play space is outdoors…

- There must be appropriate fencing to mark the boundaries of the play area.
- Care should be taken to ensure there are no pointed objects or stones on the ground, which may cause injury to the children.
- The material/equipment should be cleaned regularly and checked for damage.
- The teacher must show and explain the boundaries of the space designated for outdoor play. This is very important as this is the first step towards safety during play.
- The children must always wear footwear during play.

If the designated play space is indoors…

- The space must be cleaned regularly.
- The space must not be slippery.
- The material/equipment should be cleaned regularly and checked for damage.

Note: *It is recommended to keep a first aid kit handy. The play space should be organised such that children with special needs could be included in play.*

Following is a sample activity from the Game book:

Delivering the parcel on cycle

Requirements

- Tricycles for as many children present,
- An object that acts as parcel i.e. a ball/plastic fruit/toy etc.

Figure 20.11: *Children Engaged in Outdoor Play Process*

Copyright © Muktangan Education Trust. All rights reserved. Reproduced with permission

Developmental experiences:

Cycling, picking, bending

Procedure–

- Designated wide indoor/outdoor area
- Have the children mount their cycles holding a parcel at one end of the area

Suggested way of play–

- Children are told that they will be delivering the parcel from the start point to their friends waiting at the end point.
- Once the child delivers the parcel they get up from the cycle and give it to another classmate who then takes a turn at delivering the parcel back to the other end.
- Variations–
  - ❖ The teacher can make a zigzag line on which the child has to ride the tricycle to another child at the end point.
  - ❖ Make tracks with potatoes at equal intervals and let the child cycle his way through by picking up the potatoes till the end point.

Note

1. We would be happy to collaborate with ECCE teachers and educators more on this to share all of the toolkit contents. Feel free to contact us at toolkit@muktanganedu.org. Website: ***https://toolkits.muktanganedu.org/***

References

Heckman, J., (n.d.) *Invest in quality early childhood development.* https://heckmanequation.org/assets/2014/05/F_Heckman_Brochure_041515.pdf.

Kroeker, J., (2017). Indoor and outdoor play in preschool programmes. *Universal Journal of Educational Research 5(4)*, 641–47. https://doi: 10.13189/ujer.2017.050413.

Ministry of Human Resource Development. (2020). National Education Policy (2020). https://www.education.gov.in/sites/upload_files/mhrd/files/NEP_Final_English_0.pdf.

National Council of Educational Research and Training. (2005). *National curriculum framework (2005)*. New Delhi, India. http://www.ncert.nic.in/rightside/links/pdf/framework/english/nf2005.pdf.

National Council of Educational Research and Training. (2019). *The Preschool Curriculum (2019)*. New Delhi, India. https://ncert.nic.in/dee/pdf/Combined_Pre_school_curriculumEng.pdf.

Press Information Bureau, Government of India (2017). Cabinet approves continuation of sub-schemes under umbrella scheme 'Integrated Child Development Services (ICDS)' for the period till November, 2018. http://pib.nic.in/newsite/PrintRelease.aspx?relid=173550.

Vasal, M. (2007). *Early childhood education (ECE): Ideas, concepts and practices in rural setting of Gurgaon (Haryana).* Unpublished Master's thesis dissertation. The Maharaja Sayajirao University of Baroda, Vadodara, India.

21

Anganwadi Teacher's Handbook*

This handbook is designed to help Anganwadi Teachers become reflective practitioners, thus transforming Anganwadi Centres (AWCs) into vibrant learning centres for holistic development of 3- to 6-year-old children. The Azim Premji Foundation initiated an intervention in 2012 to understand and strengthen early childhood education (ECE) provided under the Integrated Child Development Services (ICDS) scheme, a public sector programme for children, at Sangareddy district in Telangana.

The ICDS scheme, launched in 1975, is a government welfare scheme that offers six services at AWCs for children under the age of 6 and their mothers:

1. Supplementary nutrition (for children under 6 years and pregnant and lactating mothers)
2. Immunisation (for children under 6 years and pregnant and lactating mothers)
3. Health check-up (for children under 6 years and pregnant and lactating mothers)
4. Referral service (for children under 6 years and pregnant and lactating mothers)
5. Pre-school education (for children 3 to 6 years of age)
6. Nutrition and health education (for women between 15 to 45 years of age)

While initially the focus in AWCs was on health and nutrition, in recent years preschool or early childhood education (ECE) is

---

* Correspondence related to this paper can be directed to M. Sreenivasa Rao, State Head, Telangana, Azim Premji Foundation. He can be reached at: msr@azimpremjifoundation.org.

increasingly being seen as foundational to the growth of children. Even as the overall ECE system needs fundamental structural changes, our experience shows that it is possible to improve the quality of early education by addressing first-level issues of infrastructure, curriculum, learning materials and community participation.

This handbook will help Anganwadi Teachers (AWTs) to implement a developmentally appropriate learning programme in the AWCs. This handbook has three parts. Part A is an introduction to the programme, Part B has detailed plans for each of the 14 themes that the children will explore through the year and Part C helps the teacher create teaching-learning materials (TLMs) for use in the classroom.

The excerpt here includes Part A of the handbook and within it four representational components of Good habits, Conversation, Storytelling and Play are presented.

CONTENTS
What are development milestones?
What is a developmentally appropriate curriculum?
Themes
Components
What are developmentally appropriate curriculum plans?
Annual plan at a glance
Components: Guidelines for Teachers
• Good Habits
• Conversation (Circle Time)
• Songs
• Story
• Play
• Creativity
• Pre-numeracy
• Pre-literacy
• Scientific knowledge
• Nature walk
Weekly plan: A sample

What are 'Development Milestones'?

A child in his or her first year uses crying, sounds and gestures for communication. She or he gradually learns the use of words, and later, full sentences to express herself/himself. Like language development, there is a broad sequence in the development of all the domains (physical-motor, social, emotional, cognitive) as a child grows up. The set of behaviours, skills, abilities that are observed in children at a specific age are called developmental milestones. By understanding these milestones, we can understand the progress of the development of the child. Though these milestones are indicative of the average age, each child has his/her own pace of achieving these milestones and he/she cannot be compared with other children.

The knowledge of these milestones helps the teacher, parents and professionals to know whether a child is developing various abilities as per his or her age range. It allows teachers to plan activities that provide opportunities for the development and achievement of these developmental milestones in the curriculum. It is also helpful in identifying developmental delays that can then be remediated in consultation with parents and if need be with the help of specialists and professionals.

Development milestones or objectives for small children have been clearly stipulated by the Ministry of Women and Child Welfare (GOI) in the Child Assessment Card (3-6 years old). Our developmentally appropriate curriculum is based on these guidelines. The Sangareddy ECE programme is a developmentally appropriate, thematic curriculum.

What is a Developmentally Appropriate Curriculum?

A developmentally appropriate curriculum is based on understanding of how children grow, develop and learn. The content chosen, the pedagogical approaches or methodology that teachers follow, the activities and experiences—all are based on understanding of children and their development. A developmentally appropriate curriculum also focuses on the whole child. Therefore, the preschool curriculum is based on and caters to all domains of development: physical motor, cognitive, language, social, emotional and creative.

Young children between the ages of 3-6 years learn by experiencing and doing things. In the process of learning, children are trying to make sense of the world they are growing up in. Children learn through inquiry, asking questions, discovering more about the world around—objects, people, spaces, animals and birds. To make sense of the world, children also need to draw connections between different aspects of their lives and the lives of others.

A curriculum for young children should be cohesive, should satisfy their curiosity and should be meaningful. The developmentally appropriate approach to curriculum is one such way in which all these different aspects of learning and development can be brought together.

Thematic Curriculum

In a thematic curriculum, topics or themes are chosen which are of interest to the children and are considered valuable for learning by the adults. Each topic/theme is explored in detail. Thus, children gain in-depth understanding about that topic. A thematic curriculum is planned such that through all the different components of an ECE programme the child learns about, explores and experiences the theme. In a thematic programme the conversation, story, songs, play, games all revolve round the theme. Children therefore gain understanding about a topic through these various modes and simultaneously lot of information gets reinforced.

In exploring a theme in detail, children learn new vocabulary, can learn to count, identify patterns, colours, shapes, and study how things change. Thus, a single theme can help in learning language, science and maths. Reading and writing activities get easily assimilated into such a curriculum. At the end of a theme, besides exploring it in detail, children also gain an understanding of different subject matter areas, gain experiences on different domains of development and learn or practice skills within the context.

Themes. Fourteen themes have been chosen for this curriculum that are of interest to children, which children can explore, experience and discover. These themes are from the children's immediate world.

1. Myself and my body
2. My family
3. My village
4. Fruits and colours
5. Plants and trees
6. Air, water and surroundings
7. Vehicles
8. Vegetables
9. Animals
10. Flowers
11. Birds
12. Calendar
13. Seasons
14. School

Components. Components are the actual activities that constitute a day's programme. All the active, interactive strategies, experiences, activities and pedagogical aspects which are part of an ECE programme are called Components. The nine components that we employ in our ECE programme are the following (these are described in detail in later in the document):

1. Good habits
2. Conversation (Circle Time)
3. Songs
4. Story
5. Play
6. Creativity
7. Pre-literacy
8. Pre-numeracy
9. Scientific knowledge

The Curriculum Plans

These are guided daily plans for the Anganwadi Teacher (AWT) based on the theme for the month. All components are woven into these plans. While these plans guide the AWT for various activities through the day and week, the teacher has the liberty to enhance and modify her practice, teaching-learning material (TLM) and adjust the duration of components (activities) as per the needs of her learning group.

The month of June is the transition period with new children registering in the AWCs. So, the thematic plans begin only from July. From July onwards a specific theme has been selected for every two or four weeks.

Table 21.1: *Annual Plan at a Glance*

Sl No	Theme	Month	Duration
1.	My Self and my Body	July	2 weeks
2.	My Home, Family and Food	August	2 weeks
3.	My Village	September	1 week
4.	Fruits and Colours	October	2 weeks
5.	Plants and Trees	November	2 weeks
6.	Air, Water and Surroundings	December	1 week
7.	Vehicles	December	1 week
8.	Vegetables	January	1 week
9.	Animals	January	1 week
10.	Flowers	February	1 week
11.	Birds	February	1 week
12.	Calendar	March	1 week
13.	Seasons	April	1 week
14.	School	April	1 week

Timetable: Some pointers

- The programme is planned for three hours every day.
- At a specific time, the session/activity changes. However, if the children are more interested or engrossed, the session/activity may extend by five to seven minutes.
- Activities and experiences for each day are mentioned.
- Stories and songs are repeated in that week and are recapitulated in subsequent weeks.

- The time allotted to conversation/circle time is 20 minutes. The assumption is that the Anganwadi Worker will generate responses from children by asking questions and by helping them to think and relate the discussion to their daily lives. Each child should be encouraged to speak.
- During 'free play', children should have access to learning materials, books and blackboard etc. They should be encouraged to engage with all of these materials and activities.
- Outdoor play should be under an adult's supervision.

Components: Guidelines for Teachers

Good habits. Good Habits is a separate component of the Sangareddy Curriculum as it is considered an important part of curriculum in the Telangana preschool curriculum framework. Good habits can and should be inculcated and can become a daily feature of the programme. It can also be integrated in the curriculum by selecting relevant themes of hygiene, nutrition, as well as promoting socio-emotional skills.

> Habit is a regular repeated behaviour, which requires little or no thought and is learned rather than it being innate. It can be developed through reinforcement and repetition. When we keep doing an activity repeatedly and regularly then, it becomes a habit.
>
> Habits play a crucial role and can influence the attitude and behaviour of children. In the early years, children effectively learn the habits and habits go a long way in establishing a child's personality. Good habits like bathing, washing hands, combing hair, walking in a line etc. need to be inculcated early in life.

Conversation (Circle Time). Children acquire some language abilities from their natural settings. When they join preschool, they have some ability to use spoken language. Providing listening and speaking opportunities can sharpen and extend their language ability.

i. Visits to the homes of children. Daily home visiting is an integral part of the school programme
ii. Organising social functions in the school for parents and guardians
iii. Inviting parents and guardians to observe and help in the work of the school
iv. Organising a programme of community cleanliness
v. Organising a programme of preventive health work
vi. Acting as guides and friends in times of difficulty

(N. B. These activities will also be the practical programme of adult education in the responsibilities of parenthood for trainees)

When the trainees have established friendship with the parents and the community as a whole, they can take the next step in their relationship with the village community.

The following programme is suggested:

1. *Village Survey:* A study of the village homes and village community, with a view to understand the social, economic and cultural background of the child
   (a) **Sanitation and Health**: Housing, space and sanitary conditions; arrangements, if any, for disposal of night-soil and waste; drainage and water-supply
   (b) **Professions**: Agriculture, labour, handicrafts, crafts, industries, business, and professions such as small shop-keepers, money-lenders, landlords small and big, holy-men, beggars
   (c) **Economic Standards**: Study and classification of home budget, home geography, means of income, items of expenditure, size of family, indebtedness
   (d) **Cultural**: Social status of the family and its influence, professions of the family, social habits, religious life, social and 'religious' discipline, sense of citizenship, neighbours, history of the family and its influence, contribution of the family to the community life, both beneficial and harmful; educational qualifications,

if any, (N.B. Professional skill should be considered as education) in the family, hobbies, if any, musical and artistic abilities, vices, if any, among the family members

(e) **Social and Cultural Background:** Institutions and groups contributing to the cultural life, such as temples, fairs, festivals, bhajans, religious groups, folk-dances, entertainments during social functions and religious holidays, religious functions, institutions and groups of social service in the community. Vices in the village, harmful institutions in the village and locality, presence, and influence of anti-social elements in the community, political groups and influences in the village

2. Organising co-operative life in the following departments of village life:

   (a) economic
   (b) social and cultural
   (c) sanitation and health

3. Revival and re-orientation of rural culture

Section III – Child Study—The Environment and the Child

1. *The Physical (Geographical) Environment.* Practical Work: Study of the physical environment of the locality and its possible effect on the child. A comparative study of two villages with entirely different physical environment and their possible effects on the child
Theoretical: The interrelation of the environment and the child

2. *Social, Economic and Cultural Environment.* Practical: Study of the family home and of the family, family budget, income and expenditure, means of income, items of expenditure, size of the family, animals at home, space and sanitary conditions, daily diet, clothes, furniture if any, tools of work if any, health of the family, social status, social

habits, relationship with neighbours, with the community as a whole, vices if any, cultural activities, professional skill, religious life

Economic, social, cultural (including religious) condition of the village, general health and sanitation in the village, the diet of the village

Theoretical: The social environment and the child:

1. The sanitary conditions in the village and their influence on the child
2. The industries and crafts in the village and their influence on the child
3. The animals in the village and their influence on the child
4. The festivals in the village and their influence on the child
5. The vices in the village community and their influence on the child

3. **The Influence of Heredity.**

   Practical: Study of the family histories of different types for three generations

   Theoretical: The influence of heredity

4. **The Influence of Physiological Development.**

   Practical: Study of the physical growth and development of the child:

   1. The pre-natal stage
   2. Birth to 1 year – the dependent stage
   3. 1 to 2 years – babyhood
   4. 2 to 4 years – the pre-basic stage (i)
   5. 4 to 7 years – the pre-basic stage (ii)

   Theoretical: Laws of natural growth. Effect of heredity and environment on physical growth. Importance of normal physical development in child education

The effect of malnutrition, insanitary habits and unhappy homelife on physical development

The basis of instincts and capacities in a child

Education of the emotions

Education of the imagination

Sensory-motor development (the acquisition of skills through helping parents, brothers and sisters.)

Training in responsibility and social adjustments through family life

4. *The Child at School.*
   (a) Physical development: through balanced school meals, healthy and happy environment and a life of well-balanced activity and rest
   (b) Emotional development: imagination, self-revelation, and self-expression
   (c) Sensory-motor development. Acquisition of skills
   (d) Beginning of training in citizenship through activities in the school community
   (e) Habits of co-operation

Section IV – History of Child Education

1. Child education among primitive communities
2. Orthodox child education in early and medieval times
3. Revolutionaries—Froebel, Pestalozzi, Rabindranath Tagore, Madam Montessori. The kindergarten, the nursery school, and the Montessori school movements
4. Contemporary movements and trends in child education in other countries. Contemporary movements in child education in India
5. Gandhiji's contributions in the philosophy and technique of child education

Section V – Basic Principles and Objectives of Pre-Basic Education

1. ***General***
   (a) What is true education?
   (b) *Nai Talim* as education for life and through life. The four stages of pre-basic, basic, post-basic and adult education
   (c) The new social order as envisaged by *Nai Talim*, and its relation to the all-round development of the individual personality
   (d) The meaning of 'education through work'; the conditions to be fulfilled for work to be the medium of education
   (e) The true significance of self-sufficiency in *Nai Talim*
   The meaning of Gandhiji's dictum: 'True education is that which is self-sufficient'
   Ethical and economic implications of self-sufficiency

2. ***Special***
   (a) The place of pre-basic education in the programme of *Nai Talim*
   (b) The significance of pre-basic education in a programme of national reconstruction
   (c) Close correlation between adult and pre-basic education
   (d) The necessary qualifications, personal and professional, of a teacher of pre-basic education
   (e) The place of the pre-basic teacher in the community and the role to be played by him or her in social reconstruction
   (f) The special problems of child education:
      i. in rural areas
      ii. in industrial areas
      iii. in tribal areas
      iv. in communities attached to institutions

Section VI – Content of Pre-Basic Education

1. Physical nurture
2. Medical care
3. Personal and community cleanliness
4. Self-help and self-reliance
5. Social training
6. Educational and creative activities—play
7. Speech training and children's literature, songs, stories, dramas, dialogues and conversations
8. Development of the mathematical sense
9. Development of the scientific spirit, nature study
10. Music and rhythm including voice production
11. Art

Section VII – Organisation of Work

1. How to prepare educational programme for a day, for a week, for a month, for a whole term
2. How to organise a group of children, average number of children 20 to 30
3. How to plan and organise school meals
4. How to plan medical care and its supervision
5. How to prepare educational material and equipment; the necessary conditions to be fulfilled by educational material and equipment in pre-basic education
    (a) All our equipment should be truly national i.e., evolved out of our own research and study of the requirements of a child in India
    (b) As far as possible, educational material should be prepared by the local craftsman to suit the needs of the children of the locality. (This is desirable even if such things prove more expensive than standardised articles produced in a central workshop, as it will stimulate and develop the initiative and skill of both the

teacher and the local craftsman, will be a helpful factor in adult education, and will thus raise the standard of both general intelligence and craftsmanship in the locality)
- (c) Equipment should be educational. It is a well-known fact that too much or too perfectly finished equipment stifles the initiative and imagination of the child. The pre-basic school should, therefore, be as simply equipped as is consistent with the educational requirements of the child, and there should be an 'unfinished' quality about the equipment and toys which will stimulate the child's imagination and initiative. The child should be able to take them to pieces and put them together again
6. How to conduct teachers' meetings
7. How to plan and organise excursions and carry out programmes such as festivals, meetings, study circles
8. The necessary educational records and how to maintain them
   - (a) School registers
   - (b) The time-tables and how to plan them
   - (c) How to formulate standards of development of a child in the pre-basic stage
   - (d) Progress reports, charts, etc. of the development in adult classes, and of the children in pre-basic schools at different stages
9. How to use (i) reference books (ii) technical literature
10. Technique of self-assessment of work

Section VIII – Cleanliness and Health (including Nutrition)

The principles and practices of clean and healthy living form a subject of major importance in the training of teachers of pre-basic education, as physical nurture and the formation of clean and healthy habits occupy the central place in the educational programme of children under seven.

The training will be divided into three stages:

1. ***Healthy Living in the Training School Community.*** Understanding of the importance of one's physical and mental health and organisation of the community of the training centre according to the principles of clean and healthy living. This will include:
   (a) Rules of clean and healthy living, with an understanding of the reasons for them
   (b) Elementary anatomy and physiology
   (c) Science of nutrition
   (d) The art and science of nursing ordinary diseases
   (e) Preventive health measures
   (f) Social, moral, and intellectual aspects of clean and healthy living

2. ***Healthy Living for Children at Home and at School.*** The co-ordination of the child's life at home and in school on the principle of clean and healthy living.

   The Homes
   (a) The daily visits to the homes of children both before and after school
   (b) Friendly talks with the parents on problems relating to the health and cleanliness of children, parents and home
   (c) Helping the parents in the daily routine of personal cleanliness for their children and arrangements for nursing and treatment in cases of illness in the home

   The School

   This will be the main educational programme of the pre-basic school.

   Personal Cleanliness

   There should be a morning review of personal cleanliness, and training in habits of clean living as under:

(a) Cleanliness of the hands, legs, eyes, nose, ears and mouth – why and how
(b) Cleanliness of the hair and scalp. The problem of lice; dandruff and how to cure it
(c) Care and cleanliness of the nails – why and how
(d) Care and cleanliness of the gums and teeth – why and how
(e) Answering calls of nature – when, where and why? Cleanliness in the process. Utensils and cleansing agents used
(f) Spitting and cleaning the nose – where and how
(g) Cleanliness of the clothes – washing, drying and folding
(h) Cleanliness of the bedding – shaking and airing. Washing and sunning
(i) Cleanliness in eating, washing of hands and utensils used, before and after eating
(j) Cleanliness of drinking water
(k) Cleanliness of personal possessions – articles used for personal cleanliness, clothes, bedding, toys

Environmental Cleanliness in School

(a) Classroom – cleanliness of the classroom before and after classes, with special reference to the cleanliness of the floor where classes are held on the floor
(b) Cleanliness of the school equipment, both before and after the classes
(c) Cleanliness of the school compound, roads, the space immediately round the school-building, school well, play-fields and compost-pit
(d) Utilisation of waste water from the well and kitchen; to be drained into the vegetable garden
(e) Manure – disposal of refuse, night-soil and urine. Cleanliness of urinals and latrines

(f) The hygiene of school meals, cleanliness of all materials, equipment and surroundings:

   i. The kitchen, the store-room, and the dining hall, before and after food
   ii. The vessels used for cooking and serving
   iii. The food prepared and the cooking process
   iv. Keeping milk, ghee and buttermilk
   v. Storage and preservation of food-stuffs including vegetables
   vi. Serving the food

   (g) Keeping of gardens, making artistic and geometric designs. Creepers on buildings, lining the road with plants. Clapping and cropping

   School Health Programme

   (a) Detection of the signs of illness, treatment of minor ailments in school, and the use of the child clinic and school first aid centre
   (b) Arrangement for segregation and treatment of infectious disease
   (c) The proper arrangement of school meals, activities and rest periods
   (d) Routine procedure of weighing, measuring and assessing the physical development of the children. Maintenance of individual and group records
   (e) Practical work in the child clinic

3. **Healthy Community Living.** The third and the most important stage will be co-operation with the institution and workers of adult education in the programme of sanitation and preventive health work in the community as a whole. This programme should be closely correlated with that described in Section II—Social Training.

Health Survey of the Village

With especial reference to the welfare of mothers and children.

- i. *The child from birth to the age of two*

    Sterilized dressing of umbilical cord, feeds, weight, warmth, fresh air, clothing, bathing, hours of sleep, protection from infection, care of eyes, ears, skin, defects in the system if any

- ii. *Childhood between ages of two and four*
    1. Weight and height according to the standard weight and height measurement charts to be maintained
    2. Protection from contagious infections. Sore eyes, skin troubles, scabies, measles, whooping cough, etc. Recognition of any ailment. Malnutrition, running nose, teething, etc.
    3. Good habits, personal hygiene, bathing, cleanliness in food, clothes, etc., suitable for a child
    4. Diet – quantity and quality in balanced food
    5. Social health and hygiene – collective cleanliness in school and playground described under heading (2)

- iii. *Mother*

    Age, profession, economic standard, education, health, social status

    Charts maintained: health, parental care, diet, feeds, exercises, cleanliness in bathing, clothing, treatment of ailments, such as scabies, etc.

    Examination for diseases pertaining to pregnancy, for lie of child, disproportion, etc., weekly examinations. Preparation for delivery. Clothes, antiseptics, etc. Nursing period, mother's food, modes of feed. Preparation of feeds, preventive measures against infection. Contagious diseases of child-birth

iv. *Father*

Age, profession, economic standard, education, health, social status, personal cleanliness and health. Clean habits both personal and household

v. *Home*

Standard of food, shelter, sanitation, comforts, provided for a child as regards rest, clothes, spacious housing conditions, good water-supply, health, discipline, etc.

Village Sanitation and Health Programme

Help in the formation and organisation of health co-operative movements by village people. Principles and methods of organisation. Emphasis on preventive rather than curative measures.

i. *Village Sanitation*

Cleanliness of the village pond or village tank and common well

Cleanliness of the public places, roads, public rituals, public urinals and common latrines. Disposal of the refuse and night soil. Drainage of rain-water, waste-water, sewage water. Cleaning any bushy growth, cleaning of the filthy and foul spots. Making path-ways and construction of small roads, preparation of village park, open spaces for meetings, etc.

ii. *Cleanliness in cases of emergency*

Death and diseases: washing the house, use of disinfectants, destruction of the infected clothes and bedding.

Epidemics: isolation, use of disinfectants, washing of clothes, cleanliness of utensils, cleanliness of the village tanks and common well, purification of drinking water

iii. *Cleanliness during feasts*

Cleanliness during large-scale cooking; the vessels used for cooking and serving; the dining place, before and after food; the water used for drinking and cooking. Disposal of refuse

iv. *Fairs and festivals*
Construction of temporary latrines and urinals, bathing facilities, supply of pure drinking water, cleanliness of the roads and bazaars, provision of extra dustbins, disposal of refuse

Study of Problems of Rural Hygiene and Sanitation

The physical, economic, social and moral factors involved in their solution.

i. *The village water supply* – water for drinking and cooking, for bathing and washing clothes
ii. *Village houses* – construction, ventilation, arrangements for light and air, latrines, urinals, storing of food and agricultural equipment, disposal of rubbish and waste-water
iii. *Village planning* – roads and lanes, village latrines and urinals, village dung-heaps and preparation of manure
iv. *Village health* – common communicable diseases in the village, preventive measures, immunisation. Hygienic measures for special occasions and for large crowds
v. *The village diet* – how to improve it with locally available materials

Section IX – Nature Study: The World around Us.

The object of nature study should be to develop the child's sensitiveness and to make it feel at home with nature. The teachers' role is to create the proper atmosphere and to stimulate the interest awakened in any normal child, placed in a natural environment. To do this the teacher should himself be interested in nature. He should develop his powers of observation and should have a love for animal and bird life and the life of nature.

Though the children at this stage do not require scientific knowledge, the teacher should have a scientific understanding of the life of nature around him.

Observation and study on the following lines is suggested for work with the children:

1. **Living Beings.**
    (a) *Our Domestic Animals and their Young*: The bull, the cow and the calf. The goat (or sheep in wool producing areas) and its kid, the horse and foal, the dog and its pup, cat and kittens, the buffalo and calf; cock, hens and chickens

    The love of the mother for its young. How animals look after, feed and protect their young. Their sorrow when separated. The cries of animals—in joy, in pain, in hunger, in anger, in fear. The mother's call to her young ones—imitating animal cries, nursery rhymes, animal stories and fables

    (b) *Other small animals you come across in the house*: The rat, the lizard, the scorpion, the spider
    (c) *Those that creep and crawl*: The snake, friend and foe, the humble earthworm, the farmer's friend
    (d) *Insect friends and foes*: Ants, bees, butterflies, moths, beetles, the common fly, mosquitoes, white-ants (termites)

    Get some butterflies' eggs or caterpillars and rear them. Watch them grow and develop them into butterflies

    (e) *Birds*: Hens and ducks. The crow, the parrot, the dove and the pigeon, the sparrow, the myna. Recognition of these and other common birds by colour, shape and calls. Bird song in the morning and in the evening. The nest, the eggs, the young. How the mother feeds the young. (Keep a bird bath in the school garden and boxes for sparrows to nest)

(f) *Pond Life*: The frog, the croaking of frogs. The tadpoles. The life story of frogs

Beetles that swim. Dragon flies. The fish

(g) *Plants*: They also live. They take food and they grow, they sleep. They reproduce through seeds. Watch the growth of a plant from the seed (using a glass tumbler or globe and blotting paper)

They need food and water just as we do. If you don't water them they will die. They also need sunlight. Just like us they become pale and weak if they are always kept in the dark. Simple experiments to illustrate the facts

The Parts of Plants: Similar to our organs and limbs. The stem, the roots and leaves. The stem, the body of the plant; the leaves, which help the plant to breathe and use its food. Their shapes and sizes. The roots—hands and mouth of the plant

Changes in Plants: They grow old and die. They change with the seasons. Leaves fall. Fresh shoots come. They burst into bloom. (Some in summer, others in spring, and still others in winter)

Some have sweet scents and beautiful colours. Recognition of different flowers by scent and sight. The bees and butterflies feed on their honey

From the flowers come seeds from which young plants grow. We should not pluck flowers for our pleasure but only when it will help the plant. Develop sensitiveness against plucking flowers. How to pick flowers and fruits to help plant life. We can also gather fallen flowers

Acquaintance with crops around the year: Picnic in the field during harvest time. Take the children out at the time of sowing

Threshing of corn, winnowing, etc., associate children in these activities

(h) *Trees*: Huge plants, their shapes and sizes; stories connected with trees

(i) *Trees and plants as friends of man*:

They give us food, rice, wheat, jawar, vegetables, etc.

They give us shelter and shade

They give us clothing – cotton

2. **Non-Living Beings.**

Earth, Mud, Clay

Stones, different sizes, shapes and colours, beach pebbles

Sea shells (in areas near the sea)

Metallic things – Their feel, their sound

Wood – Their feel, the pretty design of the grain. Observation of the size

Water – Uses of water; wells, ponds, streams, rivers, sea

Rain – Clouds in the sky. The dark clouds of rain, the light clouds of autumn

Lightning, thunder, showers

Puddles and slush. Streams and ponds

The rain fills our wells and waters our fields

Air – The gentle breeze, the stormy wind, and the wild storm

The skies above – The blue sky. The sun, sunrise and sunset. The moon, how it wanes and waxes. The full moon, the stars, the planets, the milky way

The shooting stars

General Science for Student Teachers. Animal life. Food and feeding habit of the animals mentioned. Carnivorous and herbivorous animals.

Chief characteristics of chewing animals. The cow – its four stomachs.

Mosquitoes and the fly. Their life cycle. Conditions which favour their growth. Fly and mosquito control, use of insecticide

How flies and rats help to spread diseases

Birds: The adaptation of their bodies for flight

Plant life: Parts of a plant, and function of each

Parts of a flower. Pollination – fertilisation

Parts of a seed – conditions for germination

Favourable conditions for plant growth

Natural phenomena: Causation of wind. Formation of clouds, and rain. The rotation and revolutions of the earth

Long and short days. The seasons

Eclipses: planets and stars and comets

Section X – Language and Literature.

Speech training.

Collection of stories, songs, dialogues, dramas for use with the children

Section XI – Music and Rhythm.

1. Art and science of music
2. Voice production
3. Collection of folk songs and folk dances, action songs, singing games, and children's operas, etc.
4. Organisation of children's *bhajan mandalis*. Children's dramatic groups
5. Collection of children's games

Section XII – Art and Handicraft

It is not necessary for the pre-basic teacher to be an artist or even a drawing teacher for organising art activities for the children of this age. Though art (drawing) is one of the main aspects of education, in the pre-basic stage children are not to be 'taught' any art or drawing by anybody. In this stage of education art has its own place. It is a very important outlet for the visual, mental, and imaginative experiences the child has in his life. It is an aesthetic activity, which involves form, colour, line and movement, etc. The child's way of looking at these things is altogether different from that of the adult. It is very difficult for the adult to feel these things in the way the child does.

The child experiences one thing. Then he expresses it on the paper or in the clay, etc. Then he compares his object on paper with the actual one. This makes him develop and thus educate his sight, observation, and sensitiveness of touch.

The work of the teacher is not to teach the child how to draw but to let him *experience and let the experience out*. But he should know the natural ladder the child climbs in the course of his art experiences. He should understand and feel also the depth of pleasure the child experiences in 'doing' especially in aesthetic activities.

In short, the teacher should understand the child as an aesthetic human being.

The second but equally important aspect is that the child should be given plenty of art materials of various kinds.

It is necessary that the pre-basic teacher should know how to prepare art materials for children.

These should be prepared out of locally available material.

It is expected that the teacher understands the child's mind in his aesthetic experiences and knows how to make equipment for the art class. An artist without these two things cannot be as good a teacher of art in a pre-basic school as an ordinary teacher who possesses these.

Course of Studies

1. Different stages of child's drawings, classification of children's drawings

Qualities of art
Problems in teaching art
Attitude of the home and school community towards it
How can parents help the child in these activities
2. Making of art equipment
Brushes out of fibrous things, like cotton, jute, hair, palm stem, etc.
Painting surface: paper, boards, and walls, mud, wood, stone, etc.
Colours: earth, stone, vegetable, and chemical colours (and their binding medium)
Water colour, chalk and crayons, charcoal, pencils, etc. Gum, glue, ricewater, tamarind seed, flourpaste, egg, and gelatine, etc.
3. Clay work and ornaments, preparation of clay, pulp for paper mache, toy making with cloth, paper, grass leaves, cardboard, etc.
4. Mask making, basketry, mat making
5. Stage preparation. With local materials like mats, bamboo, etc. Dresses and ornaments with flowers, etc. Collecting good pictures and reproduction of great works of art
6. Decoration on festivals and special days, arrangement of the classroom, etc. holding exhibitions of the works of the children
7. Lectures on the general and historical aspect of art

Note: The pre-basic teacher should know as many crafts as possible.

Note

1. The Hindustani Talimi Sangh published the first version of syllabus for pre-basic education teachers in the year 1945. The syllabus was titled, *Basic National Education: Syllabus for the Training of Pre-Basic Teachers*. Published by E. W. Aryanayakam, for The Hindustani Talimi Sangh,

Sevagram, Wardha. The text of the syllabus reproduced here, however, is of the revised edition published in 1953. The revised edition was published with the title, *Pre-Basic Education: A Syllabus for the Training of Teachers*. Published by E. W. Aryanayakam, for The Hindustani Talimi Sangh, Sevagram, Wardha.

Recommendations for Way Forward

Kinnari Pandya, Jigisha Shastri and Vrinda Datta

This volume on Early Childhood Care and Education (ECCE) profession in India provides a view on the practices for professional development being tried in the field. The papers based on perspectives derived from programmes on the ground and backed by theoretical frameworks, suggest the potential for several facets of these programmes to be scaled up for professionalising the ECCE domain in India.

It is heartening to note that several recommendations presented in the report of the conference, Re-defining Early Childhood Development Profession in India: Challenges and Potential, published by Azim Premji University (2017) have found a place in the recommendations of National Education Policy (NEP) 2020. For instance, the multimodal teacher preparation, various levels of certification, universities and higher education departments as the key institutions responsible for preparing ECCE professionals and so on, are some direct recommendations of the 2017 report of the conference that are of prominence in the ECCE recommendations in the National Education Policy.

Based on the papers in this volume, the recommendations made in the 2017 conference report, and the recommendations of NEP 2020, we provide a framework for professionalising the ECCE domain in India going forward.

To summarise the key insights and recommendations emerging from the papers in this volume:

1. The papers bring to fore the historical trajectory that ECCE as a domain has seen in the policy and higher education space, the ongoing efforts of various academic and public

institutions for pre-service and continuous professional development of ECCE practitioners, success of distance mode programmes, vocational programmes, and provide a range of models that need to be adopted for professional development. Efforts such as the Nai Talim approach of early years teacher preparation programmes, and the community-based contextual rootedness of teachers and their preparedness to work with young children are aspects central to developing early educators.

2. The key curricular aspects for preparation of teacher educators, teachers and the nature and content of curricula have been articulated in the papers. The significance of diversity and inclusion as key approaches in teacher preparation for early years education, is also elucidated in the papers, along with specific skills that teachers need to develop and practice.
3. Voluntary organisations develop unique context-specific approaches to nurture and train early years frontline professionals such as caregivers and Anganwadi Workers, and support in-service professionals. The experiences and organisations presented in this volume are representative of the kind of contribution organisations are making. There are several other organisations doing similar work.
4. Frameworks and practices for in-service teacher educator development and teacher performance act as critical references to strengthen the overall professional development practices.
5. A resource pool for teachers in the form of toolkits and curriculum for early childhood programmes, and the pre-basic teacher education curriculum as an artefact of study are included to provide a holistic view of the various components of early years teacher development.

It is evident that several unique measures are being undertaken across the ECCE spectrum in our country. Given the diversity among Indian contexts, context-specific programmes keeping basic principles of early years development and teacher preparation are of critical significance. Further, the insights from these efforts also help consolidate the learning and feed into the system for realising the several recommendations of National Education Policy 2020.

Way Forward

The National Education Policy 2020 has given a clear pathway for professionalising the domain, through emphasis on knowledge and shared understanding of curriculum, pedagogy and ethics for working with young children.

To quote, Section 1.7 of the Policy:

> To prepare an initial cadre of high-quality ECCE teachers in Anganwadi Centres, current Anganwadi Workers/Teachers will be trained through *a systematic effort* in accordance with the curricular/pedagogical framework developed by NCERT. Anganwadi Workers/Teachers with qualifications of 10+2 and above shall be given a 6-month *certificate programme* in ECCE; and those with lower educational qualifications shall be given a one-year *diploma programme* covering early literacy, numeracy, and other relevant aspects of ECCE. These programmes may be run through *digital/distance* mode using DTH channels as well as smartphones, allowing teachers to acquire ECCE qualifications with minimal disruption to their current work. The ECCE training of Anganwadi Workers/Teachers will be *mentored* by the Cluster Resource Centres of the School Education Department which shall hold at least one monthly contact class for continuous assessment. In the longer term, *State Governments shall prepare cadres of professionally qualified educators for early childhood care and education, through stage-specific professional training, mentoring mechanisms, and career mapping. Necessary facilities*

will also be created for the initial professional preparation of these educators and their Continuous Professional Development (CPD).

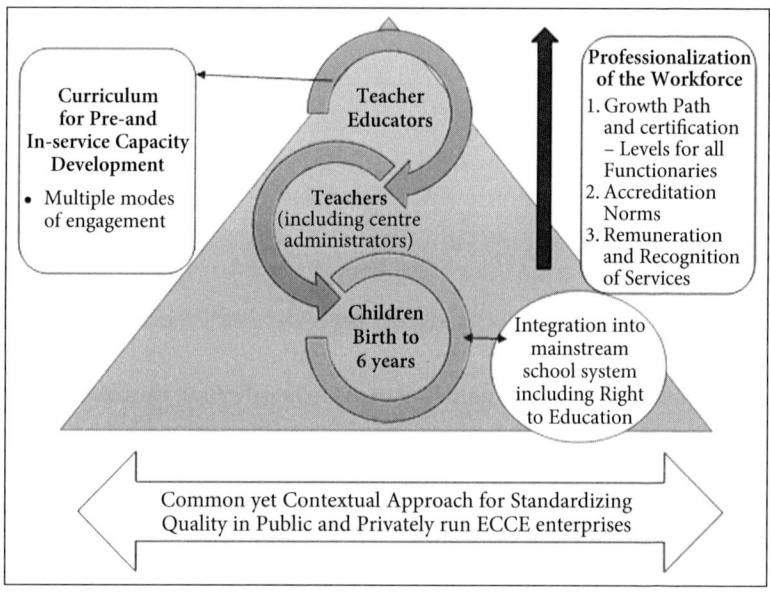

Figure 23.1: Way forward for streamlining the ECCE profession in line with NEP 2020

In order to lay a course of action with reference to the recommendations for ECCE stated above, we provide a framework to visualise the gaps and the necessary steps towards professionalising the early childhood development domain in India.

Given the current complex and layered ECCE spectrum in India, gradual yet clear steps are required to streamline and strengthen the field in India. To make this vision a reality, the framework indicates strengthening the *inter-related core of ECCE*—children, teachers and teacher educators.

Urgent attention to and implementation of the following steps is recommended:

- *Right to Early Childhood Care and Education:* Make amendments to the *Right to Education Act 2009* and bring children below 6 years of age in the ambit of this Act.

  This will ensure that compulsory provisions for access and care, development and education are made for 'all' children in our country.

  Further in this Act, ensure that a degree in ECCE is mandatory for teachers of preschools across the country.

- *Early Childhood Teacher Competency and Professional Development Framework:* National Council of Teacher Education (NCTE), Niti Aayog, National Council of Education, Research and Training (NCERT) must lay out a clear competency framework for beginner, developing and proficient teacher development. This competency framework must form the basis of pre-service and in-service programmes for ECCE teacher development.

- *Professional Development Programmes:* Range of certificate, diploma and degree programmes for early years teachers should be integrated within the overall higher education programme structure as recommended in the NEP 2020. This will ensure equalisation of rigour and preparedness of early years teachers, like primary and high school teacher preparation programmes. National Curriculum Framework for ECCE Teacher Education must be developed and should form the curricular basis of different levels of certification programmes. Further, universities must be charged with advancing ECCE knowledge base and continuous contribution to the domain of ECCE.

- *Institute an Accreditation and Norms Framework for ECCE:* This would provide a professional development growth-path for early years teachers. For instance, strengthening norms such as at least 5 years of service as a teacher before applying for supervisor position in the preschools or ICDS programme, at least 10 years of experience as a teacher, and curriculum coordinator, for becoming a school

administrator, private franchise administrators to undergo specific certification in ECCE, and so on.
- *Continuous Professional Development Programmes (CPD):* Certificate and Diploma programmes as already recommended in the Policy must be offered. Quality control measures of these programmes must be mandated to the University Grants Commission or equivalent body so that mushrooming of poor-quality teacher preparation institutions can be prevented at the outset. The curricula for these programmes must be mapped to the norms and competency frameworks for professional development suggested above in the professional development programmes.
- *Flexible, multimodal* approach needs to be recognised as an important medium for continuous development programmes and certification of teachers.
- *Provision of Professional Networks and Recognition Platforms:* The recognition of a profession is determined through its knowledge base, practices, and a sense of *community* of practitioners. It is important to provide regular opportunities to preschool teachers to network among their peers, understand practices and processes that work or do not work within different contexts. While the non-formal networks are gaining momentum, a systematic effort wherein network connections are desired for professional upgradation can be positioned within the overall professional development measures.
- *Ensure High Status and Identity of ECCE teacher:* Status is determined by qualification, remuneration as well as position in the official cadre of personnel. The idea of 'honorary' workers such as the contractual work arrangements of Anganwadi Workers must cease. Permanent position, with all key benefits of employment must be available to an early childhood teacher in the country. Protecting the rights of an early years teacher is

at the core of how we as a country see the well-being of our children.
- *Quality and Ethics Framework for ECCE Professionals:* A profession is governed by its responsibility towards society. For ensuring consistent accountability and quality of everyone concerned to work with children, a quality and ethics framework must be developed and guide the work of all ECCE professionals. In the absence of such an approach, the efforts of the individual and system at large would achieve only a limited goal of engaging and caring for children, without commitment to quality. Ensuring highest quality and standard of practice is the underlying principle of professional practice.

These eight steps provide a starting point for consolidating the various efforts of policies, programmes and practices that have so far determined the course of the ECCE domain. All sections of this volume indicate to us that much has been happening in the policy and practice sphere across public and voluntary organisations and university programmes working in the domain in the last two decades. However, there is still a long way to go before this 'half-profession' of ECCE is seen as a core 'profession' within the teacher education sphere, as well as within the larger social sphere where the ECCE teacher is regarded as the most important contributor in a child's life, and therefore receives the highest social status as that of a doctor or a lawyer.

The Constitution of India envisions an equitable childhood experience for all children of our country. Early years teachers are central to realising this vision. With the National Education Policy 2020 recognising the criticality of ECCE in children's holistic development and building strong foundations for education and life, all these recommendations can see light with political and administrative intent and consistent push from the ECCE professional community. Significant steps are being taken by various national bodies towards implementation of the Policy, and there is hope that Early Childhood Development will emerge as a full profession with all contours of the profession thriving over the next decade.

REFERENCES

Ministry of Human Resource Development. (2020). *National education policy 2020*. https://www.education.gov.in/sites/upload_files/mhrd/files/NEP_Final_English_0.pdf Accessed August 8, 2020.

Azim Premji University (2018). Conference report. *Redefining early childhood profession in India: challenges and potential.* Azim Premji University, Bengaluru.

About the Contributors

Kanika Agarwal is a Deaf educator with over 10 years' experience. Among the few Deaf researchers in India, she uses deaf-centric teaching content and bilingual teaching methodologies in her classrooms.

Mridula Bajaj is an expert on issues related to young children and has over three decades' experience in programme design, research, training and advocacy. She has contributed to the development of 'The ECCE Policy of India' to strengthen policies and programmes.

Valentine Borges is visiting researcher at IBERS Distance Learning at Aberystwyth University, UK. A qualified learning designer with keen interest in pedagogy and STEM education, he has worked at Muktangan, Mumbai, as leader of the research department and teacher educator.

Neela Dabir is an academic and social worker whose research focuses on vulnerable children, street children, women in distress and vocational education. She has held key positions at TISS including as Registrar, and Dean of the School of Vocational Education.

Vrinda Datta is the president of Association of Early Childhood Education and Development (AECED), India. She has served as the Director of the Center for Early Childhood Education and Development (CECED) at Ambedkar University, Delhi, and as Professor at the School of Human Ecology, TISS, Mumbai.

Pranjali Dev is a doctoral candidate at the University of Delhi. She has worked in areas of educational research, early childhood care and education and teacher education. Her doctoral research delves into literacy and language development during early childhood.

Karma Gayleg works with the Ministry of Education in Bhutan as ECCD Specialist and has published widely on the subject including in *ARNEC Connections*, *Childcare Exchange* (USA), *Early Childhood Matters* (BVLF) and *Scoonews* (India).

Gauravi Jadhav was associated with Muktangan Education Trust since 2007 where she was responsible for Preschool Curriculum Planning and

Development, Content Development, Teacher Education, Outreach and Advocacy initiatives.

Vaijayanti K. is Director, Research and Evaluation at the Akshara Foundation, Bengaluru, and was a member of the 2013 national panel on ECCE policy framework. She has deep understanding of macro issues including policy and planning as well as micro areas such as curriculum development and research.

Venita Kaul is Professor Emerita (Education), Ambedkar University, Delhi, from where she retired in 2016 as Director of School of Education Studies and Founder Director of Center for Early Childhood Education and Development (CECED). She is also Chief Editor of *Children First: A Journal on Children's Lives*.

Pankaj Khare is Director, Planning and Development Division at Indira Gandhi National Open University (IGNOU). He is an expert in data mining and has published two books and over 40 research papers. He is recognised as a master trainer for e-learning and open and distance learning.

Gayatri Kiran is Director of Nidhi Early Interventions in Bengaluru. A UGC Research Fellow of Delhi University, she has been a consultant in ECCE, including special needs in early years, for over two decades.

Shikha Kumari is the ECE pedagogical coordinator of Prajayatna and is responsible for curriculum development, pedagogy design and capacity building of the ECE team. She has worked with teachers and children in ECE and math education.

Ankur Madan is currently Director, School of Education at Azim Premji University and teaches courses in child development and inclusive education. Her research interests and publications focus on childhood studies in India. She is currently interrogating the concepts of inclusion and inclusive education from the practitioners' perspective in the Indian context.

Elizabeth Mehta is the founder of Muktangan Education Trust and has over 40 years' experience in teaching and teacher education. She was awarded the MBE by the British government in 2015. Her work has won recognition from the Indian government, teacher training colleges and NGOs.

Maya Menon has spent four decades in school education, with the last 20+ years working specifically with educators. She is the

Founder Director of The Teacher Foundation that offers professional development programmes and services for school teachers and principals of both public and private schools. She has written and published extensively about education and blogs at http://mayamenon.teacherfoundation.org/.

Prerana Mohite is a Vadodara-based educator with more than 30 years' experience in child/human development, with specialisation and research experience across key dimensions in ECDE. She is a consultant with the School of Vocational Education, TISS, Mumbai, and is working on developing a postgraduate diploma programme in ECCE.

Varadarajan Narayanan is with the School of Education, Azim Premji University, Bengaluru. He is also associated with the Schoolbooks Archive project to collect, digitize, curate and provide online access to schoolbooks and related documents used in the subcontinent over the last two hundred years.

Nilesh Nimkar is a founder trustee and director of Quality Education Support Trust (QUEST), a pioneering institution in rural and tribal education with presence in 27 districts of Maharashtra. He has over two decades' experience in early childhood education, elementary education, teacher capacity building and curriculum development.

Kinnari Pandya is Associate Professor at Azim Premji University, where she works on early childhood education and teacher education. Her research and practice is on curriculum for young learners, teacher preparation and their continuing professional development, especially in public systems.

Mary Punnoose is the Chief Functionary of Prajayatna, responsible for its strategic planning and programme conceptualisation. She has over two decades' experience of working closely with government schools, anganwadis and multiple stakeholders in the education system.

Yogesh G. R. led the ECE Initiative of the Azim Premji Foundation at Sangareddy, Telangana. He has been instrumental in mentoring the resource persons' team and creating a scalable multimodal engagement for capacity building of anganwadi teachers. He has worked on capacity building of primary and upper-primary teachers at the Puducherry District Institute.

Jumana Rampurawala is a teacher educator with over two decades experience in child development, school curriculum and pedagogy. She has been associated with Muktangan Education Trust since 2006, where she coordinates the teacher education resource centre, teacher trainee recruitment and management of teacher education outreach projects.

M. Sreenivasa Rao (MSR) has been with Azim Premji Foundation for the last 20 years and leads the ECE initiative in Telangana while supporting other states to implement ECE effectively. His areas of focus are working with young children, assessment and research.

Rekha Sharma Sen is Professor of Child Development at IGNOU, New Delhi. Her areas of teaching and research include ECCE, Early Language and Literacy, Disability, Sociocultural Dimensions of Creativity, and Gender in Open and Distance Learning.

Jigisha Shastri is a visiting faculty with Azim Premji University and has contributed to the conceptualization and implementation of ECE work of the Azim Premji Foundation. She has worked with UNICEF as well as the private and government sectors on ECCE. She has contributed to ECCE research, curriculum and resource development and capacity building of teachers across India.

Asha Singh is a visiting faculty the Azim Premji University and is a teacher educator with expertise in art and pedagogy. She has contributed to various ECCE and the Arts and Aesthetics programmes. She was an advisor to the preschool television series *Tarram Tu* and the international collaboration *Galli Galli Sim Sim* in visualising content for India's multiple contexts.

Rajashree Srinivasan is Professor at the School of Education, Azim Premji University. Her research interests include child development and teacher education. She anchors TeachTE, a project focusing on the professional development of teacher educators in India.

Padma Yadav is Professor with the Department of Elementary Education at NCERT, New Delhi. She is involved in Research Training, Teacher Education, and Evaluation Programmes, in addition to development and extension activities for ECCE, Foundational Literacy and Numeracy, and Elementary Education.